Includes Meditation CD

Crystal Skulls

Expand Your Consciousness

by **Jaap van Etten, PhD**

Other books by Jaap Van Etten

Crystal Skulls: Interacting with a Phenomenon

Gifts of Mother Earth

Birth of a New Consciousness

Dragons: Guardians of Creative Powers

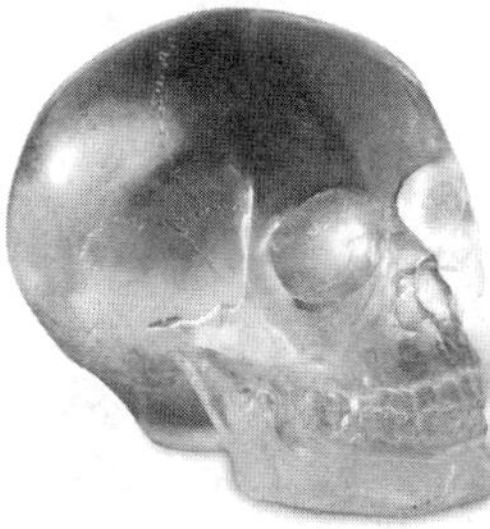

Crystal Skulls

Expand Your Consciousness

by Jaap van Etten, PhD

Light Technology Publishing

* * *

ISBN-13: 978-1-62233-251-9

Light Technology Publishing

Light Technology Publishing, LLC
Phone: 800-450-0985
928-526-1345
Fax: 928-714-1132
PO Box 3540
Flagstaff, AZ 86003
LightTechnology.com

This book is dedicated to all caretakers of crystal skulls who, throughout time, have been willing to awaken the potential of their crystal skulls, thus contributing to the expansion of consciousness into Oneness.

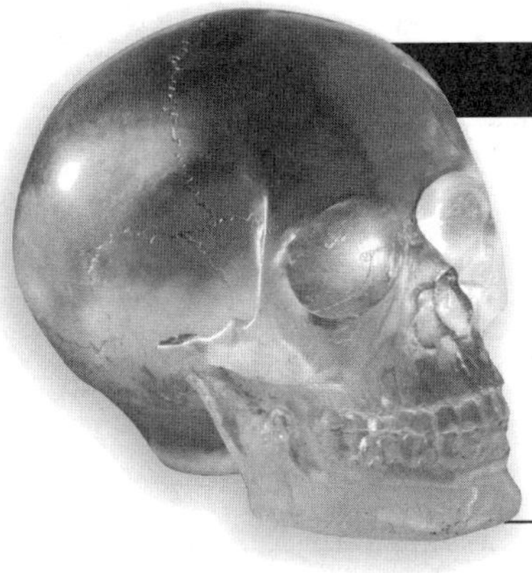

Table of Contents

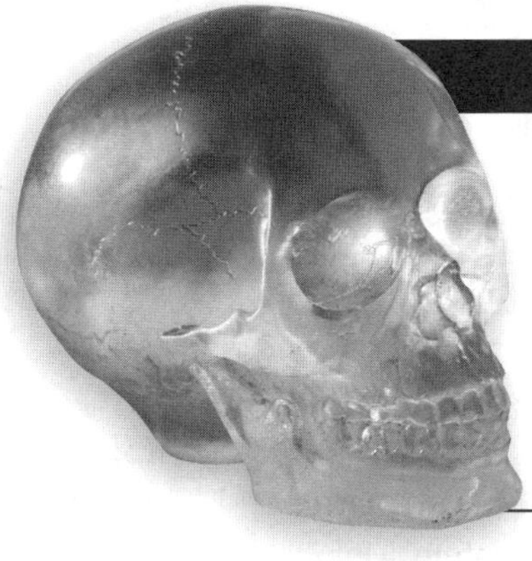

Acknowledgments

Since the writing of *Crystal Skulls: Interacting with a Phenomenon*, the number of people supporting me in the writing of this second book on crystal skulls has grown. This support comes from many different directions — people who come to our weekly meditations; caretakers of ancient, old, and contemporary skulls; and those who have listened to my lectures or attended workshops that my wife Jeanne and I have facilitated.

Due to this increase in connections, I cannot mention everyone individually. Know that I feel much gratitude for all who have supported me, whether in a small or a large way. Your support has been, and is, important to me.

There are always people who have contributed in a special way. I would like to thank Kendall Morgan, who has been the driving force behind the "triple date" crystal skull events (from the 9–9–9 to the 12–12–12). These events have helped me to share my thoughts about crystal skulls in a coherent way. The feedback during these conferences has greatly stimulated me.

I would also like to thank Jorge Lozano and Gina Leon, who organized three conferences in Mexico City. These conferences have been very stimulating and have helped me to gather information, some of which has been included in this book and some that may form the basis for a next one.

I would like to thank all organizers who have invited me to participate in their events or to present something at their centers or locations. Every verbal and written expression helps to fine-tune the understanding and presentation of the information gathered.

I would like to thank every person who has participated in our weekly crystal skull meditations. There have been so many who have attended these meditations over the past seven years that I cannot mention all of their names. However, I'd like to give the names of those who have been regulars for many years: Sandi O'Connor (who has been part of it all from the very beginning), Diana Rodriguez, Cher Lynn, Adele Sands, Daniel Maddux, Ssuzanne Grandon, Snowy and Sigrid Schrack, and Ted and Debby Mercer.

I would like to thank all the elders, speakers, and caretakers I have met during the different events. Thank you for your stimulus, direct or indirect. Thank you, Grandmother Flordemayo, Daykeeper Hunbatz Men, Carolyn Ford, Ron Irvin, Michele Nocerino, Grace and Maurice Dunner, DaEl and Lauri Walker, Jane Doherty, Arthur Fanning, Stephen Mehler, Kirby Seid, Kirk Landauer, and Raymond Tarpey.

It might seem like I have forgotten one name, but I have not. Sherry Whitfield, I have to mention you separately. We have had many in-depth discussions and have shared at a level that I consider to be unique. Our exchanges have been very important for me personally and for my understanding of crystal skulls at an energetic level. Thank you for being such a wonderful spiritual "sparring partner" and friend.

I am very grateful to Kristina Arysta and Sandi O'Connor for their willingness to read the manuscript of this book and to help to develop it into a form that I could offer to my publisher without shame. Thank you for your very valuable contribution.

I have to add a special thanks to Kristina Arysta for the many valuable discussions and exchanges we have had. Your clear mind and intuition have been of great support to me.

I'd also like to thank Evita de Vos, who again has changed my sketches into professional illustrations. Thank you for a pleasant and professional collaboration.

Thank you, Melody Swanson, my publisher, for again expressing your confidence in me by accepting this book for publication. I am very grateful for your wonderful support team who changed the manuscript into a good-looking book.

I always like to end my acknowledgments with the person who is most important in my life. Thank you, Jeanne, my beloved wife, for all your sharing, your willingness to challenge me, your support, your love, and your patience. My relationship with you has changed my life and has supported me in connecting deeper with myself. Without your support I would never have been able to write this book.

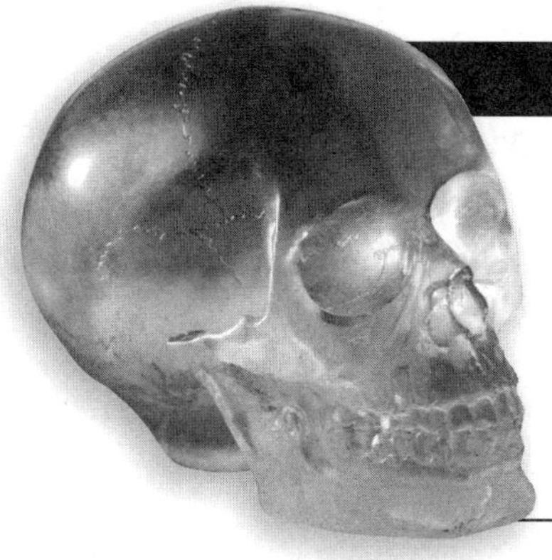

Introduction

This book is about remembering who we are: spiritual beings having a human experience. Remembering may lead to the awakening of the full potential that we, human beings, have. We do not know what this full potential is. However, increasing numbers of people feel that it is more than surviving in a physical world. This feeling leads to the decision to embark on a spiritual journey, searching for ways and tools that help to give direction and purpose to that journey.

Those who are on a spiritual journey experience that life is filled with significant change. In current times this change is often called "the shift." This shift is linked with the year 2012, which is believed to mark the end of the Mayan calendar. Some believe that this shift *will* happen on a specific date (December 12, 2012) or that it has *already* happened on a specific date (October 28, 2011)[1], while others believe that the period of the shift spans years or even decades.

Other people stress that the shift will lead to a major change in economic values whereby the separation between the rich and the poor will need to be bridged. They believe that those who control wealth, a small elite group of people who control the major banks and the global economy, need to share that wealth, and such a change will only happen when the masses of people take back their power. David Icke is one of the most outspoken people on the need for such an economic shift[2].

I do not believe that such a shift will happen on a specific date. However, a date may mark a significant point in the process of a shift. It is not difficult to see that a shift is already happening. One of the signs is increased interest in spirituality. This shift can be defined as one from a culture of scientific materialism to a more spiritual culture. An increasing number of people are beginning to realize that we are spiritual beings having a human experience. Although this is a rather vague phrase, it serves to remind us of our spiritual essence and the need for daily spirituality. People have begun to realize that the endless need for more and more "stuff" is not satisfying the lack they feel in their lives. An increasing number of people are realizing that this need, this emptiness, is actually caused by a lack of spirituality, even within religious practice. They have come to realize what they really need is love, joy, and happiness.

Looking at our society, we see that many people are stressed, fearful of the current economic developments, frustrated with governments, and afraid of the deadly aggression of random bombings, shootings, and wars that seem to rage on unabated. The key is fear. Fear divides people, making them give away their power to others who seem to lead, like institutions and governments. Differences invoke fear. Fear leads to aggression, as it seems easier to fight rather than to choose to transform fear into love.

When we are in a state of love, it is impossible to kill. Love raises our vibration and expands our consciousness to remember who we truly are: loving spiritual beings who have chosen to experience a physical reality through physical bodies we call "human." The challenge we accepted in choosing life on Earth is to remember who we are by reconnecting to our divine essence through pure love.

The purpose of this book is to share with you how I experience crystal skulls and the way they support us on this journey of remembering who we are and that we all are one. Crystal skulls are ideal tools, supporting us in increasing our vibrations, helping us to remember who we are, and consequentially helping us to express who we truly are instead of expressing who we have been conditioned to be.

Crystal skulls are such fascinating objects, artifacts, tools, and conscious beings. Having studied crystal skulls for more than eighteen years, I have hardly scratched the surface of what they are. At the same time, my fascination for them has grown. Crystal skulls have stimulated me to undertake a journey of many unexpected experiences, and fortunately the end is nowhere in sight. It's a journey of discovering and remembering not only what crystal skulls are, but also of who I am. This book describes the journey of my discovery of the nature of crystal skulls. Everyone who starts working with crystal skulls begins a similar yet personal journey.

The Journey

My journey with crystal skulls began in 1994 when I met my first crystal skull. While living in the Netherlands, I visited the Southwest of the United States. As part of that trip, I stayed ten days in Sedona, Arizona, and on my last day there I visited a woman who had many crystals. When she saw how much I enjoyed her crystal collection, she said she had a surprise for me. She asked me to sit down and close my eyes. She left the room, and when she came back I felt something cold and heavy placed in my hands. Although I did not know what I had in my hands, I started to cry. I described this experience extensively in the introduction of my first book, *Crystal Skulls: Interacting with a Phenomenon*[3]. After about half an hour of sobbing, I opened my eyes and looked at something that I would define as ugly: a clear quartz crystal skull. Needless to say, I wanted to know what a crystal skull was and what made it so special that it had made me cry. My curiosity intensified when I learned later that the skull was not one of those "special" skulls that are called "ancient" but rather a recently carved skull from Brazil.

Back in the Netherlands, I soon discovered that crystal skulls were a relatively unknown phenomenon. Hardly anyone knew about them, and I could not find anyone who had one. Even the person I usually bought many crystals from, who had sold crystals for over thirty years, had never heard about crystal skulls. However, this has changed completely and now crystal skulls are very popular in the Netherlands.

I was determined to find out more about crystal skulls, hoping to understand my emotional reaction. So I looked everywhere to collect as much information as possible. At the time, only a few books were available. The most informative book I found was *Mysteries of the Crystal Skulls Revealed*[4]. The other books focused mainly on the Mitchell-Hedges crystal skull, which was, at that time, the most famous and well-known crystal skull.

In the first phase of my research, I obtained most of my information on crystal skulls from the Internet. One important website was that of the Society of Crystal Skulls International, founded in 1940 by Nick F.R. Nocerino. Nick was considered a master on the subject of crystals and crystal skulls. Even today no one has seen as many "special" crystal skulls as Nick did during the fifty years of his research. He developed techniques that helped to define skulls, their ages, and — to some degree — their purpose. When Nick passed away in 2004, the website was removed from the Internet, but the extensive information he collected is still privately archived by his family.

Another informative website was created by Joshua Shapiro. This website still exists[5] and has remained a popular source of information on crystal skulls.

It is difficult to identify what induced the sudden expansive interest in crystal skulls. No doubt the activities of Nick Nocerino, Anna Mitchell Hedges, JoAnn Parks (with Max), Joshua Shapiro, and many others have contributed to this increase. However, their activities alone seem an insufficient explanation. Toward the end of the nineties, the interest in crystal skulls grew exponentially, and it has taken on a surprising form during the first twelve years of the twenty-first century. People attribute the increased interest to changes in human consciousness, the so-called new age. As we will see, crystal skulls help us to expand our awareness (consciousness), and people searching for ways to increase their awareness have realized how helpful crystal skulls are in this evolutionary process.

Initially I was focused on understanding my emotional reaction during my first encounter with a crystal skull. People suggested that it might be related to past-life experiences. My focus is not on past lives but on the here and now; therefore, I was more interested in understanding their relevance for me in this lifetime. Because my reaction was not caused by what my five senses told me (that is, I had no clue what I held in my hands), I assumed that my reaction was based on sensing energies. I assumed that my emotional reaction was a subconscious reaction to the experience of these energies. Therefore, I shifted my focus to understanding the subtle energies connected with crystal skulls.

The study of subtle energies was not unknown to me. I had studied intuitive development and applied these skills to the study of human energies, using this knowledge in sessions with people. I also used these intuitive skills in my study of Earth energies. However, when you embark on a journey of studying the subtle energies of a system, in this case crystal skulls, it is helpful when similar studies are available. Unfortunately, not much helpful information was available on this topic. Therefore, the first phase consisted of trial and error, excitement and frustration, and expansion and contraction. I began to understand that working with crystal skulls was literally working with myself and being confronted with issues I had not yet dealt with. Studying the energies of crystal skulls turned out to be a journey of understanding myself.

Beginnings

In 2006 my wife, Jeanne Michaels, and I met Sherry Whitfield and the ancient crystal skull Synergy. Although I knew of Sherry and although we live only a four-hour drive from each other in Arizona, we met at a crystal skull event in the Netherlands. This meeting was very important. Although we instantly felt a deep connection, it took more than a year before we started to meet more regularly. The exchanges with Sherry and my connections with Synergy have been very important for my journey of understanding crystal skulls and myself.

In 2010 Sherry and I were both presenters at a crystal skull conference in Mexico City, organized by Jorge Lozano and Gina Leon[6]. One of the attendees was Bec Campbell who had organized a trip for Sherry and Synergy in Australia. She made an interesting comment to me. She said, "Your book is for people who have had more experiences with crystal skulls. What is missing is the basic information on crystal skulls — information for those who are just starting on their journeys. After that they may be ready to read your book." This comment was a bit shocking for me, but it brought up the idea of writing a basic book on crystal skulls. Sherry and I thought of collaborating by each writing a part of the book.

As soon as I started to write, I realized that I could not resonate with the idea of being restricted to a "basic book." I am only able to write on subjects I am passionate about, like the evolving deeper understanding of the energies of crystal skulls. So I include some basic elements as the foundation to the ongoing discoveries and understanding of the energetic dynamics of crystal skulls — how these energies help us remember who we are, how they transform, and how they help us release all that we are not. When I shared my thoughts and feelings with Sherry, she understood me, so I embarked on a journey to write the book you now hold in your hands. It is part of a greater journey, and the plan is to follow up with at least one more book. After all, studying crystal skulls is a continuous journey.

At this point, it is important to acknowledge Nick F.R. Nocerino as the founder of the research on crystal skulls. He dominated this field of research for almost fifty years. With his enthusiasm and passion, he stimulated many people to work with and study crystal skulls. When he passed away, he left behind a field that has gained increasing attention. His legacy should not be forgotten, but at the same time, it is important to move forward with the research on crystal skulls, exploring new avenues and seeking new approaches. This book is a manifestation of these new pathways of discovery.

A Metaphysical Book

This is not a scientific book. I discussed in my previous book how crystal skulls cannot be understood with the current beliefs held by the majority of the scientific community. Science has the tendency to compartmentalize, and that creates separation. There are signs of a change in attitude as some famous scientists recognize the importance of subtle energies — like David Bohm, who believes that subtle energies are part of the implicate order, the world of subtle energies and the unmanifested[7]. Hermann Oberth, one of the fathers of rocket technology, said that the future of science in general mostly depends on the progress of parapsychology[8]. Not long before he died, Nikola Tesla said, "Once science starts researching immaterial phenomena, it will make a more significant progress inside a decade than it did in all the previous centuries of its existence"[9]. However, these bold statements have not yet reached mainstream science.

Denying that crystal skulls induce consistently reliable experiences in people is very unscientific. We no longer have to wait for science to catch up with what people have known and sensed for eons of time. Many believe that crystal skulls have been used for a long time. There have to be reasons for such a widespread belief, and to discover what these reasons are, we must be willing to open up to our experiences and share them with others.

The only way to understand the universe is through the harmonious integration of the logical and mental masculine perspective of knowing, understanding, and applying knowledge, with the intuitive and sensitive feminine perspective of experiencing the crystal skulls and their effects on us. This integrated masculine/feminine perspective is the only way to understand the role of crystal skulls in human spiritual evolution. By now it must be abundantly clear that this is a metaphysical — not scientific — book.

The Importance of Age

The age of a crystal skull (that is, is it "ancient" or not?) seems to be important to many people. I hope to make it clear that age is unimportant. What is most important is the journey that you take with your crystal skull. Yes, we can learn from those who have worked with crystal skulls in the past. Those that were carved and worked with in the past invite us to reconnect and rediscover the gifts they offer. This allows us to work with our contemporary crystal skulls in an optimal way, which is independent of the age of the crystal skull. Our state of awareness determines what is possible, whether the skull is old or contemporary.

The experience of crystal skulls can be quite personal, so it is important to never compare yourself with others. No one will be able to master all aspects of crystal skulls. Be happy wherever you are in your ongoing journey with crystal skulls, and share and explore with others.

If we accept that the journey is the goal, we can journey with any crystal skull that we are attracted to. Let go of the need to own an ancient crystal skull. People with such needs often encounter confusing and even painful situations, such as being tricked into buying an ancient skull that is not ancient at all. Many of these ancient skulls are not made of natural materials but of resin, which is artificially made. As we will see, from an energy point of view, these skulls are not *real* crystal skulls.

Sometimes people buy crystal skulls that are not sold as ancient, but because they have very profound experiences, they deceive themselves into believing that their crystal skulls must be ancient. They even search out psychics who will confirm their misbeliefs.

Purpose and Focus

This text is intended to be an addition to my first book, but it can also be read independently. Therefore, a few aspects from the first book have been repeated, often within a different context. I also have included a more extensive list of old and ancient crystal skulls and their energies based on the latest insights (see Addendum I).

The main focus of this book is to provide information that will help people understand how crystal skulls support us on our journeys of spiritual development and help us make this journey more efficient and easy. Crystal skulls help us to raise our vibrations to limitless levels. They also help us to be in the here and now, because they always are fully who they are and reflect that state to us.

The role of crystal skulls becomes even more important when we realize that the predicted shift may force us to make choices on a level beyond what most people realize. One of the people writing about this is Dolores Cannon.

Dolores has become well known for her method of bringing people into a deeper state of hypnosis than most other hypnotists can. This allows people to connect with information that otherwise would be inaccessible. During her sessions, it became clear that at this time in history, many souls have come to Earth specifically to help with a shift in consciousness that, as they say under hypnosis, inevitably will happen. In order to be part of this shift, people need to raise their vibration. There are many souls who have come to Earth at this time to help increase the vibrations of people to allow as many as possible to be part of this shift. In their hypnotic state, many people talk about Earth separating into two realities: one based on fear and duality and the other one on love and oneness[10]. In 2010, five different crop circles appeared that seemed to indicate this possibility that Earth will split into two realities, supporting the information and ideas shared by Dolores and others[11]. Whatever happens, crystal skulls can support us as we go to the Earth of love and Oneness. This Earth can be an experience or may be a real Earth.

This book contains a wealth of information that leads both the beginner and non-beginner on their journey to Oneness. It contains information that may stimulate you, ignite new impulses, and assist you on your journey to Oneness. Enjoy this journey with the crystal skulls. Let yourself be guided by love and curiosity, and make every step a celebration.

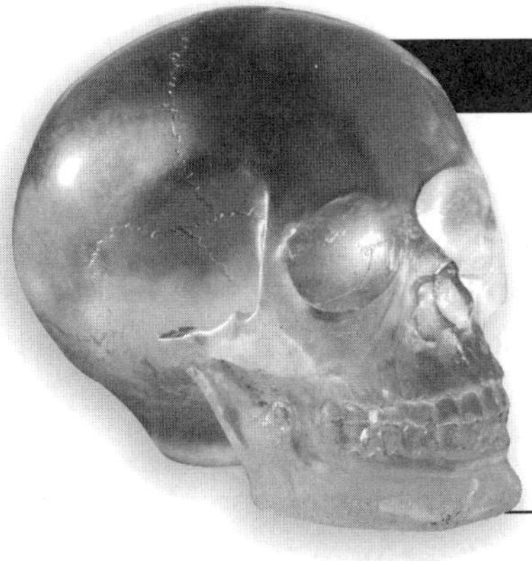

CHAPTER ONE

Crystal Skulls and Their Characteristics

This book will take you on a journey from basic questions about crystal skulls to an understanding of the energies of crystal skulls, leading to an understanding of the contribution of crystal skulls to our personal and collective spiritual evolution. This chapter starts with a basic question and then looks at the qualities and characteristics of crystal skulls.

The most common question people ask about crystal skulls is also the simplest one: *What is a crystal skull?* Although the interest in crystal skulls is rapidly expanding, most people have never heard of them and therefore will ask such basic questions. There is also curiosity as to why people would have any interest in something as "scary" as crystal skulls. For many people, a skull is still a symbol of death or danger; for example, the use of skull and crossbones is a symbol for something that is poisonous. With the growing interest in crystal skulls, engaging answers to these questions are needed. An answer like, "It is a piece of crystal or stone carved in the shape of a skull" is correct but not very satisfying.

It is interesting that even people who work with crystal skulls often are unable to give a good description of what a crystal skull is. This is not surprising. We do not yet fully understand the materials (crystals and stones) crystal skulls are carved from — even though some people claim they do — and we definitely do not understand all aspects that the shape of a skull adds to the qualities of those materials.

My belief is that crystal skulls are the most powerful tools to support us on our journey of remembering and expressing who we are. To help you understand why I believe this, let us start at the very beginning by looking at two aspects of crystal skulls: the crystals they are carved from and the skull shape.

Crystals

When I observe people working with crystal skulls, I notice that there are three main ways people connect with them. Therefore, we can separate people who work with crystal skulls into three groups.

The first group consists of people who mainly connect with the crystal aspects of a crystal skull. Consciously or subconsciously, these people focus mainly on the healing of the physical aspects of their being as a basis for their spiritual journey.

People in the second group, which is much smaller, connect mainly with the skull aspect of a crystal skull. These are people who focus mainly on the development of their consciousness. As we will see in chapter 5, the energies of the skull shape offer different qualities from those of the crystals they are carved from. By bringing focus and conscious intent to our understanding of these different energies, we can use them in the optimal way.

The third group consists of people who connect with both the crystal and the skull shape aspects at the same time. They work with both healing and expansion of consciousness. Often these people move between these two aspects, continuously growing, expanding, and changing. This is the optimal way to work with crystal skulls.

In general most people connect more easily with the crystal aspects of a crystal skull. It seems that most people need the crystal energies most. As we will see, the skull qualities amplify the healing qualities of the crystals even more. When a person works mainly with the crystal aspects, the skull aspects act as an amplifier but also offer a permanent opportunity to expand even more. Because the crystal aspects are so important, we will share more about them in several chapters.

Many people who buy a crystal skull tend to forget the origin of the material it is carved from. They are so focused on the object itself that they tend to forget that the crystal or stone is a gift of Mother Earth. When a crystal has been carved into a form that alters its natural shape, it becomes more difficult to remember that the material comes from the Earth. However, every crystal and stone is part of the large crystalline being that we call Mother Earth. When we work with crystals and crystal skulls it is important to feel gratitude for these wonderful gifts. Working with crystal skulls has an effect on Earth because we are working and interacting with a piece from her and thus with her.

The key reason that skulls are made from crystals and stones, materials from Mother Earth, is to remind us that all basic materials in our physical bodies come from Mother Earth. It reminds us that in order to develop spiritually, we also need to take care of our physical system. The total mass of Mother Earth, with all her variations in stones, crystals, and minerals, creates the energy fields, vortexes, lines, and grids that support us in creating a healthy physical system[1]. Therefore, crystals have been used for healing for eons, and crystal skulls can be used in the same way (see chapter 4). Allow yourself to feel which crystal skull resonates most with you when you are selecting one. In chapter 2, we will look at the selection of crystal skulls in more detail.

The Skull Shape

Besides the question, "What is a crystal skull?" another popular question is: *Why are they in the shape of a human skull?* As mentioned earlier, people in modern Western society perceive the human skull as a symbol of death. It is associated with pirates (who flew flags with skulls and crossbones on them), secret societies (like "Skull and Bones"), and biker gangs. For many people, it is not a symbol that creates a feeling of warmth and joy. But in other cultures, especially those that do not fear death, a skull is celebrated because it is a symbol of rebirth, of transitioning into another life.

The skull is especially important in the Mayan culture. The symbol of the skull is present in this culture in many ways. Their respect for the skull shape may be a reason so many people associate crystal skulls with the Mayan tradition. This association is strengthened by authors like Drunvalo Melchizedek, who describes in his book *Serpent of Light: Beyond 2012* a ceremony that he and his group conducted in Chichen Itza. Suddenly Mayan people came out of the jungle with thirteen crystal skulls and joined the ceremony[2]. Also, the book by Morton and Thomas[3] and the books of Patricia Mercier[4] have greatly contributed to this association of crystal skulls with the Mayan people. Therefore, in many events focusing on crystal skulls, Mayan Elders have been included[5].

These stories, however, do not explain the importance of the shape of the human skull. To understand the importance, it is helpful to listen to what some carvers share about their experiences carving crystal skulls. In 2008 during an event in Sedona, both a famous carver from Brazil, Leandro Souza, and an indigenous carver who lived in Colorado, the late Gary Butler, shared the same information. They both felt a shift as soon as the eye sockets were brought into the rough shape of a crystal skull. My book *Crystal Skulls: Interacting with a Phenomenon* has pictures that show the shape just after this

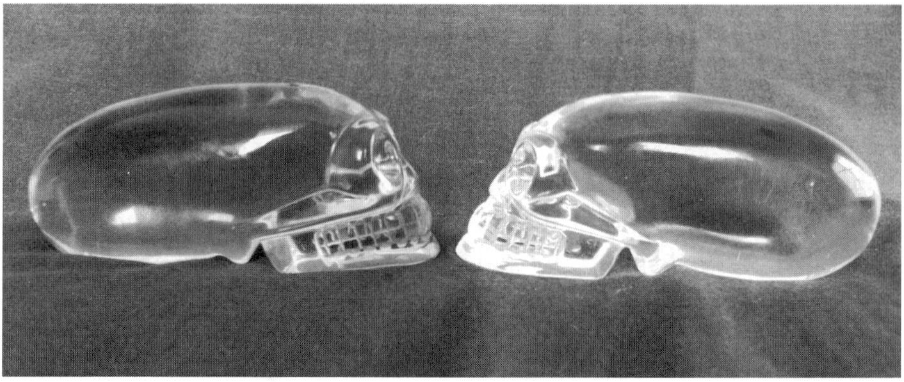

Two "alien" skulls with elongated craniums. These skulls do not have the energies of human-shaped crystal skulls.

shift (color plates 12-14). Gary Butler shared that he created the eye cavities early in the carving process because it helped him to stay connected with the energies of the skull during the carving process[6].

These carvers give an important message: There is a shift in energy when you carve a crystal into a crystal skull. This suggests that there is a difference in energy between a crystal skull and the crystal it is carved from. In general, it is not easy to experience this shift, because it occurs during the carving process before you buy a crystal skull. The skulls are carved in Brazil, China, or other distant places, so it is difficult to have an opportunity to experience such a shift. Nevertheless, those who work with crystals and crystal skulls will agree that the skull shape does something to a crystal that creates an energy system that goes beyond that of the crystal itself. We will look at these energies in more detail in chapter 5.

With the increase in interest in crystal skulls, we see that carvers increasingly make different shapes like alien skulls, dragon skulls, and animal skulls. Those who are sensitive to energies will notice that all of these skulls are powerful tools but that they do not have the type of increase in energy that the shape of a human skull offers and that is needed to affect human consciousness. The shape needs to be close enough to a human skull to induce this type of shift in energy. For example, alien skulls with a very elongated cranium (image 1.1) will not create the same energy shift as the human-like crystal skulls. Alien skulls are very powerful and connect with a particular energy field. However, this field is energetically very different from the field of crystal skulls based on the human shape.

We see a similar situation when, for example, a skull is carved at the end of a crystal (image 1.2). In such cases, there is no energy shift that connects such a carving with the human crystal skull field. Does this mean that a crystal skull needs to be anatomically identical to the shape of a human skull? The answer is no. Fortunately there is room for variation; otherwise, many crystal skulls would not have the crystal skull energies. It seems that a crystal skull needs to have a shape that without a doubt represents a human skull. There are exceptions though. A crystal skull like Lucy (image 1.3) is obviously closer to a monkey skull than a human one but nevertheless holds all the energies.

We do not yet have the ability to explain the addition of crystal skull energies when a crystal is carved in the form of a human skull. It seems that the shape of the human skull

1.2 A crystal with a small skull on top is energetically not a crystal skull.

1.3 Lucy, a crystal skull that looks more Simian than human

functions as a trigger that "plugs" the crystal into an energy (information) field that induces this shift. Could this field be a gift from our ancestors so that we can create tools that can truly help us on our spiritual journey? Could these tools have been created for the purpose of helping us to remember who we are? Any answer to these questions may seem speculative, but when you go through the different chapters of this book, you may understand that the answer to these questions is undoubtedly yes.

There is one more aspect to the skull shape: The human skull holds the brain. The brain has many functions, one of which is to help us to translate experiences and information that we receive through our senses, and other ways, into awareness. Awareness helps us to understand ourselves and our interactions with the world around us. Crystal skulls have characteristics that may induce many experiences, and the brain is the place that helps us to translate them into awareness. The skull shape may be an invitation to use our brains more optimally to be able to expand awareness.

One of the characteristics of crystal skulls is that they have the ability to store information. We will look at that in the next part of this chapter. In order for information contained in crystal skulls to be utilized, it first must be accessed. Once accessed, it needs to be translated into something that teaches us or helps us to connect more deeply with ourselves. Again, it is the brain that helps in that process.

Our ancestors who initially carved crystal skulls may have done so with a clear purpose in mind. They wanted us to remember who we are by providing us with clues. These clues may help us to tap into a system that holds that information. The shape of a skull may help us in this process of remembering.

The skull shape is a symbol. Even the ancient Egyptians knew that symbols are the language of the real (higher) consciousness that works through the heart instead of the brain[7]. The ancient Egyptians defined a difference between what they called the cerebral (brain) consciousness, which is meant to function as a survival system in our daily life, and the real (higher) consciousness that works through the heart and with symbols. In their tradition, the shape of the skull would be a symbol that speaks through our hearts and connects us with our higher consciousness. We now live in a time when people are reconnecting with their hearts, and this may explain the growing interest in crystal skulls — through our hearts, we subconsciously or consciously recognize the importance of this symbol.

The Basic Qualities of Crystal Skulls

Crystal skulls have basically the same qualities as crystals. However, these qualities express themselves more strongly in crystal skulls than in crystals. Crystal skulls amplify the existing qualities and characteristics of crystals. As was mentioned earlier in this chapter, the energies of crystal skulls manifest differently from those of the crystals they are carved from. It seems that the energies induced by the skull shape amplify the intensity of the characteristics of crystals. These particular characteristics are rarely described when discussing crystals, but they are more easily recognized when we work with crystal skulls.

There are apparent differences in the descriptions of the characteristics of crystal skulls. In the past I defined five basic characteristics: crystal skulls reflect, refract, transmit, attune, and store information. These characteristics have been described in *Crystal Skulls: Interacting with a Phenomenon* (6-11). Sherry Whitfield, caretaker of the ancient crystal skull Synergy, mentions eight or nine characteristics[8]. She adds the following characteristics to the five just mentioned: crystal skulls focus energy, amplify energy, transform energy, and may act as witnesses.

I still prefer the five basic characteristics I mentioned earlier, although nowadays I have accepted one additional characteristic as a main one: crystal skulls amplify. Initially I believed that amplification was solely an aspect of reflection. However, I now accept that amplification is an additional aspect induced by the crystal-skull energies.

The characteristics are mostly dormant in recently carved crystal skulls. When we work with a crystal skull, we awaken its potential and therefore increase the power of its characteristics. This is the reason why fully awakened crystal skulls, those we call "ancient," are so important: because they help us to connect with these characteristics and teach us how to work with them. Through the dedicated work of their caretakers, contemporary crystal skulls increasingly express these characteristics as well. In other words, awakening a crystal skull is important. Even more important is the awareness that we will experience the characteristics of a crystal skull only when we direct our awareness to that skull, be it consciously or subconsciously. We are the ones in power — not the crystal skulls. Only through our focused attention will the potential of a crystal skull be awakened.

The characteristics of crystal skulls are so important that they are summarized here (image 1.4). Although this information has been presented in my first book, often in a more extensive way, some new information is included here.

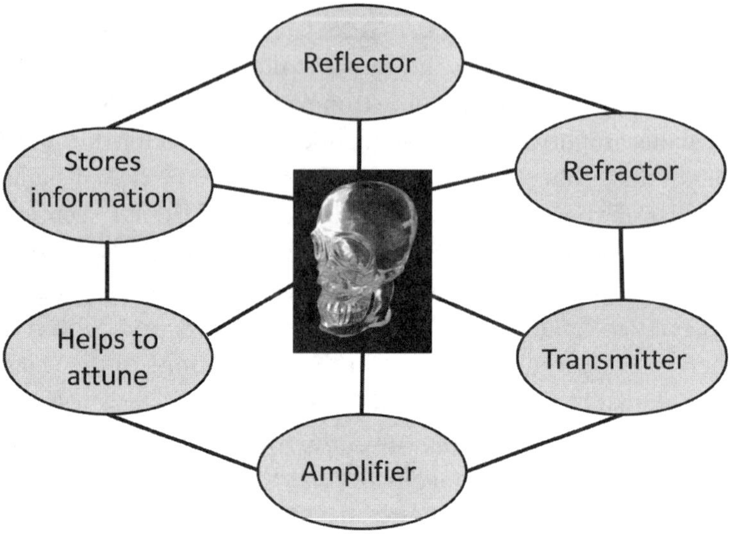

1.4 The six main characteristics of crystal skulls

Crystal Skulls Reflect Energies

As reflectors, crystal skulls help us to see who we are. They help us to remember our essence and the purpose of our lives on Earth. Remembering is essential for those on a conscious journey. The quality of reflection is important in helping us in that process. Crystal skulls give clear reflections — like a mirror. Working with a crystal skull is like looking into a mirror. Of course, we need to make the decision that we want to look in the mirror. Nothing is forced on us; it is a free choice.

Crystals are believed to hold the purest consciousness in physical form (*CS*, 4) and therefore are the most perfect reflectors of our state of consciousness. Crystal skulls amplify this reflection even more. They reflect the state of our awareness. When we are aware of what we want to change and open ourselves for the crystal skull energies, we have the opportunity to change what no longer serves us. Crystal skulls help us to connect with what purity in physical form means.

My earlier research showed that crystal skulls take on the electromagnetic energies of their environment. Crystal skulls showed different frequencies when placed in environments with different ambient frequencies. The frequencies of the crystal skulls came very close to those of the environment they were in, and this result was initially surprising and disappointing. The expectation was that crystal skulls made of different materials would have frequencies that characterize them in a unique way, but I found that their energies, although slightly different, all reflect the energies of the environments they are placed in (*CS*, 62-70). It took a while for me to realize the importance of this finding. Because crystal skulls do indeed reflect their environment, when we hold a crystal skull, it takes on our energies and reflects them back to us. In that way, it gives us an opportunity to be grateful for what is and change whatever no longer serves us.

The characteristic of reflection can also lead to experiences that may be defined as negative. Within the world of those working with crystal skulls, sometimes ego is strongly reflected. This leads to competition and a need to own an ancient crystal skull to be "important." Crystal skulls reflect this need and amplify it. Some sellers, especially from China, like to use this need and sell fake ancient crystal skulls. This creates even more negative energy.

To reflect where we are on our journey is truly a great gift. However, we have to be willing to really look at what is reflected to us in order to learn from it. Then we can use this gift to help us transform anything that does not support us on our journey of remembering who we truly are.

Crystal Skulls Refract Energy

We may remember the term "refraction" from basic physics. When white light shines on a prism, the light will be refracted into different colors. We also see this phenomenon when sunlight shines through rain and the light of the sun gets refracted into a rainbow.

From a metaphysical perspective, we can say that a crystal skull refracts our light into different aspects. This enables us to see aspects that otherwise are not so easy to see. This allows us to explore aspects of our past — and maybe even future — lives. We also can explore the idea of being a multidimensional being. In general, we see that this characteristic is not actively used by many people. However, people may spontaneously have experiences that are consequences of this characteristic. Being aware that crystal skulls help us to see aspects of ourselves other than psychological and emotional aspects may help us to accept everything we perceive and receive as valid and valuable. Interpretation of such experiences may be more difficult. However, we can obtain clarity only when we accept whatever we experience as valuable and are willing to explore the meaning further. This can be done through sharing and receiving feedback. Make sure that you feel from your heart which feedback feels true and which does not. Of course, we can continue to explore more deeply with the crystal skulls, trusting that we will receive insights when the time is right. It is important to not become frustrated, to hold no attachments, and to always trust in divine timing.

Crystal Skulls Transmit Energies

A transmitter receives and sends out energies and information. The most commonly known transmitters are radios, televisions, and cell phones. Anything that sends and receives signals or energies may be called a transmitter. In a sense, we — human beings — are transmitters, and so are crystal skulls. Being a reflector also requires that a crystal skull be a transmitter. The skull needs to receive the signals and energies that we send out and broadcast them back. That makes it seem like the function of transmission is a consequence of being a reflector, but there is more to it.

Many people share the experience of their crystal skulls speaking through them. A very good example of this is described in the book *The Skull Speaks*[9]. The information that was received by Carole Davis came through the Mitchell-Hedges crystal skull that was used by a consciousness to transmit information. We see this as an increasingly common phenomenon. It is pretty common to hear, "My skull says ...." As valid as this may be, it is important to realize that the fact that a crystal skull can be used as a transmission station does not define who or what is using it as a transmission device. Sometimes what seems to be a transmission may be a reflection of a longing of the skull's owner that is sent back by the skull, and this may be mistaken for a message coming through or from the crystal skull.

While this characteristic of transmission holds great potential, it is also rather tricky. Unless we are well trained, it is not easy to discern what truly comes through the skull and what comes through our own systems and is based on longings that we hold subconsciously. When information comes through crystal skulls, we often ask, "Who is actually sending the message?" We are the ones who determine what frequency the crystal skull is attuned to, and that in turn determines who can use the crystal skull as a transmission station. Again, the key is to approach the crystal skull with love to ensure that it is activated to the highest possible frequencies so that the messages we receive come from a source that reflects love and respect for us. Therefore, activation is a very important subject, and we will look at that in detail in chapter 6.

It seems that crystal skulls, especially ancient skulls, become connected to a specific consciousness that uses the skull as its transmission station. When lecturing about their experiences with ancient skulls, caretakers speak factually that they communicate with the crystal skulls as if they were beings. Most likely they communicate with the consciousness that is connected with the skull. For most people, it is more difficult to know for certain if they are communicating with a being, so they simply accept that they talk with the skull.

This phenomenon of a consciousness connecting through a skull does not seem to be restricted to ancient or old skulls. There are many caretakers who establish deep connections with their contemporary crystal skulls. In the process, they activate their skulls to such a level that higher spiritual entities are able to connect with them. They may establish relationships with guides that transmits information through the skull to the caretaker. The characteristic of transmission opens doors that, for many people, may seem to be "a bridge too far." For others, however, it forms a powerful support system on the journey in becoming who they truly are.

Crystal Skulls Attune Energies

When higher spiritual beings choose to connect with the caretakers of crystal skulls, they activate the energies in a skull that are attuned to the caretaker. Such an activation enables an easier connection and communication. In the same way, it is possible for a caretaker to use a crystal skull to attune to certain energies, certain beings, or a certain consciousness. In a sense, crystal skulls help us to focus on a particular source we want to connect with. People use this characteristic to connect with guides, angels, dolphins, and even plants. This attunement makes it easier to channel with a crystal skull than without. However, attunement is not the most commonly used characteristic of crystal skulls. Some crystal skulls are more suitable than others as attuning systems. If this is a characteristic that is important to you, it is likely that you have been attracted intuitively to a crystal skull that strongly holds this particular characteristic.

Crystal Skulls Store Energy and Information

Storing energy and information is considered a major aspect of crystal skulls. Many of those working with crystal skulls believe that this is the major reason for the creation of crystal skulls. They believe that our ancestors stored information in crystal skulls to allow us to have a source of information that would help us during transformation.

The fact that information can be stored in crystals is applied in current technology. For example, storing information with lasers is called holographic imaging. This technology stores information in a three-dimensional way using crystals as a storage device. Generally, they use artificially grown crystals because they are flawless and can avoid interference when the information is retrieved. How this process works is very technical[10] and beyond the scope of this book.

Using a laser to create a holographic image demonstrates that it is possible to store electromagnetic frequencies in a crystal. As this works with light, it will work with other electromagnetic impulses, like our thoughts and intentions. Crystals have been used in this way for healing. With intent, information can be stored in crystal skulls, and it is believed that this has happened in the past. It is our task to learn how to access this information.

In technology, holographic imaging has not yet been perfected in such a way that it is available as a usable device. However, it does demonstrate that information can be stored in a crystal skull.

We use other technological systems that transfer information using electromagnetic frequencies as carrier waves — for example, radios, televisions, telephones, and computers. All these systems use certain electromagnetic frequencies to bring information from point A to point B. We need an apparatus to send the information via that frequency and one that receives and translates it into something we understand. All energy frequencies can be used to carry information; therefore, all energies that are connected with crystal skulls may be carriers of information. This is also true for energies connected with human beings. The fact that crystal skulls are transmission stations means that a lot of information can be passed on to and through a crystal skull. We will look at that in more detail in later chapters.

In summary, we can say that crystal skulls are linked to information in several ways. We are invited to learn to work with these different systems to be able to receive and work with information that is connected with crystal skulls to help us in our spiritual evolutionary process.

Crystal Skulls Amplify Energies

Crystal skulls are able to amplify energies, and most people who work with crystal skulls experience this phenomenon. The amplification is in part a consequence of the reflection of energies. The principle is simple: If you are working with your crystal skull from a place of love, the crystal skull will reflect love to you. As a consequence, you are able to love even more, which is reflected again to you. During a meditation, especially when you can stay focused, the energy will increase to such a degree that you may experience love beyond anything you have experienced before. The energy of love that you sent out initially will have been amplified to a deep and even ecstatic level.

To the extent that positive feelings can be amplified, so can negative ones. For example, if you meditate with your crystal skull and you think about something that gives you a feeling of importance, this need to be important will be amplified, and as a consequence, you even may act on it. Crystal skulls simply amplify whatever is present — for the better and for the worse. When you work with crystals skulls, be aware that they reflect and amplify so that you can use these qualities to grow, heal, and expand instead of pulling yourself deeper into ego.

Besides amplification through reflection, there is another aspect of amplification that is unique to crystal skulls. As I mentioned previously, there are energies that specifically belong to crystal skulls beyond the usual crystal energies. These crystal skull energies amplify all the characteristics of crystals, including amplification. This makes crystal skulls even more powerful amplifiers than crystals. Therefore, it is important to always be aware of the energy you send out, because it will return to you much stronger.

Other Qualities of Crystal Skulls

The six characteristics that are mentioned above are unique to crystals and crystal skulls. However, there are characteristics that are not unique to crystal skulls or crystals and are, to various degrees, a consequence of some of these main qualities. We will discuss some of the most important of these characteristics.

One quality is the ability to focus. We can use almost anything to help us to focus, such as music, a candle, a stone, a mantra — actually, any object. However, a crystal skull is the strongest tool to support focus because it reflects, refracts, and amplifies. Focusing is important because it allows us to use a crystal skull in the most optimal manner.

The importance of focusing energies, awareness, and attention is so great that although it is a consequence of earlier-mentioned characteristics, it deserves its own attention. The quality of focusing energies also helps us to focus our brains. In modern times, our brains are overstimulated by the noise of cities, radio, television, computers, and cell phones. Our brains are trained to shift focus continuously, and as a consequence, it becomes increasingly difficult to calm the brain and focus on what we choose to focus on. We can only truly change if we have the ability to focus and thereby become aware of what we are doing, how we are doing it, and what compels us do it. Only then can we connect with what is and is not in alignment with our true selves, which enables us to choose what we want to change. This gift from the crystal skulls to help us focus is of major importance.

Another quality that is attributed to crystal skulls is transformation, which is not unique to them. There are many energy systems that support transformational processes. In fact, any harmonic energy system can contribute to transformation, as can crystal skulls. Their ability to transform depends to a large degree on the level of activation. However, more important for the process of transformation is the fact that crystal skulls are reflectors, amplifiers, and points of focus.

Transformation takes place mainly when we are clear about what we want to transform. Once we know what to transform, we can set an intent for a transformation. (See more about intent in chapter 8.) Crystal skulls will amplify this intent to transform. Crystal skulls are also able to bring hidden issues to the surface. Once we are aware of these issues, we can transform all that no longer serves us on our spiritual journey.

Another characteristic of crystal skulls is that they can function as witnesses. You can use crystals and crystal skulls to record events due to their ability to store information. People who have developed the gift of psychometry — the ability to read what has happened with an object — can access the information of what a crystal skull has witnessed. This information can also be transferred to other crystals or crystal skulls. This ability to act as a witness is greater in crystal skulls than in crystals. The witness ability is not the same for all crystal skulls, as some are much better witnesses than others. To find which crystal skull is best as a witness requires a high level of sensitivity.

In summary, it can be concluded that crystal skulls have characteristics that make them very important tools for personal transformation, the development of various skills, and the expansion of awareness. They stimulate us to focus in meditation; they help us to develop the full potential of our brain (see chapter 4), and consequently our psychic abilities; and they help us to heal and balance. What amazing tools we been gifted by our ancestors! Crystal skulls are such important tools that it is truly worthwhile to explore the full extent of their potential.

CHAPTER TWO

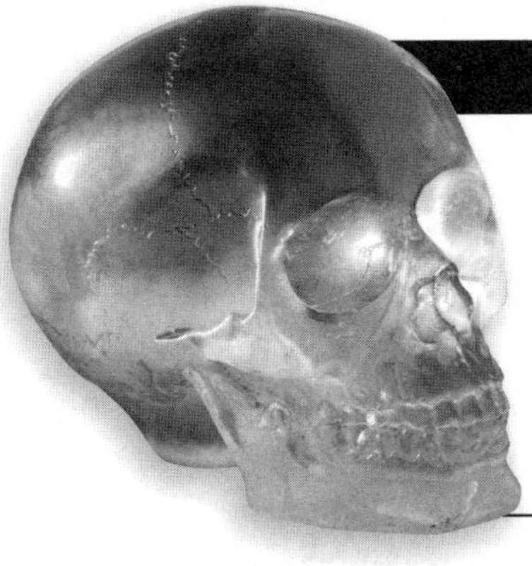

Choosing a Crystal Skull

The purpose of the first chapter was to help you to understand that crystal skulls are powerful support systems for your evolutionary progress. This second chapter is focused on a different general question: *How do I find a crystal skull that will help me most optimally on my journey?* There is a short answer to this question, while at the same time there are several aspects you could consider.

The short answer is that the best crystal skull for you is the crystal skull that you are most attracted to, that you resonate the most with, that makes you happiest, and that gives you the most immediate connected feeling. Such a crystal skull will give you what you need in the phase of your life when you meet it. Sometimes people are quite overwhelmed when they meet the first crystal skull they resonate with. However, make certain that you are connected with your heart; otherwise, the strong feelings may come from your mind and ego. The mind/ego has even guided people to buy "ancient" skulls that are not even made of natural material.

Most people believe they are not sensitive enough to perceive the feelings that guide them, and consequently they will have difficulty recognizing these sometimes-subtle feelings. In addition, most people have powerful minds that are used to doubting what is felt. In order to give the mind something to play with, I will give a more lengthy answer to the question along with some information that may be helpful in selecting your crystal skull(s).

General Considerations

Before even thinking about buying a crystal skull you may want to ask yourself a basic question: *Why do I want to have a crystal skull?* Even if the information in chapter 1 makes you curious, it still is important to ask that question. Without a deeper longing to work with it, a crystal skull will most likely become another object that will catch dust or, as many people joke, a rather expensive paperweight.

Let us assume that it feels right for you to work with a crystal skull. The next question is: *What do you feel the purpose of having a crystal skull is?* Do you have it because you want to achieve something, or for meditation, or for healing? Ask yourself — in all honesty — as many questions as you can come up with and see whether you receive some insights. To the best of your ability, listen to the messages you receive while you are connected with your heart. The more clearly you understand the reasons for your attraction to crystal skulls, the more powerful your work with them will be.

You do not need to go through these questions, of course. The simplest reason people buy crystal skulls is that they feel attracted them and want to find out why and what that attraction is. As I mentioned in the first chapter, the shape triggers our subconsciousness and awakens a longing that we need to explore. There is no doubt that this is a very good reason to get a crystal skull and explore that attraction.

For some people, a crystal skull is a meditation tool. They have observed friends or people at an event having profound experiences while meditating with crystal skulls. It is almost logical that the next step is to have your own crystal skull to explore the gifts that meditating with one brings.

Some people are already aware of the potential of crystal skulls. They are on a spiritual journey and want a crystal skull to help them understand who they are and remember the essence of their being. They know that crystal skulls can help them on their quest. This often is a very strong motivation that easily leads to a more in-depth exploration of these wonderful tools.

Another reason I often hear is that people want to help "heal" Earth. I strongly believe that this is an incorrect motivation. Earth does not need healing. If she needs healing, she is quite capable of taking care of herself. It is human beings who need healing, and there is no doubt that crystal skulls can help with that. The first step of healing may be transformation of the idea that we believe that we need to heal Earth and/or know how to do that. However, we can use crystal skulls to transform the low-vibrational human energies that we have left in many places and in many of the grids on Earth. We need to transform such energies to clear an area and allow it to fulfill its function again. That is not healing Earth but taking responsibility for what we, human beings, have created.

People also like to have crystal skulls to use them in ceremonies. These ceremonies can be personal or done with groups. Based on the characteristics of crystal skulls, it is obvious that they can greatly amplify the power of a ceremony.

Another reason for working with a crystal skull is almost inherently built into the way people work with their crystal skulls, and that is using them for personal healing. All crystal skulls are able to contribute in various degrees to the process of healing the person who works with them. However, crystal skulls also can be used to help others in their healing processes. Some crystal skulls have been used almost exclusively for that purpose during certain periods — like Max, the Texas crystal skull, when he was with Norbu Chen, a Tibetan healer (see Addendum I, skull 5). Nowadays several of the caretakers of crystal skulls that are considered ancient or old use their crystal skulls, at least partly, to support people in their healing process.

There are other personal motivations. Some people are researchers who have a deep longing to understand the energies of these wonderful tools. Their motivation can be to collect and share information to help people to use these tools more optimally on their journey of exploring who they are. This book is an example of that. For most people, there is not one single reason, but a mixture of reasons. Often the way they work with their crystal skulls changes over time, depending on the changing needs during their personal, spiritual journeys of expanding awareness.

It rarely happens that people restrict themselves to working with only one crystal skull. Caretakers of ancient or old skulls seem to do that more often than those of contemporary crystal skulls. Some even gather large groups of crystal skulls (image 2.1). People may do this for different reasons, one of which may be that working with different crystal skulls is helpful in the process of exploration, as was the case with caretakers of the crystal skull in image 2.1 and with my wife and I. Each of these crystal skulls gives different types of support and understanding.

Another reason may be that contemporary crystal skulls often are not very active and therefore do not give the same support and satisfaction as ancient skulls. Consequently, people continue to search for "the right crystal skull," because they subconsciously know that they are not yet having an optimal experience. However, it would be more helpful to continue the exploration of the crystal skull(s) they have. The intent of this book is to stimulate people to go further and deeper into their explorations.

Crystal skulls have something magical, and once you are hooked, they keep calling, "I want to join you ...." Some people call this the "crystal skull

2.1 A beautiful layout of the crystal skulls of caretaker Adele Sands (© Adele Sands)

bug" — easy to catch, difficult to get rid of. In such a case, simply enjoy the journey, but never forget to keep looking at the deeper motivations for your expansion.

Crystal Skulls of Different Crystals and Stones (Materials)

Another question that often arises has to do with the type of material the crystal skull has been carved from. "What is the best material for me? What kind of crystal skull shall I choose?" These are big questions for many people. Most people are attracted to skulls made of certain material, but they have heard that quartz is the best material for crystal skulls. As we will see, quartz is special in many ways, but that does not mean that it is the optimal material for you. Again, the most important aspect is to feel which type of crystal or stone attracts you, because that is always the best guidance.

There are a few aspects to consider. We are continuously changing, even when we try not to change. Change is inherently built into life in this reality; therefore, our needs for support on our journey will change as well. Different materials give different types of energy and the material you are attracted to may provide exactly the energies and support you need at that phase in your life. It is safe to say that every crystal skull, independent of age and material, is important and always provides support on a journey of discovering who you are. Therefore, in most cases, any discussion about which material is more important is irrelevant. Trust your journey and go with what feels best.

Many people feel that it is important to know what the properties of each material are. This question has validity — knowledge can be of support. However, it can also prevent us from exploring our personal experiences. There is a tendency to believe that "they" know better, so we dismiss our experiences when they are seemingly different.

Information can work as a sort of "programming." If information tells us that a certain crystal has certain qualities, our tendency is to see whether we will be able to feel what we are supposed to feel. If that does not happen, we may feel that we are doing something wrong.

The effect of certain energies on our system can be rather complex. For example, if it is said that a certain stone works on the heart chakra, we do not necessarily feel it there. We may feel it in areas that prevent us from opening our hearts. If we deny these feelings because they are seemingly not connected to the heart, then we may miss some very important information. Looking at the qualities of gemstones and earth stones is useful to help you to understand what you have experienced — not to get an expectation of what you need to experience.

When you compare the opinions of different authors about the qualities of certain earth stones and gemstones, you may find quite a lot of differences. At the same time, there are standard lists of qualities that people spread on the Internet that have become "truth." That is another reason to be careful in accepting what people say about gemstones and earth stones. Over time I learned to forget what people say about the qualities of the different crystals and stones. I simply acknowledge my experience, learn from it, and feel gratitude for it. I know that my experience of a certain crystal has changed over time, and I know it will keep changing. We are still in an initial phase of understanding the true nature and qualities of crystals. If you would like to "know" the qualities of crystals and gemstones, there are enough books on the subject, and the Internet also provides a lot of information[1]. However, I believe that it is better to learn to trust and honor what you experience than to follow others.

Carving Style

Contemporary crystal skulls are carved mainly in China and Brazil but also in Nepal, Mexico, and Germany. Some high-quality crystal skulls have also been carved in the United States. People talk a lot about the quality of the carving style and also about the quality of crystal skulls carved in China versus the ones carved in Brazil. Certain master carvers, like Leandro Souza from Brazil, have become popular. Since carving crystal skulls is an art, certain styles become popular and more expensive. Although you may prefer a certain style of carving, it is not fundamental for your journey and the understanding of crystal skulls.

Carvers influence the quality of the skulls they make. Many carvers can be considered artists who are able to sense the form that best expresses a particular piece of crystal.

The attitude of a carver is also an important influence on the initial quality of a crystal skull. Is the carver dedicating his full craftsmanship into what he is making? Does a carver like what she is carving, or is she just filling the day to make money? However, this hardly ever makes enough of an impact that it cannot be compensated for with heart-centered work with your crystal skull.

In most cases, people will not be able to sense consciously the differences between carvings, but sometimes they will know subconsciously. Therefore, it is important to trust that a crystal skull you are attracted to most likely is the right one for you: at least there is a high likelihood that that skull resonates with you and will support your journey.

Some people believe that crystal skulls that are machine-carved by Chinese carvers do not have souls while hand-carved crystal skulls by Brazilian carvers do[2]. This is an unfair and offensive generalization, as there are masterful carvers in both countries. Some of the Chinese work is masterful and made with true dedication while some of the Brazilian skulls lack basic energy. It is important to realize that often a crystal skull made by a master carver has involved work done by other people, often apprentices.

When people start working with crystal skulls, they begin to see them as beautiful and begin to choose skulls based on their visual aspects. There is no doubt that the visual appeal of a crystal skull will help to deepen your connection as a basis for the activation of that crystal skull. However, buying crystal skulls to create a collection is contrary to the true purpose of crystal skulls — they need to be worked with and, as we will see, activated to fulfill their purpose.

Sizes of Crystal Skulls

The size of a crystal skull is another consideration for many people. Often people ask, "Does size matter?" The answer is a cryptic no and yes. No, size does not matter when you use a crystal skull for personal use. For example, a crystal skull of 1 inch (2.5 cm) offers all of the characteristics and all qualities of the material it is made of and all of the energies you need.

People refer to size in relationship to the amount of information that can be stored in a crystal skull. Of course more material will give more storage capacity. The question is, however, whether you need that extra storage space. The information that can be stored in a skull that is 1 inch in size is already more than what people can process in a lifetime. Because we are unable to process all information that we receive, we select only the information we want to process — often subconsciously. We only need to connect with information that helps us to understand who we are, and a small crystal skull can help us to do that.

All of the information held by all crystal skulls is available in the crystal skull field. Any crystal skull can connect us with that field — the size of the skull is irrelevant. What is important is the level of activation (see chapters 6 and 7).

Then why is the answer also yes to the question of whether size matters? The size of an energy field around a crystal skull depends on the size of the crystal skull. Other determining factors are the type of material the skull has been carved from and, more importantly, its level of activation. The largest fields are created by quartz.

Table 1 summarizes data about the relative sizes of crystal skull fields. It estimates the fields of energy around various quartz crystal skulls, both from when they were purchased and after they were activated to thirty-six layers (for an explanation of layers, see chapter 6). Sam is my and my wife's clear quartz skull; Synergy is an ancient crystal skull (see Addendum I, skull 3). See image 2.2 for Synergy and Sam together.

The data in this table clearly shows that activation is a major factor determining the size of a field around a crystal skull. Size is a secondary factor. The table only shows crystal skulls that have thirty-six activated layers. Even Synergy, a fully activated crystal skull, still has the ability to expand its field. Apparently we are not yet able to use the full potential of a fully awakened crystal skull. There is still much to learn.

You may wonder what the importance of a larger field is. It is only important when you have certain goals in mind. For example, for a large ceremony,

Size or name of skull	State	Size field
2 in (5 cm)	just carved activated	1.3 feet (0.4 m) 58.3 yards (52.5 m)
3 in (7.5 cm)	just carved activated	4.6 feet (1.4 m) 220 yards (198 m)
4 in (10 cm)	just carved activated	13.2 feet (4.3 m) 0.7 miles (1.1 km)
5 in (12.5 cm)	just carved activated	30.4 feet (9.3 m) 3.9 miles (6.3 km)
6 in (15 cm)	just carved activated	163 feet (49.3 m) 8.5 miles (13.6 km)
Sam	just carved activated 2009 2011	192 feet (58.2 m) 13 miles (20.8 km) 16.2 miles (25.9 km)
Synergy	2011	19.9 miles (31.8 km)

Table 1 Sizes of the radiuses of the energy fields of quartz crystal skulls of different sizes after carving and activation

it may be wise to have a skull of a larger size to create a powerful supporting field. Also when people clear energies of past human activities that do not support the spiritual evolution of humankind, like the energies of wars or destruction, larger crystal skulls are more beneficial.

Follow Your Heart

The information given in this chapter may be helpful in choosing your crystal skull or skulls. However, I would like to repeat that the most important consideration is to follow your heart, following what feels most right for you in the moment. We can plan whatever we want with our minds, but the journey of remembering may guide us in all kinds of unexpected directions. We will never know beforehand all aspects of our journey. It will unfold when we are willing to move forward one step at a time. It is impossible to plan

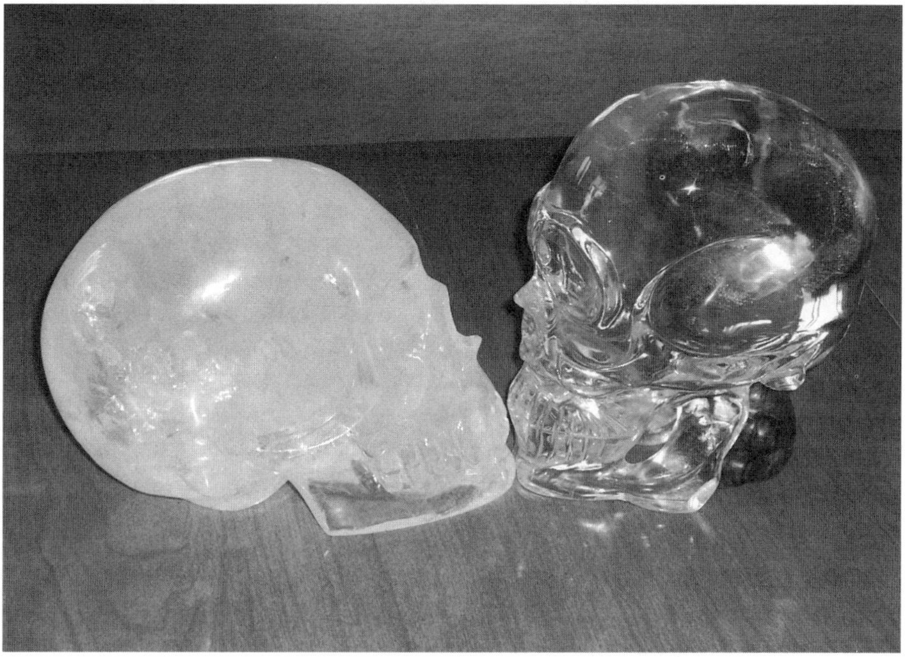

2.2 The ancient crystal skull Synergy (left) of caretaker Sherry Whitfield and the contemporary crystal skull Sam (right) of the author and his wife

with certainty in each moment what we will need in the future. Therefore, it is not important what we "think" when we select a crystal skull but what we feel. Feeling will always lead us to situations that will stimulate us to move forward on our journey in the easiest way. At the same time, do not make your choices too serious. Enjoy the process and trust that it will always lead you to where you need to go. Realize that the next step on our journey always involves making another choice.

CHAPTER THREE

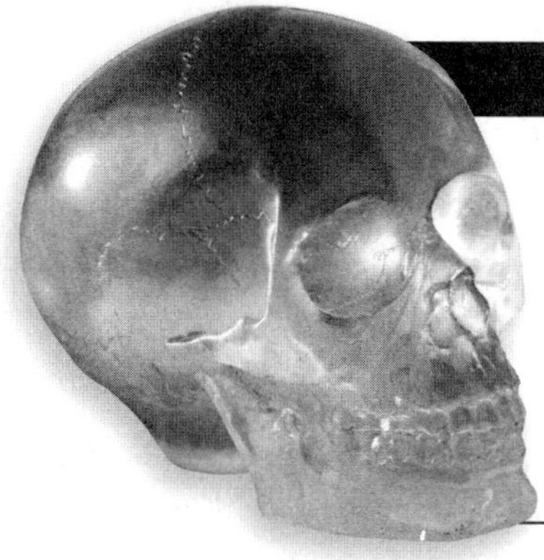

Preparing and Maintaining Your Crystal Skull

When people acquire their first crystal skulls, a common concern arises as to whether it needs to be cleansed, especially if it has arrived through the mail or was from a shop. Those who have explored the topic are aware that there are almost as many different opinions about cleansing as there are people who offer those opinions, which vary from "no need" to "absolutely." While most people believe that crystal skulls need to be cleansed, the ways to cleanse them may vary. Maybe the question is not so much which method to use but more about how efficient each method is and which one resonates with you. Even when a suggestion has been given, we still have a tendency to ask about other methods, indicating that people have doubts about the efficiency of the different methods. That is especially true when people do not have the ability to energetically check the effectiveness of a certain method. They prefer to use multiple methods "just to be sure." Unless you have a crystal skull that has been programmed negatively, any method used with love, clear intent, and trust will do the job effectively.

There is a lot of information about cleansing that comes from people working with crystals. Most of these methods are applied to crystal skulls. Given the fact that there is so much information available, I will restrict this discussion to summarizing the effectiveness of different methods as they apply to crystal skulls.

In the first chapter, I already mentioned that, from an energy point of view, there is a difference between a crystal and a crystal skull. These differences will be discussed later, but it is important to mention that crystal skulls have different needs than crystals have with respect to cleansing. The need for cleansing also changes when a crystal skull becomes more activated. Therefore, you may find or hear comments that may sound incorrect for crystals but are quite proper for crystal skulls because of the different energies.

Cleansing after Receiving Your Crystal Skull

It is highly unlikely that you purchased an ancient or old crystal skull. The energetic condition of an ancient crystal skull is so different from a recently carved contemporary crystal skull that the caretaking and cleansing of such a skull is totally different. Independent of age, every crystal skull likes to be cleaned physically when arriving in a new environment to remove dust and grease from transportation and people handling it.

Unless people have worked with an ancient or old skull in a negative way, used it for black magic, or used it as part of dark ceremonies and human sacrifice, no special cleansing is needed. If such a crystal skull has been used in a negative way, its cleansing is beyond the ability of most people and needs to be done by an expert in such techniques. In the unlikely event that you encounter such a skull, the best advice I can give is to stay away from it or to ask advice from a specialist. Working with those energies is beyond the purpose of this book, especially because each case is unique and may require different techniques.

When negative energies are a consequence of being a witness of negative situations, the energies are easier to remove. The optimal methods will be discussed below.

Most people obtain contemporary crystal skulls. After a physical cleansing with mild soap and water (with exceptions we will discuss later), basically all cleansing is energy cleansing. There are different methods that can be used that can roughly (and arbitrarily) be separated into a few groups. The first group consists of methods that use ceremony. The second group uses outside forces, the third uses Mother Earth, and the last is cleansing through energy work.

Ceremonial Methods

It is possible to design your own ceremony to cleanse your crystal skull. You can use methods you have learned from traditions you are familiar with. All of them will have a certain value, and when done from the heart and with clear intent, they will work.

The method that is most commonly used is smudging. Smudging is generally seen as a Native American tradition, but different forms of it have been used over eons of time and across many traditions. Many churches use incense with the same principle: Something is burned — like herbs (sweetgrass and sage), trees (cedar, Juniper), incense (many different types; follow your heart), or copal[1] — and the smoke, which contains the energies of the burned material, is used to clean spaces, objects, and people. It often is the first part of a ceremony to create an optimal energetic state in the people who will participate and in the environment in which the ceremony will be performed.

There is no doubt that smudging works. However, it works mostly on the ambient energy fields and the energy fields that we can summarize under the term aura; the fields around people, animals, plants, crystals, and objects. It often gives a feeling of well-being and relaxation because it brings the energies around us into a better balance. In general, smudging does not go deep into the energy system of people or living beings.

For crystal skulls, smudging works on the energies that have attached themselves to the skull during carving, transportation, and being in a shop or other places. Smudging is a good cleansing method for starting a relationship with your crystal skull.

Outside Forces or Energies

I place the majority of recommended methods for cleansing in this category. An example is placing a crystal skull in or under water. Not all material can be placed in or under water. Some material will get damaged or even dissolve in water, such as selenite, calcite, and halite. Many people believe that placing your crystal skull under tap water is a good method to cleanse it. Other than cleaning the dirt off of it, I do not believe this to be true. Water from a tap is "dead" water and actually is not really good for anything (not even to drink). It can have a draining effect energetically. If you would like to use water to cleanse your crystal skull, use living water — like mountain streams or the ocean. However, if you decide to place your crystal skull in the sea, make sure that there are no big waves or strong currents. Several skulls have been lost to unexpected waves. Cleansing with water that is alive — especially if it is salt water — also helps to balance energies within the crystal skull. However, there are more crystals that are damaged by salt water than fresh water. Allow the skull to dry naturally, preferably in the sun, to be charged with great energies.

If you are too far from the sea, you can give your crystal skull a salt bath. But be careful, as salt can be detrimental for certain crystals — like alabaster, calcite, carnelian, hematite, labradorite, lepidolite, moldavite, opal, and turquoise, to name a few. The concentration of the salt will vary, depending on the type of energies you would like to remove. The darker the energies (that is, the lower the vibrations), the higher the concentration of salt you will need. In almost all cases, a solution of one half pound of sea salt in a gallon of water will do[2]. You also can cover the crystal skull with sea salt for a couple of days.

You can place your skull in the sun or in moonlight. Placing crystal skulls in the sun and moonlight actually contributes more to charging them with energies than to cleansing. However, the more activated the crystal skull is, the fewer the negative energies that remain in the skull — unless programmed in special ways. So activation to increase the vibration is the best way to create optimal protection. If you decide to place your crystal skulls in sunlight, be aware that the colors of certain crystals will fade, like amethyst, celestite, opal, aragonite, and turquoise.

Another good cleansing method is to place your crystal skull in a large quartz crystal cluster. Make sure that your quartz cluster is activated sufficiently and cleansed; otherwise, you may end up with two objects that need cleansing. You can also place your new crystal skull within a circle of activated crystal skulls.

A last method I would like to mention is the placement of your crystal skull in a bowl of flower petals, particularly roses. Make sure that you express gratitude to the flowers from which you obtain the petals. Even when no cleansing is needed, the placement of crystal skulls in petals is an uplifting and wonderful experience.

Realize that whatever method you use, the most powerful effect comes from your belief in the method. Therefore, it is important to be convinced that the chosen method works and then work with it from your heart and whole being.

Bury the Crystal Skull in the Earth

Most of you will not prefer to bury your crystal skull in the earth, especially since many of you have just acquired new skulls and it is hard to part with them. Burying your crystal skull is a method that you do not need to use unless other mentioned methods have failed. It is especially effective when the crystal skull contains heavy dark energies and is used for those that have been part of ritual killings or black-magic rituals.

The duration of the burial of a skull is experimental. It seems that, for most cases, a period of one month is sufficient. This method is often seen as part of a larger ritual to cleanse negative energies. The most optimal time to bury a skull is when there is a full moon, and the burial and the timing are often part of this larger ritual[3]. If you decide that you want to bury your crystal skull, be sure that you properly mark the place. If you don't do this, you will not be the first person who has had to dig around in the yard to try to find your crystal skull (or crystal).

Whether or not you want to use this method will depend on what you feel guided to do. I can repeat this statement over and over: Always follow your heart. When you feel — not think — that you are doing the right thing, it always will be reflected in the results.

Clearing through Intent and Energy Work

Another method is available for those who work with energy modalities. This method is based on the idea that human beings can create powerful energy fields that can heal, balance, and cleanse other systems. The key is to have a clear intent. With a clear intent in mind, most people who work with crystals and crystal skulls can cleanse them energetically. The ability to transform or clear energies from a crystal skull depends on the training and the experience of the person. Because intent is so important, I have included a whole chapter on the subject (chapter 8).

Personally, I always use the energy-clearing method for everything I clear. I consider it a part of learning to sense, feel, recognize, and work with energies. I have learned from failures and successes, both of which I consider to be experiences that guide me in life.

Other People Working with Your Crystal Skull

Another common question is: *Is it okay to let other people work with my crystal skull?* Such a question is only asked when there is the idea that others can do harm to your crystal skull. The answer is simple: If it feels right to let somebody hold your crystal skull, then trust that it is all right to do so. If you are connected to your heart and it does not feel right, you have to stick to your truth. However, when the reason you do not let people hold your skull is based on fear, it is important to work through your fears and determine their source. This is especially so because these fears will be amplified by your crystal skull.

Sometimes we worry that most other people do not have a high vibration and can "mess up" the energies of our crystal skulls. Or maybe we are afraid that a person may have an ominous agenda and will do something to our crystal skulls that we do not like.

The key is the level of activation and, consequently, the overall vibration of your crystal skull. All energy exchange is based either on resonance or on intent. The intent of almost all people is to experience your crystal skull. With such an approach, the law of resonance will come into effect. When your crystal skull is sufficiently activated, it will have a powerful energy field. The object or person that is most powerful will determine the resonance vibration. A less strong system will begin to resonate with a stronger system. Therefore, people will resonate with an activated skull instead of the skull resonating with the person. We see this phenomenon most clearly with the fully activated — or ancient — crystal skulls.

There may be people with a strong ego who would like to do something with your crystal skull, sometimes solely to demonstrate how powerful they are. Therefore, if you are uncomfortable, do not let such a person work with or hold your crystal skull. Make sure that people understand that they can work with your crystal skull only with your permission. Fortunately most people are aware of the need to ask. When a person does not ask you may need to be more careful and follow your inner guidance and intuition. If you doubt, choose the safe path and say no to such people.

I have a lot of experience in allowing other people to work with our crystal skulls. My wife, Jeanne, and I are the caretakers of over 230 crystals skulls. Every week we open our home to host a crystal skull meditation. People work with these skulls during the meditation, and we have never experienced our crystal skulls being affected in a negative way. On the contrary, actually, over time the field around the crystals created during the meditation has become so strong that only positive experiences are created, and the few challenging situations were transformed easily into positive ones.

Allowing someone to hold your crystal skull is easy. Allowing a person to take care of your crystal skull for a certain length of time is quite different. Many people will not easily allow another person to take care of their crystal skull(s). However, if you trust a person enough to do so, it may be beneficial for the skull and for all involved. We often have crystal skulls of other people stay in our circle for shorter or longer periods of time.

It is important to realize that no object really belongs to us. If things belonged to us, we could take them with us when we transit this dimension/world. Crystal skulls have the same purpose as human beings: to share their essence with this world and to support everyone who comes in contact with them during their journey.

Your Ongoing Relationship with Your Crystal Skull

What do I need to do with my crystal skull when I have it for a longer period of time? That answer is simple. The key point is to love your crystal skull and work with it regularly. Placing a crystal skull on a shelf is not the right way to take care of it and build a relationship with it. Anybody who has crystal skulls knows that they need to be worked with. That in and of itself could be a reason to let other people work with your crystal skull, especially when you have more than one of them. It becomes difficult to pay attention to all of them. It is helpful to organize crystal skull meditations, because that will create an increasingly powerful field that one or two people alone cannot create. It may sound surprising to some, but the best way to maintain an ongoing relationship is to treat your crystal skull like a person you love. This means that you will interact with it as often as you can. It is the only way to get to know your crystal skull in an increasingly intimate way and create the most optimal relationship.

Assuming that you can approach your crystal skulls in this loving way, you will create a situation in which no maintenance is needed other than cleansing them from dirt and grease because they are frequently being held in your or other people's hands.

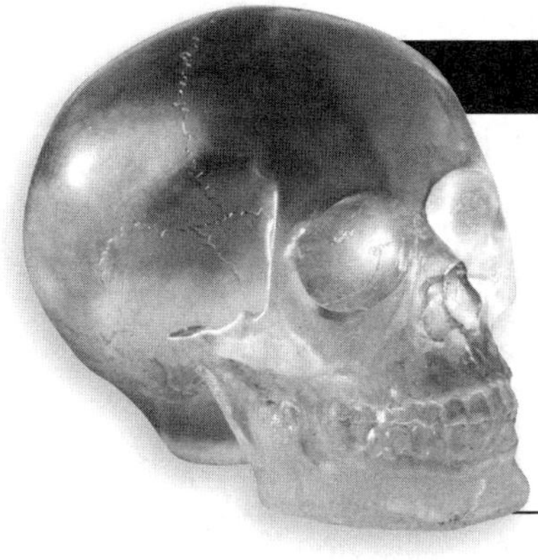

CHAPTER FOUR

Working with Your Crystal Skull

Some people seem to have clear motives to start, but once they have a crystal skull, they wonder, "Now what?" We mentioned in chapter 2 several different reasons why people may buy crystal skulls, but a lot of people buy their first crystal skull simply because they are excited to do so in the moment.

This chapter will describe a few ways in which crystal skulls can be used. This is by no means a complete overview of what you can do with your crystal skull. Once you start working with it, you will find your own unique way. If you are heart-centered, everything you do with your crystal skull will support you personally and will also support the larger whole. Therefore, the key in working with crystal skulls is *love*. Without love, crystal skulls will not awaken to their full potential, so the support for our growth will come to a standstill. With love we keep growing, independent of the way we use our crystal skulls.

Meditation

Most commonly, crystal skulls are used for meditation. Many people say that they find it difficult to meditate. They believe that meditation is useful only when you have no thoughts. If that were the case, many people who meditate regularly would be failures, because for most people it is very difficult, if not impossible, to quiet the mind longer than a couple of minutes. If the mind becomes quiet, people often feel that they are no longer really awake. They have no clue where they are and what they are "doing." This is a consequence of a change in their brain frequencies, and it is best to accept such experiences as part of the process of meditation.

The comments people make about meditation raise the fundamental question of the nature of meditation. For some people, the answer seems to be clear, but for many it is not. From my perspective, meditation is a technique to train the brain to quiet itself so that we can listen to the heart — our connection to our soul. For some, the purpose of meditation is to master a technique, but I believe the main purpose is to support us on the journey of remembering who we are. To receive answers to the question of who we are, we cannot rely on our minds. The mind will only tell us what we already know, as its function is directly coupled with the brain. As simplistic as it may sound, the function of the brain is to survive. The function of the heart is to help us remember who we are — to reconnect with our essence, our soul, our multidimensional self.

In order to understand meditation, we first have to understand something about the brain. The brain, its functions, the brain waves, and the relationship between the brain and heart are more extensively described in *Gifts of Mother Earth* (6-12). Even though I do not wish to be repetitive, it is important to highlight a few principles within the context of this book.

The brain is always active, and these activities can be made visible with an electroencephalogram (EEG). An EEG registers the electric impulses of brain activity. The brain has a number of recognizable frequencies that reflect brainwaves during different activities. These brain frequencies are grouped into five frequency ranges that are defined by Greek letters: beta, alpha, theta, delta, and gamma. Because the five types of brain waves are important in understanding some of the effects of crystal skulls, we will describe these five groups (for further information, see *GME*, 7-8).

The Five Brain States

The five different brain states can be described as follows:

Beta state. The brain waves have a frequency range from 12 to 36 Hz. This is the most active state. The patterns are generally very irregular. These are the brain waves of alertness, concentration, and cognition. They are associated with focused attention, peak concentration, clear thinking, processing visual information, and hand-eye coordination, but also with anxiety, worry, and fight-or-flight activity (heightened alertness). For most people, this is the dominant state of the brain during the day when the eyes are open and we are listening and thinking during analytical problem solving, judgment, decision making, and processing information about the world around us.

Alpha state. The brain waves have a frequency range between 8 and 12 Hz with a peak in activity around 10 Hz. The patterns are more regular than with beta waves. The keywords for this state are relaxation, visualization, and creativity. Its attributes are deep relaxation, detached awareness, non-drowsiness, alertness, reflection, introspection, and contemplation, with an open mental focus. Alpha is the link from the conscious beta state (focused attention) to the subconscious theta and the higher-conscious delta states (deeper states of awareness). The frequencies of your brain activity most likely move into the alpha state when you quietly watch the sun set or watch water flowing in a creek.

Theta state. The brain waves in this state range in frequency from 4 to 8 Hz. Key descriptors of it are meditation, intuition, and memory. It is also called the dream state. Some refer to this state as the functioning of the subconscious mind, as it is found in meditative states, prayer and spiritual awareness, dowsing[1], drifting off to sleep, and dreaming, as well as after we come out of the delta state. This is the subconscious connection to the higher consciousness and the akashic records. It is the state that leads to self-healing. The theta state has been identified as the gateway to learning and memory. You need this state to connect on a deeper level with Earth and crystalline energies. This is a natural state in children until they are thirteen years old. It is also a state that gives feelings of oneness and knowing.

Delta state. This is the state with the lowest frequency, ranging from 0.1 to 4 Hz. The delta is defined as the higher conscious mind. It acts as a radar or unconscious scanning device for intuition (hunch, sixth sense), instinctive action, inner knowing, and deep psychic awareness. Some people call it the gateway to the soul. Normally this state is only found in deep dreamless sleep or in trance, but it can also be induced in a very deep meditation and even during dowsing. Neurons, which are not involved in the processing of information, all fire at the same time. Certain frequencies in the delta state also trigger the release of human growth hormone, which is beneficial for healing and regeneration. It is the dominant rhythm in infants up to one year of age.

Gamma state. The gamma state has the highest frequencies — above 36 Hz. Recent research showed that these frequencies can go up quite high, to about 200 Hz. Initially the gamma state was defined as the frequency range of 36 to 44 Hz, and this remains a popular definition. Higher-frequency ranges are called hypergamma (up to 100 Hz) and lambda frequencies (100 to 200 Hz). Others define the gamma range as 36 to 70 Hz. Basically, the gamma frequencies are the ones that represent the simultaneous processing of information from different areas. This can be called "high-level information processing." Also, precognition is connected with the gamma state. Research shows that long-term meditation develops a high level of gamma frequencies and high levels of brain synchrony and coordination[2].

Brain States and Crystal Skulls

When a person meditates with a crystal skull, assuming this person is able to stay focused, the first three brainwave states will be part of the brain activity. The meditation starts in the beta frequencies, the state we are in most of the time. This is the time to prepare yourself for meditation — for example, setting up the space, selecting a crystal skull you want to meditate with, selecting music, or lighting candles. Often this preparation can be relaxing and helps you activate alpha brainwaves. These alpha brainwaves become more powerful when you sit down and begin to relax. When you relax deeply and bring your awareness to a crystal skull, a shift to the meditative brainwaves, the theta waves, takes place almost automatically. You can sit in that state for as long as it feels comfortable. Whenever thoughts come up and begin to take over, take a deep breath and refocus on the crystal skull you are meditating with. Never get frustrated, because you will move immediately into the beta frequencies, bringing yourself out of the meditative state.

The theta state is very important because it connects us with our subconscious during dreaming and meditation. In this state, everything we perceive is symbolic. The symbolic meaning can be close to the meaning we would give it in a beta state, but it also can be quite different. Therefore, it is important to be careful with how we interpret what we perceive in a meditative state, and similarly so in the dream state.

Ultimately, we want to go to an even deeper meditative state, moving through the theta into the delta state. The delta state is our doorway into higher consciousness and therefore our connection with the Infinite Source — the place of all possibilities, the place from where we will remember who we truly are.

When we are in a theta or delta state and are fully awake, we are in a state that is called "psychic." In a psychic state, we are able to receive and perceive information beyond that of the five senses and translate it into something that can be shared. Meditation with our crystal skulls stimulates the shift of our brain into theta and ultimately delta, and, therefore, we can say that crystal skulls stimulate the development of our psychic abilities. I have observed this phenomenon with many people.

It is possible to program our crystal skulls to help us to move at will into any of the three frequency ranges below beta. That is our goal because it allows us to access information from different sources in the moment we choose.

What follows is a meditation that has its basis in a visualization that is taught in a remote viewing course given by Gerald O'Donnell[3]. It is adapted for those who work with crystal skulls.

The Crystal Skull Brainwave Training and Programming

Before you start this meditation/visualization (see also meditation CD), first select a crystal skull that you would like to program during this visualization so that it becomes the designated crystal skull that you use to go to any brain state you wish. Preferably choose a smaller skull (around 2 inches is ideal) because it is easier to take such a crystal skull with you when you travel. If you want, you can program one to take with you and a larger one you can use at home. Hold this crystal skull in your hand or hands during the whole visualization journey.

> *Take some deep inhalations and exhalations to help you begin to relax. Stay alert. Do not go into a meditative state. This visualization is to help you recognize the different brain states so that you can go there at will. Therefore, do not move ahead of the directions for the visualization.*
>
> *Imagine that you are a tall crystal building with many levels. The number of levels is not important; you will see the building in your imagination exactly as it is supposed to be. Now, imagine that you are standing on top of this building. The top represents the normal level of brain activity, the beta frequencies. Looking around from the top of your building, you see many other buildings around you that belong to other people. You notice that all these buildings look at least slightly — sometimes even quite — different from each other. You are aware that you can see and even study these other buildings, but true connection with them and access to them is not possible at this level.*
>
> *On top of the roof of your building you see a little structure that turns out to be access to an elevator. Above the elevator, you see your name in golden letters helping you to realize that this is your elevator into your building.*
>
> *Step into the elevator, close the door, and press the button to go down. The elevator begins to move down. Feel yourself sinking deeper*

into yourself. As you count down from 5 to 1, you will sink deeper and deeper into yourself, 5 ... going down ... 4 ... going deeper into yourself without going too quickly. Enjoy the ride ... 3 ... deeper, but move only with the speed of the elevator ... 2 ... still deeper ... and 1 ... the elevator stops. Open the door and step out.

You see a large sign that reads: Level deep alpha. This is the floor that represents the deep alpha level. You see a chair, and you can choose to sit on it or walk around. The purpose is to explore this floor that represents your deep-level alpha. Take time to sense and feel how this floor feels — what impressions you get — and to see what it has to offer you.

*When you feel that you really have connected with this floor, become aware of your skull. Move to the chair — if you are not already sitting on it — and from a connection with your crystal skull and a deep connection with the floor you are on, say, "**Deep-level alpha**." You have now programmed both yourself and your crystal skull with the experience of deep-level alpha. From now on, whenever you say "deep-level alpha" while holding this crystal skull, you will move immediately into this state.*

Take a deep breath, get out of the chair, and walk back to the elevator. The door is still open. Step into it, close the door, and again press the button to descend. Feel yourself sinking deeper into yourself. Count from 5 to 1 while you sink deeper into yourself ... 5 ... going deeper with the speed of the elevator, not faster ... 4 ... still deeper ... 3 ... feel how you are changing and relaxing more deeply into yourself ... 2 ... deeper ... and 1 ... the elevator stops again. Open the door and step out.

As soon as you step out of the elevator, you see a sign that reads, "Level deep theta." This is the floor that represents the state of deep-level theta. Again there is a chair for you to sit on to explore how this level of deep theta feels. Or you can choose to walk around. The key is to experience as optimally as possible this state of deep-level theta.

*When you feel complete, focus on your crystal skull and move to the chair — if you are not yet sitting on it. From a deep connection with your skull and the floor you are on, now say, "**Deep-level theta**." Be totally convinced that you and your crystal skull are fully programmed so that anytime you hold this skull and say, "Deep-level theta," you will be immediately in that state. Feel the trust that your crystal skull will always help you to experience this state.*

Again take a deep breath, get out of your chair, and walk back to the elevator. Step in, close the door, and push the button to go down. As you count down from 5 to 1, you will again sink deeper into yourself, moving into the deepest depth of your being ... 5 ... deeper ... 4 ... deeper, you begin to realize that you are entering levels you rarely or never visit ... 3 ... deeper, and while you may think that it is hardly possible ... 2 ... you still go deeper, and then at 1, the elevator stops. You are at the lowest level — the ground floor — the place where you can connect with all other buildings you saw at the top. You have reached the deepest levels in yourself, the level that gives you access to All That Is in a natural way. Open the door and step out.

You see in front of you the lowest level, the ground floor of your building. There is a sign that reads, "Level deep delta." By now you know your preferred way of exploring a floor. This is an unfamiliar or even totally unknown territory, so it is exciting to feel, sense, and explore this level, this state. Take your time.

*When you feel complete, focus on your crystal skull. Move to your chair and, from a deep connection with your crystal skull and the ground floor you are on, say, "**Deep-level delta**." Feel the trust that your crystal skull will always bring you back to this level whenever you desire by saying, "Deep-level delta."*

You now have explored the three deeper levels of your building, of your brain. It is time to go back to the beta state, the state in which you are in at the top of your crystalline building — the state of your daily activities. Step into the elevator, close the door, and push the button to ascend.

The trip up goes much faster than the trip down. Count from 1 to 5, and at 5 you will be back again at the top level of your building ... 1 ... the elevator speeds up. You can feel that you begin to come slowly out of the depth of your meditative state induced during your journey down ... 2 ... higher and higher up ... 3 ... you begin to become more awake, realizing the wonderful journey you just made ... 4.... you realize that you will always be able to go back to the three levels you have visited, especially with the help of your crystal skull ... 5 ... the elevator stops at the top of your building. Step out of the elevator feeling completely alert and completely vibrant, active, and alive.

This meditation/visualization may work the first time, but most likely it will be helpful to do this a few times. Make sure you always use the same crystal skull so that the program is clearly and powerfully induced into your crystal skull of choice.

Oneness or Basic Meditation

While it is very helpful to work with the brain states, it is at least equally important to address the heart and to practice a meditation based on love and oneness. This is a meditation that trains you to go to love anytime you wish and to make this a part of your daily life. Again, it is very helpful to use a crystal skull during this meditation that can assist you in going to this state anytime you wish. When Jeanne and I give workshops, we always start with this meditation.

The Oneness Meditation is a basic one that can be used in combination with other meditations, especially as an introduction to other meditations. Once you are connected with Oneness, you can create powerful intentions. We will offer other meditations in this book (it is planned to make a CD that includes all meditations given in this book[4]) and will always suggest that you start with the following meditation.

Sit in a comfortable and relaxed position. Feeling comfortable will support your meditation better than trying to maintain an uncomfortable "ideal" position. Start with some deep inhalations and exhalations. At every exhalation, relax a little bit more. Feel yourself sinking into the here and now. Realize that by choosing to meditate, nothing else matters right now.

When you feel relaxed, realize that your brain has become less active. This means your system is beginning to align itself more with your heart. Now fully shift your awareness to your heart area, the area behind your breastbone. With every inhalation, activate the heart center even more and feel the energy of love expanding throughout your body. For now, restrict this flow to your physical body.

Be aware that the love energy is spreading into every little corner, into every cell. That means that love is beginning to become the directing force. This allows every cell to work optimally and lets them begin to synchronize with each other. This helps the physical system to heal and balance.

Now allow the energy of love to expand beyond the physical body and let it fill the whole room (when you do this outdoors, define the area — for example, create a bubble of love with a radius of 100-150 feet or 30-45 meters). If you are in a group, each person present will now sit in the love energy of everyone else. Feel how that creates a strong connection with everyone present and how this field becomes a coherent field of love.

In this field of love, supported by each other in a group, we come closer to unconditional love and consequently to an optimal heartbeat. That frequency will be closer to the heartbeat of Mother Earth, so we begin to resonate with her, helping ourselves feel connected and one with her.

When we are connected with Mother Earth through love, it becomes natural to connect with Father Sun and the other planets of the solar system, because they are in harmony with each other through love, through the same heartbeat.

When we resonate in love with the solar system, we will by definition also resonate with our whole galaxy and consequently also with the whole universe. Feel your connection with the whole universe, with all universes, the multiverse, with All That Is. Feel the Oneness.

Take a deep breath, bring your awareness back to the room, feel your feet or your butt on the ground, and slowly open your eyes again.

Note: From the place of Oneness, you can connect with anything you choose, like a crystal, a crystal skull, a sacred place, a tree, or an angel, providing you with a much deeper experience.

This meditation — and the same is true for almost all meditations — can of course be done with or without music, with or without incense, and with or without candles burning. It is a matter of choice and a matter of what feels best for you. Never be rigid but follow what feels right in the moment. Always remember: The key to everything we do is *love*.

People believe that we can basically meditate with any tool and that each tool is equally efficient. Without denying that every tool can help, with meditation I believe that crystal skulls, due to their unique qualities, are one of the best, and most likely *the* best, meditation tools that exist. This will become increasingly clear when you read through the coming chapters.

Crystal Skulls and Healing

Like crystals, crystal skulls are also seen as healing tools. However, while there are many books and articles on the healing properties of crystals, this subject is hardly mentioned in books on crystal skulls. There are a few exceptions[5] and there are reports of some research in *Crystal Skulls: Interacting with a Phenomenon* (88-93) and *Kristallen Schedels*[6]. Working and meditating with crystal skulls has a direct and positive effect on the human energy system, (*CS*, 88-93) and for that reason alone, it is worthwhile to work and meditate with them.

"Healing" is a word that is used in many ways. It means "becoming whole" and is part of the process of remembering who we are. We have seen that crystal skulls work on our brains, and preliminary research indicates that crystal skulls also work on our meridians[7] and our chakras (*CS*, 88-93).

Besides having a physical system with connected physiology, it is recognized that the human system has a few subtle energy systems. They are defined as meridians, chakras, and subtle energy bodies. The subtle energy bodies form the aura. Many books have been written about meridians as the basis of acupuncture and about chakras. Introductions to these subjects have been given in *Gifts of Mother Earth*[8].

The Seven Chakras

Chakras have become an increasingly important part of understanding ourselves, our challenges, and our journey to Oneness. They have become part and parcel of the work of those working with alternative healing modalities and of those on their spiritual journey. This is not surprising because, once understood, they help us to understand the processes and challenges people experience. Chakras reflect where we are in our development and what types of issues we still are invited to deal with in order to become who we truly are. Here I will summarize some of the key points. For more details, I refer you to *Gifts of Mother Earth*.

There are seven chakras that are connected with our physical bodies. They connect us with our subtle bodies and with the outside world. These seven chakras can be grouped in different ways as is shown in image 4.1.

The first group includes the first, second, and third chakras. These are the chakras that reflect how we interact with our physical world. The fifth, sixth, and seventh chakras reflect how we interact with spirituality. The heart chakra (the fourth chakra) is the bridge between the two groups. When your heart is in "survival mode" and directed mainly by the condition of the first three chakras, you are living in conditional love. That means that you can only love a person when that person is sufficiently fulfilling your needs. This is most clearly expressed by children who do not love you when you refuse them the ice cream they want. The first three chakras are related to the needs we have in order to feel happy, joyful, safe, and accepted. However, when the heart is directed by the fifth, sixth, and seventh chakras, it is easier to move into a state of unconditional love. This is the state that reflects greater spiritual stability, which is achieved by learning to deal with the issues of our lower three chakras. This is our evolutionary goal, and the crystal skulls support our journey.

Image 4.1 also presents another way to view chakras — by combining them in pairs. Each set of pairs includes a chakra from the lower three chakras and one from the upper three. This shows that there are similarities in function between the lower three chakras and the upper three chakras, and it indicates that we are invited to deal with certain aspects on both a physical and a spiritual level. The third and fifth chakras both deal with expression. When we express ourselves from a lack of self-worth and self-esteem, we express from survival mentality in our experience of a challenging world (third chakra). But if we come from a place of love, we are able to express from a

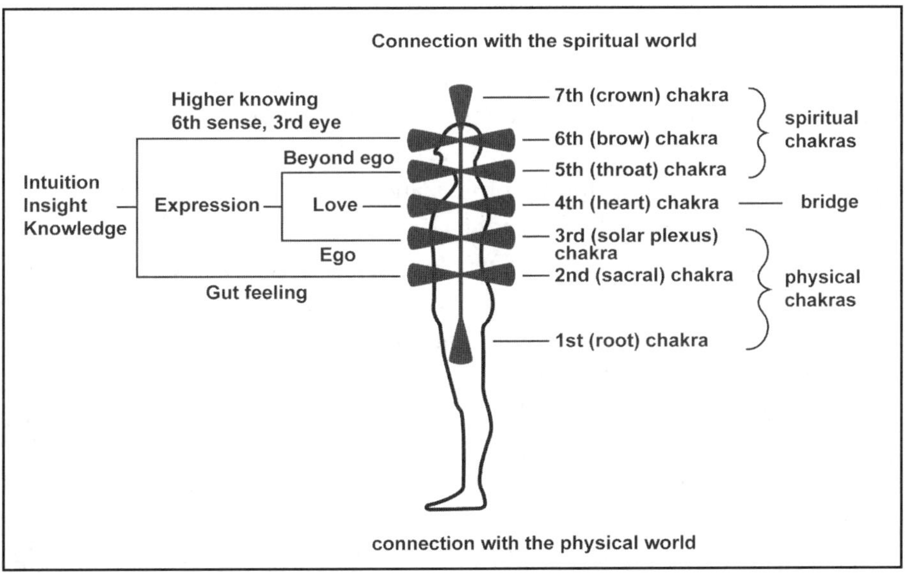

4.1 The seven chakras, their relationships, and their functions. Created by Evita de Vos.

higher and spiritual perspective — from a place of who we truly are (the fifth chakra).

The second and sixth chakras deal with intuition, insight and knowledge. The second chakra deals with the gut feeling — knowing intuitively how to relate to the physical world we live in. The sixth chakra is the chakra of higher intuition and knowing — knowing intuitively on a spiritual level what to do in and with our lives.

The first and seventh chakras deal with the experience of oneness. The first chakra is about feeling and experiencing that we are an intricate part of the physical world we live in (Earth), and the seventh chakra helps us to experience that we are one with All That Is.

Because the chakras are so important, I will give a short description of each of the seven chakras. An overview of the seven chakras, their Sanskrit names, their locations in the body, the hormonal glands they are connected with, their associated colors, and the elements they are connected with are summarized in table 2.

The **first chakra** is the root chakra that is located at the base of the spine. This is the chakra that deals with feeling safe and accepted. If we truly feel part of the world we live in, we will feel safe, protected, supported, and accepted. It is the chakra of the inner child. Because this chakra mainly develops in the first seven years of human life, all issues that a child experiences as "negative" have an effect on the functioning of this chakra. The color associated with this chakra is red.

The **second chakra** is the sacral or navel chakra and is located about two fingers below the navel. This chakra deals with the way we relate to the physical world around us. This is not restricted to people, but refers to everything, like work, money, housing, food, clothing, and nature. When our first chakra is out of balance and the world does not feel safe, we will develop all kinds of distorted patterns that we believe will enable us to relate to the unsafe world. We begin to give our power away in order to feel safe and liked. If we have a more balanced second chakra, our intuition (gut feeling) helps us to safely and appropriately relate to this world. The color associated with this chakra is orange.

The **third chakra** is called the solar plexus. It is located just under the breastbone. It is the chakra that reflects how we see ourselves, the chakra of self-esteem, self-worth, and deserving. It is also called the seat of the ego, although the ego is determined by all three lower chakras. The condition of this chakra is strongly influenced by the condition of the first and second chakras, and its associated color is yellow.

	Chakra	Sanskrit name	Location	Glands	Color	Element
1	Base or root chakra	Maludhara	Base of spine	Gonads	Red	Earth
2	Sacral or navel chakra	Svadistana	Below the naval	Certain cells in gonads	Orange	Water
3	Solar Plexus	Manipura	Just below breastbone	Adrenals, pancreas	Yellow	Fire
4	Heart chakra	Anahata	Center of breastbone	Thymus	Green	Air
5	Throat chakra	Vishuddha	At the throat	Thyroid	Blue	Ether
6	Third eye or brow chakra	Ajna	Slightly below mid-forehead	Pituitary gland	Indigo	
7	Crown chakra	Sahasrara	Just before the top of the head	Pineal gland	Violet and/ or white	

Table 2 Overview of the seven chakras, their Sanskrit name, their location in the body, the hormonal gland they are connected with, and their associated colors and elements.

The **fourth chakra** is the heart chakra and is located behind the center of the breastbone. As was mentioned earlier, this chakra reflects the quality of love — the degree a person loves conditionally or unconditionally. It tells us whether we are directed by the chakras of survival (how to function in the physical world) or the spiritual chakras. The associated color is green.

The **fifth chakra** is the throat chakra and is located in the throat area. This chakra reflects the degree to which we are able to express who we truly are. Many believe that this is the chakra of speaking our truth, but it is far more than that. However, if we are afraid to express ourselves on the level of the third chakra, we will neither speak our truth nor will we express who we truly are. The associated color is light blue.

The **sixth chakra** is located between our brows and is called the third eye, or the seat of the sixth sense. The sixth sense is also located in the second chakra. However, the sixth chakra is the chakra of the higher spiritual intuition, knowing, and wisdom. It is important not to confuse this with psychic abilities. In many cases, psychic abilities are a consequence of brain functions. The sixth sense is a higher function of psychic abilities that develops when spiritual abilities are unfolding. In most people, this chakra develops when we learn to deal with the issues within the first five chakras. In the current times, this chakra seems to be developing increasingly faster. The color associated with this chakra is indigo.

The **seventh chakra** is located at the top of the head, the crown. It is our connection to the higher spiritual realms and ultimately to All That Is. It is the chakra of Oneness, the feeling of being one with all. This is a chakra that opens up when we transform the issues that disturb the optimal functioning of our lower chakras. In this process, the seventh chakra begins to unfold as a beautiful flower. The associated color is purple, but during a kundalini experience, when all the chakras will align, the color of the seventh chakra will be perceived as white.

Because of the importance of the development of the chakras and the transformation of all that prevents them from functioning optimally, I am including a crystal skull chakra meditation here.

Crystal Skull Chakra Meditation

It is possible to create many different types of chakra meditations. I have worked many times with the meditation presented here (see also the meditation CD), both on an individual level and in groups, and it has worked very well.

After preparing your environment the way you prefer, sit down with your crystal skull. Depending on how big and heavy your skull is, you can hold it in your lap or place it on a table in front of you. Hold the crystal skull between both hands. Start with a few deeper inhalations and exhalations, allowing yourself to sink deeper into yourself.

Bring your awareness to your heart area, and with every inhalation, activate your heart center even more. Once you feel love or feel that you are connected, you are ready to continue.

Bring your awareness to the area of your heart chakra, behind your breastbone. Send a clear intent to your crystal skull to fill your heart chakra with the most optimal energy for you at this moment. Feel the energies flowing from your crystal skull through your arms into your heart chakra. Allow the energies to heal and balance your heart chakra to the optimal state for you at this moment. Feel how the experience of love increases in the process. When you feel ready, move to the next step.

Move your awareness to the throat area, the fifth chakra. Set the intent for your crystal skull to fill the throat chakra with the optimal energies to help this chakra go to its optimal condition for now. Feel the energies flowing through your arms to your throat area. Allow healing and transformation to take place in the optimal state for this moment. Feel the longing to express yourself more fully. When you feel ready, move on.

Move your awareness to the next chakra, the sixth chakra, located behind the middle of your eyebrows. Again allow those energies to move from your crystal skull through your arms to this area to bring the sixth chakra to its optimal condition. Feel the area behind the middle of your eyebrows, and feel your intuition awakening and further expanding. When you feel ready, move to the next step.

Next bring your awareness to the top of your head — the seventh chakra. Allow those energies to move from your crystal skull through your arms to this area that can help to create the optimal state for the crown chakra. Feel your connection with the spiritual realms. Feel the Infinite, the All That Is.

Once completed, move your awareness down your spine until it reaches the base at the root or first chakra. Imagine that from your crystal skull and through your arms those energies will flow to this area, helping the first chakra to reach its optimal condition for now. Feel completely safe and accepted in this world to support the process of healing and transformation in this chakra.

When you feel complete, move your awareness up to the second chakra, located about two fingers below the navel. Allow the energies that bring this chakra to its optimal state to flow from the crystal skull through your arms to the location of this chakra. Feel that it becomes much easier to connect with and relate to the world around you in all ways and on all levels. Once you feel complete, move to the next step.

Now move to the level of the third chakra, or the solar plexus, just under your breastbone. Allow the energies that will help this chakra to go to its optimal state to flow from your crystal skull through your arms to this area. Feel your self-esteem increasing — your trust and belief in yourself, your self-worth, and the feeling that you truly deserve happiness, love, and abundance.

Finally, move your awareness to the place where you started: the heart chakra. Allow those energies that can bring the heart chakra to its new optimal state to flow from your crystal skull through your arms to your heart chakra. Feel an even further expansion of love.

Once this feels finished, sit in meditation for as long as it feels comfortable to allow adjustments to take place in your whole system.

When you feel ready, take a deep breath, slowly bringing back your awareness to the room. Feel your feet or butt on the ground, and when you feel ready, open your eyes again.

When you do this meditation alone, take some time to feel what the journey has done with you. What do you feel? What changed? What issues came up? Which chakra was easy? Which one difficult? And so on. When you are in a group, you can choose to share. It will help to translate the experiences into awareness. Writing in a diary will have a similar effect.

Crystal Skulls and Ceremonies

There are many gatherings in which crystal skulls are used in a ceremonial way. Mayan leaders like Hunbatz Men actively perform ceremonies during crystal skull events. Hunbatz claims that this is part of Mayan tradition. Don Alejandro shared in 1999 during a gathering with Max, one of the ancient skulls, that he believes that crystal skulls are sacred Mayan objects that need to come back to where they belong so they can be activated together.

As mentioned earlier, Drunvalo Melchizedek mentioned in his book *Serpent of Light: Beyond 2012* that during a ceremony in Chichen Itza, Mayan people with crystal skulls joined the ceremony he and his group were performing[9].

The use of crystal skulls in ceremonies is not limited to the Mayan people. There are many stories about other tribal people using crystal skulls. One of these stories is well documented by Morton and Thomas in their book *The Mystery of the Crystal Skulls* (239-257). In one story, one of the Navajo people shared his experiences with a crystal skull they use in their ceremonies.

Many believe that some crystal skulls are still hidden because the indigenous people are afraid that the energy of the modern people will pollute their sacred objects. There also is a fear that their sacred objects may be stolen. Their fears do have a basis — history, in that sense, is on their side.

In modern times, many ceremonies have been performed by both indigenous and nonindigenous people. Ceremonies are different from rituals. Rituals are repeated actions that easily become like patterns that no longer are performed with passion, and thus their energy diminishes. Often rituals become mainly mental constructs. A ceremony, however, is something that is alive. It comes from a deep connection with what is happening in each moment. Even though it may have a basic structure, it is always dynamically changing, depending on what is happening energetically. A ceremony is always in alignment with the moment and with those who are participating. Crystal skulls amplify the energies that are generated during the ceremony. They also can be used to set a clear intent and support those who are doing the ceremony.

Ceremonies are alive. They are created through a chosen intent, through those doing the ceremony, through the location of the ceremony, and through those present. Therefore, I will not describe a specific form. The key point has been mentioned: Do a ceremony with love and respect for All That Is and allow it to unfold based on the flow of the energies.

The Study of Crystal Skulls

Everything described so far discusses ways to experience crystal skulls and observe how they can support us on our journey. Experiences often raise many questions. People wish to understand their experiences and the role of crystal skulls. They ask about the nature of activation, the differences from crystals, and so forth. There are several books about experiences with crystal skulls, about discoveries and legends, but there is limited information that helps to understand crystal skulls from an energetic perspective.

Crystal skulls cannot be understood in terms of accepted science. In order to understand them, we need to study them metaphysically. In the next chapters of this book, results from metaphysical studies of crystal skulls will be presented and discussed. Particular attention will be given to energy systems connected with crystal skulls and how these energies affect the energy systems and awareness of human beings.

The study of crystal skulls is an ongoing process. Many areas are still under investigation. The results of these studies will be presented in future books and articles.

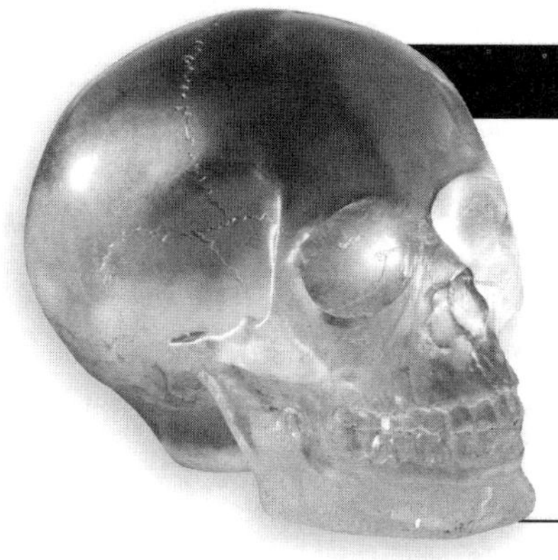

CHAPTER FIVE

Crystal Skull Activation and the Basics of Crystal Skull Energies

The first four chapters have provided some basic information about crystal skulls. It seems logical to continue with descriptions of the different classifications of crystal skulls that generally are defined as ancient, old, and contemporary crystal skulls, but I have chosen not to do that. Although I do not deny that there are crystal skulls that are contemporary and crystal skulls that have been carved earlier or even much earlier, I see these classifications of ancient, old, and contemporary as rather arbitrary. The basic definition of these terms comes from research done at The Society of Crystal Skulls International, of which Nick F.R. Nocerino was the founder and director. According to Stephen Mehler, the society made these classifications in the 1980s[1]. Because there is no scientific way to determine the moment a crystal skull was carved, they estimate the time when a crystal skull was carved psychically. There is no formal or scientific information to support the estimated age of the old and ancient skulls. Given different estimations, it becomes clear that these classifications may not be the ideal way to categorize crystal skulls. This is also true because the term "ancient" has lead to many false claims and people taking advantage of others by selling "ancient skulls" that have been carved recently.

The division of crystal skulls into the three groups — ancient, old, and contemporary — most likely will remain popular. However, by studying the energies of crystal skulls, it is possible to come to a more useful system of classification that may reflect the history of crystal skulls in a better way. The results of this approach may not differ from the society's system. In fact, in many cases the two systems agree. However, classification based on the energetic conditions better reflects what crystal skulls are and what you can do with them. This system of classification is based on the way people have used crystal skulls and to what level the skulls have been activated or awakened their potential. In order to understand this system, we need to explore in more detail the nature of activation. We also need to look at the energies that become part of a crystal skull through the process of activation. Therefore, I will give the definitions of the different groups of crystal skulls in the next chapter after we have looked at the process of activation and the energies that are awakened during an activation process.

A Definition of Activation

Activation is the process of awakening the full potential of a crystal skull. Therefore, "awakening" would be a better term than "activating." However, the term "activation" is used more commonly and will therefore be used here as well.

We do not know what the full potential of a crystal skull is, but as long as we have the intent to activate it, we are exploring what that means. Activation may mean a process that lasts a lifetime. We know so little about the potential of crystal skulls that we have no idea of the possible end result. Therefore, it is important to focus on the process and not on the end result.

The process of activating the full potential of a crystal skull is also a process of activating the person who does the activation. For the activator, it is a process of connecting with increasingly higher frequencies. And in order to be able to do so, something needs to change in the activator. Many people start with an intent that comes from a mental perspective, which allows the activation of a crystal skull to a certain level. But to activate a crystal skull further, we need to come from the heart, from a place of love, a place of true connection. If we want to go even further in the activation process, we need to learn to let go of the barrier between the crystal skull and ourselves and become one (image 5.1). Once we have learned to be one, we will keep growing through the process of reflection and amplification that will help us to see what we need to change to expand our awareness and energies even further. Through this process we can activate the crystal skull to even higher levels. This shows that the process of activation is an inherent part of the journey to Oneness through crystal skulls.

In my book *Crystal Skulls: Interacting with a Phenomenon*, I mentioned that in the process of activating crystal skulls, the number of polyhedral fields increases. At the time the book was written, the maximum number seemed

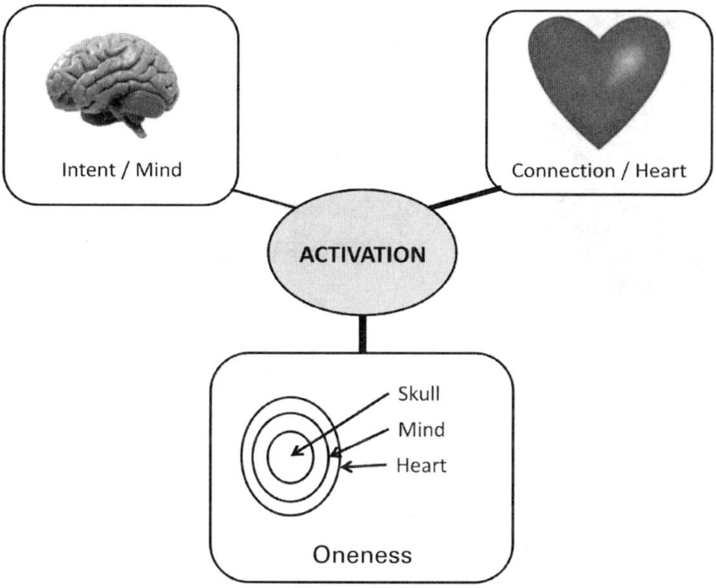

5.1 Three ways of activation: through intent (mind), through connection (heart), and through oneness

to be eighteen (71-83). Because "polyhedral fields" was a confusing and complicated term for most people, even though it was correct technically, it was replaced by "energy layers." This also is a correct term but is much easier to understand. Therefore, this term is the one used in this book. Every stone, crystal, and crystal skull has these polyhedral energy layers. As I mentioned in *Crystal Skulls: Interacting with a Phenomenon*, every layer has sublayers. Each layer has a total of twelve of these sublayers. Each sublayer increases in frequency, the twelfth being the highest. This means that each layer is characterized by having twelve sublayers. During activation, we move first through all twelve sublayers before we move to the next layer.

When we awaken the potential of a crystal skull, two processes take place (image 5.2). One process increases the number of layers and sublayers. This is expansion — with every addition, the field expands. It seems logical that each higher layer would hold higher frequencies, but that is not the case. Each layer is like the awareness of certain qualities. With this type of activation, we can experience the feeling of expansion. Although I can feel that each layer has certain qualities, I have not yet been able to define these qualities. At this moment there is an understanding of the quality of certain groups of layers, as we will see later in this chapter.

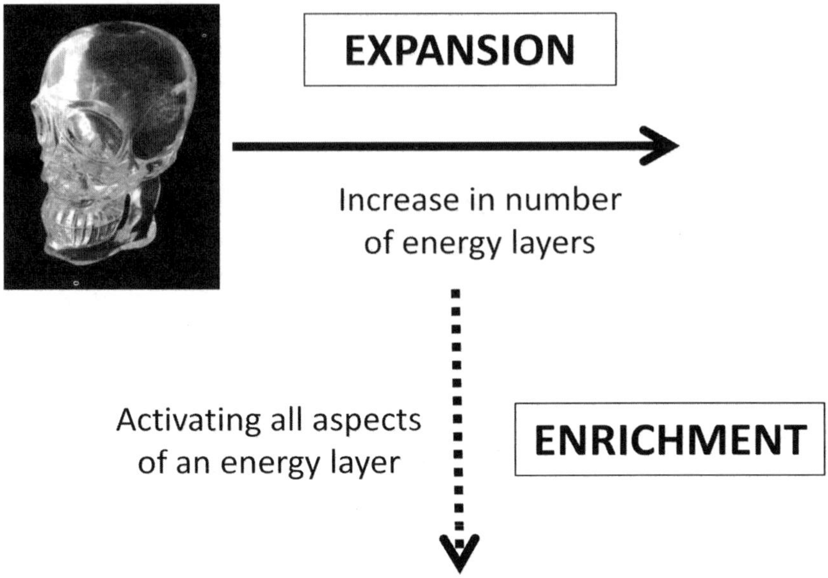

5.2 Two processes of activation: through expansion and through enrichment

The second process awakens the elements of the potential of each of the layers and sublayers. I call this the process of enrichment. It enriches the quality of a crystal skull and, as we will see, this aspect of the awakening, of the activation, gives the feeling of a truly activated crystal skull.

To help you understand these activations better, let us use an analogy. You can see your crystal skull as a house. The house has a corridor, but you cannot see from the beginning of the corridor how many doors there are leading to different rooms. Expansion is like walking through the corridor, becoming aware of the doors, and opening them. You can see the rooms, but they are dark. Enriching is like switching on small spotlights that help you to see the different parts in the room. Once you have seen all the parts, the main light switches on and the function of that room can be seen and used. Once you have seen all the rooms and their functions, the whole house lights up and the full use of the house becomes available for you.

The focus people have during activation can fluctuate considerably. Some people focus mainly on expansion. Initially this way works very well. However, after a while people have stretched so much that they cannot go any further. This may create a feeling of "getting stuck" that may even result in losing interest in working with crystal skulls.

Those who follow the three-step activation approach — brain (intent), heart (connection), and becoming one — will generally focus mainly on enriching. This gives the feeling that the power of the crystal skull increases continuously, which results in a feeling of growing in unison. This is the best and most satisfying way to activate your crystal skull, partly because the continuous growth diminishes the chance of losing interest. Every time a layer has been fully enriched, you automatically expand the energies of the skull as well, and you then continue the enrichment of the next layer. This is a natural flow experienced without effort. Focusing on expansion to get as many layers activated as possible may feel like an effort and is in fact an attempt to force a process.

In my attempt to understand activation, I focused initially on expansion. I forced the process and became ill. It took me weeks to recover. Therefore, I can say from experience that forcing through expansion is not the way to go. Activation is a natural process, and you cannot force the timing of a natural process without dire consequences.

The Energy Layers of Stones, Crystals, and Crystal Skulls

We have defined activation and the process of unfolding energies during activation so that we can review the results of this process as it is currently understood. In *Crystal Skulls: Interacting with a Phenomenon* (81-83), I mentioned a maximum of eighteen energy layers. However, this number came from the limited understanding of the energies that I had at that time. My current understanding has evolved and most likely will continue to evolve further.

To describe the energy layers of crystal skulls, we have to look at the energy layers of crystals. It was mentioned earlier that carvers feel a shift in energy when the eyes of the skull are brought into the rough shape of the skull. Initially it was believed that this shift was caused by an increase in the number of energy layers that the crystal already had. Crystals always have a minimum of four energy layers. Apparently, a crystal cannot exist unless it has this minimum number of energy layers. It was found that when the eyes are brought into the rough shape of the crystal skull, suddenly there was a minimum of six energy layers (*CS*, 7). At the time, it was assumed there was a simple addition of two layers. That turned out to be incorrect; there was an addition of six extra layers. To understand this, we need to look again at the energies of crystals and of crystal skulls.

A crystal has a certain potential that can be expressed in a maximum number of layers. When that potential awakens through activation, we see that an increasing number of these layers begin to appear. It always starts with a minimum of four layers. The maximum number of layers that will exist after activation depends on the type of crystal. The energies connected with crystals are called the "crystal harmonic frequencies." They are called *harmonic* frequencies because the energy layers can exist at different frequency ranges that are always harmonics of each other.

The potential of a crystal skull can also be expressed by a certain number of energy layers. However, crystal skulls have two sets of energy layers: those that belong to the crystal and those that are induced when the basic skull shape appears. These skull energy layers are different from the energy layers connected with crystals. They have a different harmonic frequency range that I call the "crystal skull harmonic frequencies." This may explain why people increasingly prefer to work with crystal skulls instead of crystals — crystal skulls have more to offer than crystals of the same type of material. This in no way diminishes the value of crystals; it only says that when we have a crystal in the form of a skull we have something additional. This "something additional" is very powerful and helps us on the journey of remembering and expressing who we are, and it helps us to expand our awareness and consciousness.

What is the purpose of these two different harmonic frequencies? I believe that the crystal harmonic frequencies help us to master the physical third-dimensional reality. Through healing and balancing, they help us to create harmonized physical, emotional, and mental bodies that work in alignment with the spiritual body. Crystals help us to live in this dimensional reality in an optimal way, enjoying and loving physical life. They invite us to listen when they "sing their song." They help us to reconnect and resonate again with Mother Earth, to feel our connection with her and all her children.

The crystal skull harmonic frequencies help us to expand our awareness to such a degree that we master the consciousness potential of the third- and fourth-dimensional realities. Their focus is on the development of our consciousness and awareness. Even the skull shape reminds us that they, like our own skulls, help us to focus on awareness — which is experienced and processed to a large degree through our brain — and the expansion of it.

The only crystal carving shape I have seen that has another set of harmonic frequencies is the skull. Other harmonic frequencies do exist, but the ones I have encountered are not connected to a specific form. We will look at some of these harmonic frequencies in the next chapter.

All the qualities of crystals are also available in a crystal skull of the same material. Therefore, when we need healing or give healing to others, we may choose to use either a crystal or a crystal skull. However, not everyone is ready to work with crystal skulls. Because the primary goal of crystals is healing, many people will continue to use crystals. However, crystal skulls are stronger amplifiers than crystals. If a person is open to working with crystal skulls, healing with them may be more powerful and effective. Always be aware of what works best for the person you work with.

The Crystal Harmonic Frequencies

In order to understand the energy complex of a crystal skull, let us start with the harmonic frequencies of crystals. While discovering the nature of activation of crystals and crystal skulls, it became apparent that different crystals have different energy systems. This statement in itself is not surprising, but it was a surprise to see that these differences were reflected in the number of energy layers associated with different crystals and stones.

The basic conclusion was that every stone and every crystal, once optimally activated, had a minimum of twelve layers, each with twelve sublayers. Every stone and every crystal can be activated to this energy state. However, not every type of stone and crystal has the ability to go to a higher number of layers (see image 5.3). Only quartz, some silicates (like carnelian), some agates, calcite, nebula stone, kambaba jasper, some fossilized materi-

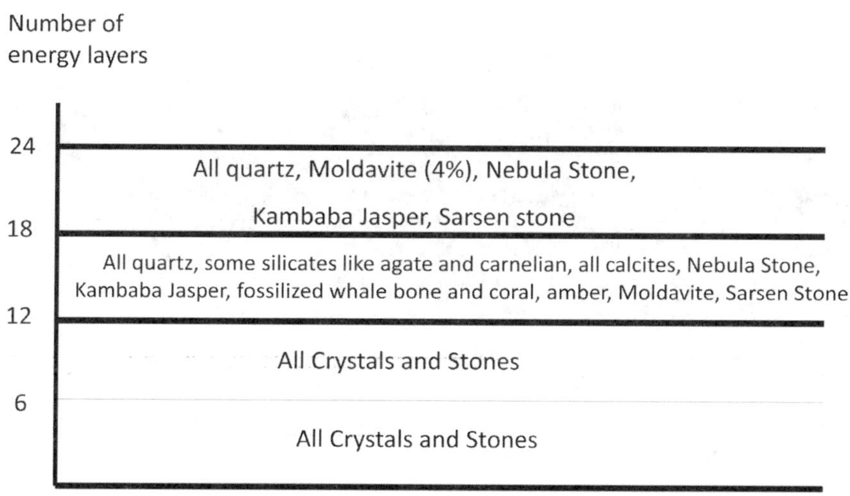

5.3 Overview of the number of energy layers connected with different stones and crystals

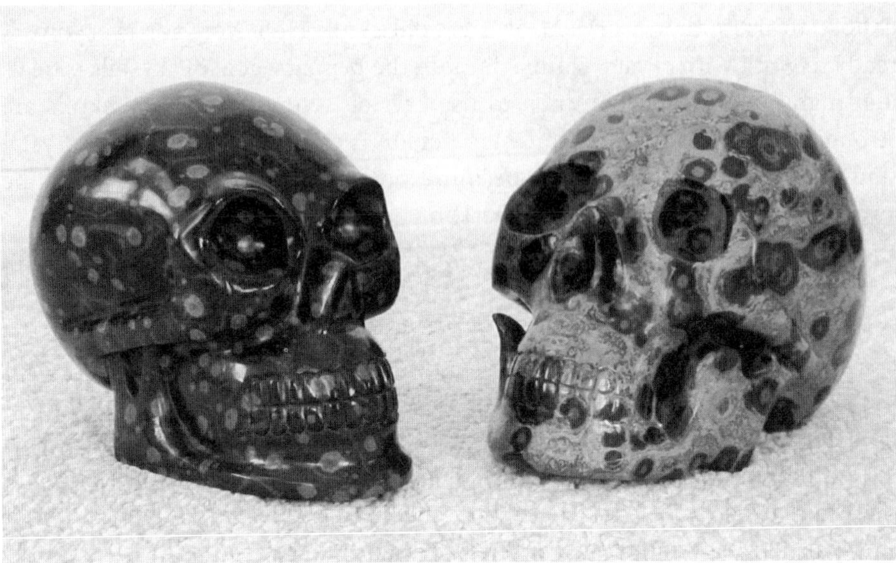

5.4 (Top) Crystal skulls carved from kambaba jasper (right) and from nebula stone (left)

5.5 Stonehenge. The inner and outer rings are made of sarsen stones. Photo © Scubabartek | Dreamstime.com

als (like whale bone, coral, and amber), moldavite, and sarsen stone are able to express their potential in eighteen energy layers. Quartz, nebula stone, kambaba jasper, and only about 4 percent of the moldavites are able to go to twenty-four energy layers, which seems to be the maximum state. Since everyone may not be familiar with nebula stone and kambaba jasper, a picture of a crystal skull of each type is shown in image 5.4. Sarsen stones are mostly known from Stonehenge. The inner and outer ring of Stonehenge (image 5.5) has been made from sarsen stone that, in a limited way, is found in the area around Stonehenge. There is no doubt that ancient people knew which stones to use to create a structure with powerful energies.

The energies of nebula stone and kambaba jasper are amazing. It is unusual for stones that are a mixture of different chemical components to have such high-energy frequencies. However, nebula stone consists mainly of quartz[2]. Sarsen stones, also mainly quartz, are the post-glacial remains of a cap of tertiary stones that once covered much of southern England. They are dense, hard rocks created from sand bound by silica cement, making them a kind of silicified sandstone[3].

From an energetic point of view, there are two types of moldavite. Although they look the same, a small percentage of them hold higher frequencies. There are no explanations for why a small group of moldavites is different energetically, and there are no systematic studies to identify their original location. The moldavites were bought, seen in shops, or seen in personal collections, and no one had information about the specific locations where their moldavites were found. I have dowsed that only about 4 percent of the moldavites hold these higher frequencies.

In addition to crystals and stones, there are a number of fossilized materials that have up to eighteen energy layers. These are fossilized whale bone, coral, and amber. It is fascinating that other fossilized bones do not seem to have the additional six layers; all other fossilized materials I have seen only have twelve energy layers.

Finally, there are a few silicates that have the ability to hold energies in eighteen layers. Silicates are related to quartz in that the main component is silicon dioxide. However, the crystal lattice of silicates is different from quartz and silicates do not have the same energetic qualities. The silicates that can develop eighteen layers are carnelian, and some agates also have similar qualities.

We are familiar with the idea of activating crystals. However, most people are unaware that every stone can be activated as well. Almost all stones have a maximum number of twelve energy layers. Whenever a stone structure is made, it is possible to activate each stone in that structure. That is what people did in ancient times. For example, each stone in the great pyramid of Giza in Egypt has been activated to its optimal level, and so have the stones of the pyramids of the Sun and the Moon in Teotihuacan near Mexico City (image 5.6). During the restoration of these pyramids, stones have been used that are not activated. Fortunately, that is only an estimated 10 percent of all the stones, so it hardly affects the overall energy. However, it does reveal our current lack of understanding of what the ancient people knew. An interesting aspect of Teotihuacan is that all major buildings are built with stones that have been fully activated.

There are other places in the world where ancient people have activated the stones for their buildings, like Tiahuanacu (Tiwanaku) and Puma Punku in Bolivia, and many of the pre-Inca structures like the walls in Cusco and in Sacsayhuamán in Peru. However, over time the Inca seem to have forgotten the ability to activate the stones they used in their constructions. The energy of activated stones undoubtedly supported the activities in and around these structures.

5.6 Pyramid of the Sun, Teotihuacan, near Mexico City

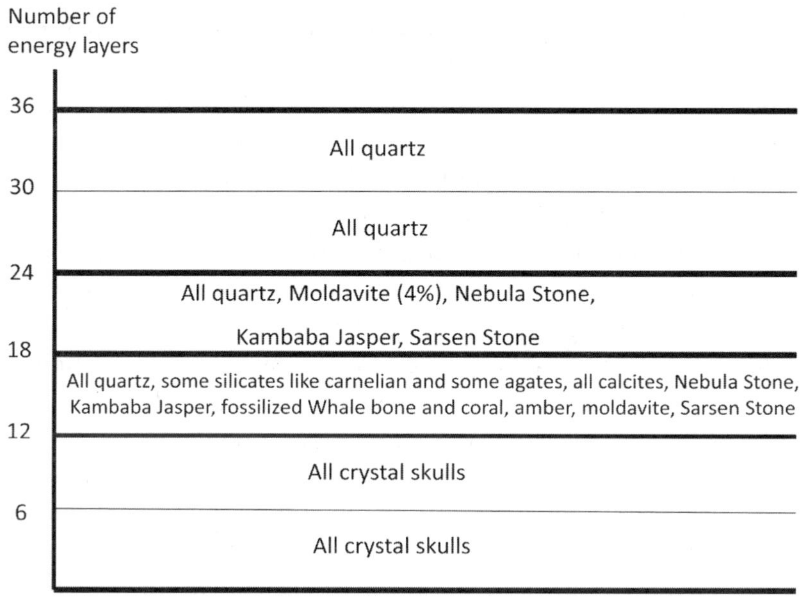

5.7 Overview of the number of energy layers of crystal skulls carved from different materials

Crystal Skull Harmonic Frequencies

Crystal skull harmonic frequencies are held in energy layers that are similar to the crystal energy layers. Basically, crystal skulls and the crystals they have been carved from have the same maximum number of energy layers. However, the frequencies of these layers are different. The frequencies of the layers of crystal skulls are all higher and distinctly different from those of the crystals of the same material.

Quartz forms an exception in many ways. Quartz crystal skulls have twelve more energy layers than quartz crystals (image 5.7). To be clear, quartz crystals have a maximum of twenty-four layers, while quartz crystal skulls have a maximum of thirty-six layers. This is true for all quartz, unless there are too many foreign inclusions that may have a disturbing effect on the energies. Quartz crystal skulls hold the widest range and the highest frequencies, which explains why all known "ancient" crystal skulls are made from quartz.

Crystal Skull Harmonic Frequencies and Consciousness

Earlier it was stated that crystal skull harmonic frequencies help us to master consciousness of the third and fourth dimensions. There is a relationship between the mastery of consciousness of these two dimensions and the number of energy layers. Both third- and fourth-dimensional consciousness belong to physical reality. Third-dimensional consciousness is the consciousness of duality. It is the consciousness in which we think by comparing one aspect to another by thinking in opposites, such as good versus bad, beautiful versus ugly, positive versus negative, and so on.

Fourth-dimensional consciousness is the consciousness of Oneness. It is not about good versus bad because they are both aspects of one thing — two sides of the same coin. Duality does not exist in the fourth dimension, and there is one interactive system in which everything works together. In Oneness, we are not separate from the environment we live in but are an integrated part of it.

When we move into this aspect of consciousness, we notice that the time lapse between thoughts and manifestations becomes increasingly shorter. It no longer takes much time for a thought to manifest. For that reason, it is good that most people still live in third-dimensional consciousness, because in this consciousness, the period between thought and realization can be quite long, giving people the possibility to change their thoughts in time to prevent them from becoming reality. Figure 5.8 summarizes the relationship between the energy layers and consciousness.

The first eighteen energy layers hold frequencies that help to master the third-dimensional dualistic world. This is a process. Even when your crystal skull has all eighteen layers activated, it does not mean that you will be a master of third-dimensional reality just by sitting with it. You are fully responsible for all the changes you need to make to get to the state of mastering of this reality by taking full responsibility of all your feelings, thoughts, words, and actions. You need to change all that is no longer in alignment with the state of mastering third-dimensional awareness. A crystal skull activated fully over eighteen energy layers provides you with the vibrational framework to make this journey easier. The vibrations of your crystal skull will help you to realize whether or not you are in alignment — that is the function of a perfect reflector and amplifier. Your responsibility is to actually live in that state to the best of your ability.

The second group of eighteen energy layers, nineteen through thirty-six, holds the frequencies that help us to master fourth-dimensional conscious-

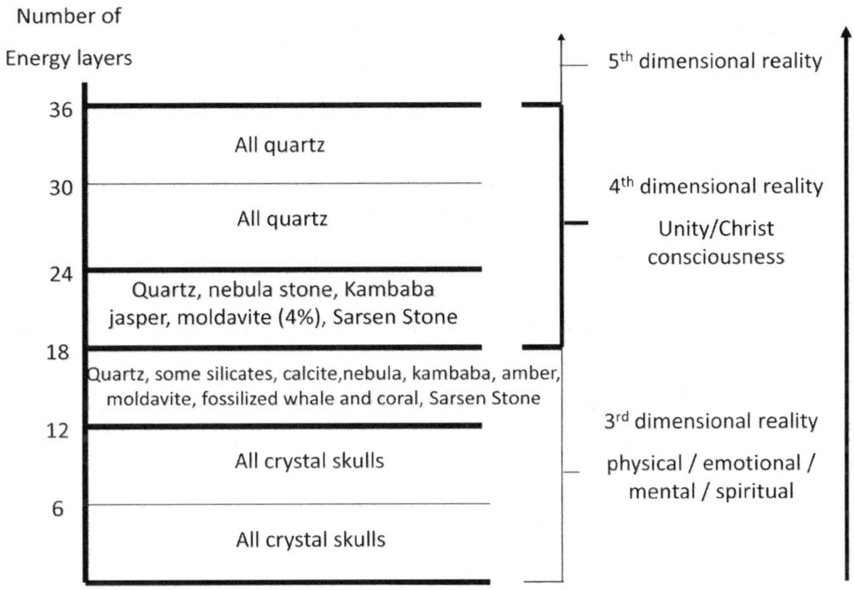

5.8 The relationship between consciousness and the number of layers of crystal skulls

ness. Within this range are two steps. The first step is connected to energy layers nineteen to twenty-four. This step is important because it bridges third-dimensional consciousness and the consciousness of Oneness. In this phase, you are sometimes more in Oneness but can still fall back to duality. I call this the "in-between phase." Many people who are on their spiritual journeys get glimpses or even periods of Oneness experience. They move for shorter or longer periods into this in-between phase. Third-dimensional consciousness is not yet fully mastered, but there are moments when Oneness is experienced.

When we start living in alignment with the energies of layers twenty-five to thirty-six, we move into the experience of living in Oneness most of the time and ultimately all of the time. This is the aspiration of many people on their spiritual paths.

Even when you have activated your crystal skull to thirty-six layers, you do not necessarily live in that state, expressing yourself permanently from that level. It also does not mean that the enrichment of the layers has been completed, even though there are thirty-six activated layers. Nevertheless, it is clear that crystal skulls do invite us on a journey to Oneness.

Crystal Skulls with a Lower Number of Layers

The fact that certain crystal skulls have a lower maximum number of layers does not necessarily mean that they also hold the lowest vibrations. Let us look at an example of a crystal skull that has a maximum of twelve layers and has been fully activated. It may seem like this is the end of the journey, but it is not. When your consciousness and vibration increases, you can raise the vibration of all of the twelve layers together. This rise in vibration does not feel like a linear process; it moves in jumps, like a sudden expansion. It has the same feeling when a layer is added. While the number of layers stays the same, the energy feels enriched. It is not clear yet what this all means, and it is not possible to give a good description of the process. It is an indication that there is still a lot to learn about the energies of crystal skulls.

The above description refers to the layers connected with the crystal skull harmonic frequencies. The layers of the crystal harmonic frequencies can also be raised in vibration, and it seems that the increases in the frequencies of these two systems are connected to a certain degree. When the crystal harmonic frequencies increase, so do the crystal skull harmonic frequencies.

The main point is to realize that crystal skulls of any material have great gifts to give as long as their material is natural. Nowadays there are also crystal skulls that are made of resin. Resin is not a crystal — even though carvers can make it look very natural — and does not possess the crystal harmonic frequencies. This makes it impossible to add the crystal skull harmonic frequencies. Because powdered quartz is usually added, most of these resin skulls may hold certain energies, but they do not have any of the frequencies that characterize crystal skulls.

Activity Levels

I previously mentioned that the true power of a crystal skull is not only determined by the expansion of the number of layers but by the combination of expansion and enrichment of the layers. Actually, we experience the power of a crystal skull more through the enrichment of the layers. Expansion makes the energies of a crystal skull visible. You can perceive layers that previously could not be perceived — simply because they were not yet awakened. Enrichment brings the potential within a layer to a fuller expression. The combination of these activations allows us to increasingly experience the quality of a crystal skull. This quality, like the frequencies in the brain, has frequency fields that again can be expressed in levels. It is difficult to define these levels because we are referring to complex frequencies. However, we can learn, through experience, to feel these different levels, which become more distinct after working with them for a while.

Recently another phenomenon connected with the subject of activity levels was discovered. When activity levels have reached an optimal state, that changes the last layer. This seems to only happen in quartz crystal skulls or skulls that hold a lot of quartz. Several of the quartz crystal skulls that have been activated earlier (the "ancient" ones) show this change in the last (thirty-sixth) layer, which widens and has a bluish shimmer. I have not seen this phenomenon with contemporary crystal skulls, even when they have thirty-six layers. Ancient crystal skulls that have thirty-six layers, a widened thirty-sixth layer, and a bluish shimmer are the Mitchell-Hedges crystal skull, Synergy, Max, Einstein, Sha Na Ra, the amethyst skull Ami, an amethyst skull from Mexico, and Lucy. The Mayan skull and ET have only a slightly wider thirty-sixth layer and a light-blue shimmer. We will look at them in the next chapter and in Addendum I.

In the next chapter, we will look at different crystal skulls. There I will mention a group that has twenty-four layers optimally activated and explain that the twenty-fourth layer has characteristics similar to the thirty-sixth layer — a widened layer with a bluish shimmer. However, when there are thirty-six layers fully activated and the thirty-sixth layer is widened with a bluish shimmer, the twenty-fourth does not have this characteristic. This suggests that the activation of only twenty-four layers to an optimal level was a conscious choice. I consider these skulls to be ancient. Examples are Ixchel, Madre, Pancho, and Paco. We will also look at these skulls in more detail in the next chapter and in Addendum I.

Activity levels have yet another interesting aspect. When people stop working with a crystal skull, its activity level will go down. The number of energy levels of a crystal skull will not change, but the quality within the layers — the enrichment — will. A level of activity will only stay when we, or others, continue to work with a crystal skull. This means that when a quartz skull is found in a ruin, assuming it is an ancient skull, it may have thirty-six layers; however, it will not have a high activity level because it has not been worked with for a long period of time. This is a very interesting aspect. There is no explanation for this phenomenon, although it may work as a protection device. Only those who really can activate a crystal skull to a higher activity level can use the full potential of a crystal skull. This prevents the possibility that when an ancient crystal skull is found it will "overcharge" the energy system of an untrained human being.

In general, overcharging will not easily happen for individuals. The consciousness of the person working with a crystal skull will determine which aspects of that crystal skull that person will connect with. Because crystal skulls are reflectors, they will reflect the energies that a person can handle. However, I have seen people overcharge themselves because they did not choose to pay attention to the discomfort that functions as a signal warning them to stop. Crystal skulls amplify this discomfort, which may lead to an overcharge.

It is not possible to define with certainty whether crystal skulls have reached their maximum activity level. However, I believe that it is highly unlikely that such crystal skulls are around. We are still learning, and therefore the skills to go to the optimal state are not yet present. Otherwise, we would be able to create contemporary crystal skulls with a bluish shimmer. In addition, there may be energies we have not yet discovered. I believe that there is still much to explore.

Ancient and Contemporary Crystal Skulls and the Journey of Activation

By now it may have become clear that activation is a key element in working with crystal skulls. We live in a time of remembering. We are beginning to remember who we are and what our place is within the physical reality we call Earth. We are also beginning to remember the true power of every living being and of every stone and crystal. As part of that, we are beginning to remember what crystal skulls can do for those who choose to work with them on their spiritual journeys.

On this journey of remembering and rediscovering, contemporary crystal skulls and crystal skulls carved in earlier times (old and ancient) play different roles. A contemporary crystal skull can be compared to an empty notebook — there is nothing written in it yet. This means that the caretakers of contemporary crystal skulls can fill notebooks with their stories and experiences. It is a journey of discovering through interacting with your crystal skull. It is a journey in which both you and the crystal skull expand your abilities. It is a journey full of excitement and new experiences. It is a journey that may have no end, and it does not need an end. It is a journey that is part of the larger journey of exploring infinite consciousness.

A crystal skull that was carved in earlier times was carved for a reason and therefore has been worked with to fulfill the needs of the time in which it was carved. It is like a book that has been written, so of course we can learn from it. Often, these "books" were written by people who had a different way of thinking; therefore, the information may not always be easy to understand — or it may not be understood at all. Still, it can be very stimulating and life-changing to "read" that book. Although I believe that most of the "book" of an ancient skull is inaccessible, there is enough available to help us awaken and to expand our awareness.

The crystal skulls that are the "older brothers and sisters" are like beacons on a road — they tell us in what direction we can go and give us something to work toward. Many people start their crystal skull journey because they connected with one of the ancient crystal skulls. It triggered a remembering and awakened their passion to start working with crystal skulls and explore their gifts.

While we let ourselves be stimulated by the older crystal skulls, especially by those that are generally accepted as being ancient, the true journey for all other caretakers is with their contemporary crystal skulls. These contemporary crystal skulls may be some of the most beautiful gifts available to work with. Understanding this may help to diminish the need to have an ancient crystal skull. It is a mistake to think that you only have an important crystal skull if it has an "ancient" sticker on it. The truth is, working with contemporary crystal skulls can make them energetically equally important as ancient skulls, even though the information connected with an ancient crystal skull may be different. Every crystal skull, independent of age, can tap into the collective information field of crystal skulls (see chapter 7). Therefore, be proud of your contemporary crystal skull, and let yourself be stimulated by both the ancient ones and the gatherings of the contemporary ones.

Activation by Light and Sound

It is generally believed that crystal skulls can be activated by light and sound. This technique has been used to research crystal skulls[4]. One method people use involves light boxes that either have constant or changing colors. The idea of working with light and sound has been developed to a great degree by Kirby Seid's Light Labyrinth[5]. There is no doubt that this type of technology supports our journey with the crystal skulls. In addition, it is very beautiful to see the play of light of different colors, especially in quartz crystal skulls. The question is: "Do light and sound activate crystal skulls in different ways, and if so, to what level (which layer)?"

When we talk about light and sound, we refer to visible light and audible sounds. Both light and sound are electromagnetic frequencies that obviously have an effect on us, because we are able to receive these frequencies and our brain is able to translate them into a perception. We perceive the light and the sound and are able to tell ourselves and others whether we like it or not. That is also the case when we shine light of different colors through a crystal skull.

When we define activation as an increase in the potential of a crystal skull being reflected in the increase of the activity level, light and sound do not directly activate a crystal skull. This is not so surprising because activation happens through conscious intent and connection. However, light and sound have quite an effect on the observer. This strong effect may increase the vibration of the observer, and *that* may lead to higher activation of a crystal skull. This will be especially true if you believe it. I like to think of working with light and sound as a way to stimulate a person to open up and become more connected. It is the effect on the observer that may help the observer to activate a crystal skull to higher levels. However, it is my experience that light and sound do not directly activate crystal skulls.

To be clear, we are talking about the light that we can observe. There also is invisible light and light connected with higher-dimensional beings. This light is a reflection of a higher-vibrational state, which means higher-dimensional consciousness. That type of light, if directed to a crystal skull, will of course increase the activation of a crystal skull.

Light and sound may have been — and still can be — part of programming information in a crystal skull. If that is the case, light and sound of the same vibration used to program the information is also needed to retrieve the information. To find out whether light and sound of a certain frequency have been used requires a high level of either perception or technology. If this interests you, I invite you to explore it yourself.

Activation Meditation

To help you activate your crystal skull to awaken its potential, the following meditation is helpful. You can adapt this meditation in any way you wish, and you can also use it to activate stones and crystals. However, as presented here, the meditation focuses on crystal skulls. My suggestion is to always use this activation meditation as a start to meditating with your crystal skulls. When you first focus on an optimal awakening of your crystal skull, you create the most optimal condition for your meditation. Sitting in an optimal energy during your meditation will help you to expand and awaken more of yourself (see also the mediatation CD).

Before starting the meditation, select the crystal skull you would like to activate or to bring to a higher level. Create the space you prefer.

Make yourself comfortable as much as possible. Start with some deeper inhalations and exhalations, and with every exhalation, allow yourself to relax a little more. Feel yourself sinking into the here and now. Realize that by choosing to meditate, nothing else matters right now.

When you feel relaxed, realize that your brain is less active. This means your system begins to align itself more with your heart. Now fully shift your awareness to your heart area — the area behind your breastbone. With every inhalation, bring more energy to your heart center and feel the energy of love expanding throughout your body. For now, restrict this expansion to your physical body. Inhale and let the love expand even more.

While staying in this state of love, open your eyes and look at your crystal skull. Look at it as if you see it for the first time. Look at it as if you meet a person you immediately feel a deep connection with and a deep love for. Allow yourself to feel that deep connection and love for your crystal skull.

Being in this place of love and deep connection, imagine that you and the crystal skull begin to merge. Feel how the separation between you and the skull begins to disappear. It does not matter how you experience this as long as you imagine the separation disappearing.

In this state of being merged with your crystal skull, allow yourself to expand into the highest frequencies possible. Feel this expansion taking place. It will take place because you have chosen to allow it to take place. You do not force but simply allow this expansion to happen naturally. While you expand, your crystal skull will be activated for you at that moment to the highest possible level in alignment with the expansion you are going through.

Sit in this energy of expansion for as long as it feels comfortable for you.

In summary, we can say that stones, crystals, and crystal skulls can be activated to levels that make their full potential available. This activation is a journey in which a person who activates a crystal or crystal skull grows, balances, and shifts awareness. Activation of crystal skulls helps a person to go to higher states of consciousness and supports them on their journey to fully remembering who they are. This is a journey that requires patience and persistence, but it is a journey with great rewards.

It is possible to work with supporting systems like light and sound, but the true activations come from the intent, level of awareness, and the imagination of a person who works with crystal skulls. Be aware that you determine the activity level of a crystal skull, and never give your power away to any crystal skull.

CHAPTER SIX

Crystal Skulls and Age

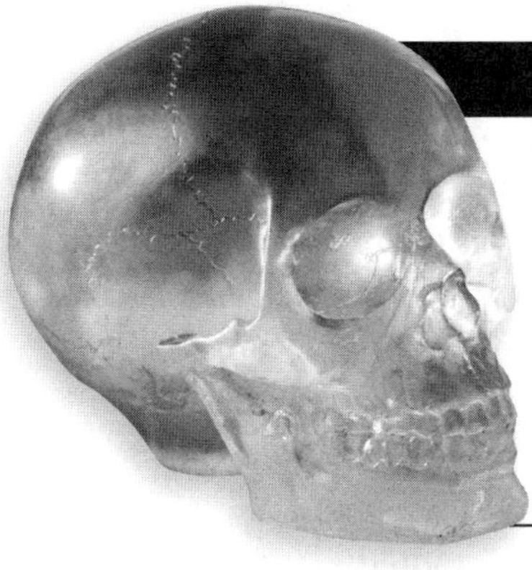

Most articles and books about crystal skulls refer to crystal skulls that are "ancient" or "old." As I mentioned in the previous chapter, this terminology has been chosen by the Society of Crystal Skulls International and has been adopted as a generally accepted definition of the age of crystal skulls. If a crystal skull was carved more than 1,500 years ago, it is called ancient; between 100 and 1,500 years ago is old; and in the past 100 years is contemporary. The problem is that there are no methods that can *accurately* determine when a crystal skull was carved. Even if it were possible to determine the age of the crystal, we still would not know when the crystal was carved into a skull. In general, it seems easy to determine whether a crystal skull was carved recently and thus is contemporary; we can recognize styles, and these styles are reasonably well recorded and known. However, it is not always that easy. There are crystal skulls that are defined as ancient by some people but that others say are fake or contemporary. We mentioned already that there are even skulls made of resin that are sold as ancient skulls[1]. People create stories about crystal skulls for a variety of reasons, which confuses the whole matter[2].

There are no scientific techniques that can easily determine the age of a crystal skull. One of the scientific methods looks at the surface of a skull to determine whether a skull has been carved and polished using rotary lapidary tools. This is based on the assumption that those who carved ancient skulls did not possess such techniques. It is believed that most ancient and old crystal skulls came from Central America and that the people there, mainly the Maya, did not possess rotary tools in pre-Columbian times. Not everyone agrees with this statement (*MCS*, 226). There are a few possible explanations.

The first explanation is that the ancient and old skulls were carved by Mayan people. If that is true, then the presence of rotary tool marks indicates that a skull is not carved by Mayan people and should be considered modern or at least post-Columbian. Another possibility is that crystal skulls were made by older cultures that had techniques like those executed with rotary tools. A third possibility could be that the Maya did have rotary tools, as Professor Coe suggested (*MCS*, 226). It is increasingly recognized that ancient cultures such as those of ancient Egypt and Puma Punku in Bolivia may have had far more advanced technology than has been recognized[3].

Jane Walsh of the Smithsonian Museum has studied crystal skulls to determine whether rotary tools were used to carving them. Together with others, she published a scientific paper that clearly demonstrates that the British Museum crystal skull and the Smithsonian crystal skull were not pre-Columbian artifacts[4]. This conclusion was based on the authors' discovery of marks from lapidary rotary wheels on both crystal skulls. They also found hard abrasives like corundum, which has been used only in modern times, on both crystal skulls. Research of the British Museum skull shows that the quartz it is made of originated in either Brazil or Madagascar. That makes it likely that the skulls were carved at a time when it was possible to obtain this material from these sources. The study concluded that the British Museum skull was most likely carved in Europe in the nineteenth century and that the Smithsonian skull was carved in 1960 shortly before it was bought in Mexico.

The conclusion that Madagascar and Brazil were the source of the quartz for the British Museum skull is interesting. In 2010, carvers in Idar Oberstein carved a crystal skull specifically for museum display. The purpose was to bring awareness that they were master carvers of crystals over long periods of time, even though their work was not known by the general public. An article published in the German magazine *Der Spiegel* stated that there are records from the past, indicating that carvers worked with quartz from Madagascar and Brazil[5]. That makes it possible that Jane Walsh was right and that the British Museum skull could have been carved in Europe. However, the article did not make any reference to information from the archives that stated crystal skulls have been carved in Idar Oberstein. The article suggested, however, that many carvings were made secretly for clients, opening the possibility that crystal skulls may have been carved on special request. In these cases, the skulls could have been carved from quartz from Madagascar and Brazil.

In an article in *Archeology* published in 2008, Jane Walsh stated clearly that none of the crystal skulls are old[6]. It is an interesting article in the sense that it is more assumption than solid scientific research, as was the case with the paper on the British skull and the Smithsonian skull.

Walsh's perspective does not align with that of all archeologists. There was agreement from the archeologist Michael Smith relative to the larger skulls. However, he believes, based on his personal experiences, that there are genuine pre-Columbian Aztec small crystal skulls. His claim is confirmed by some of his colleagues[7].

Also, Michael Douglas Coe, an American archeologist, anthropologist, and epigrapher, who is especially known for his studies on the Mayan civilization, does not agree with Walsh. I have not been able to find an article, but his opinion was presented in *The Mystery of the Crystal Skulls* (226). According to Professor Coe, evidence of wheel markings on crystal skulls does not prove that these skulls are modern. He and his colleagues have found rotary ear-spools that could have been made only by using rotary carving equipment. These ear-spools definitely are dated back to the Aztec/Mixtec period. According to Coe, "people need to re-examine their beliefs" (*MCS*, 226). So the tests at the British Museum and those done later by Walsh do not necessarily prove Walsh's beliefs. Coe's view was reinforced by other Mesoamerican experts, such as Dr. John Pohl of UCLA (*MCS*, 226).

Jane Walsh was already involved with research in 1996 at the British Museum, and that research has been described extensively by Morton and Thomas (*MCS*, 209-226). Although she was present during the research, she apparently has forgotten some of the results in her later statements and conclusions. In the tests at the British Museum, they used a crystal skull that belonged to the Redo family. This skull is an interesting one because a cross has been placed on top of it. Also included in the test were a goblet from Monte Alba, Max the crystal skull from Texas, Sha Na Ra from Nick F.R. Nocerino, the Smithsonian skull, and the British Museum skull. The goblet was known to be over 1,000 years old. They found that the skull from Norma Redo had marks that showed that it was carved and polished in pre-Columbian times, although the details of the teeth and the area around the insertion of the cross seem to have been done later with a lapidary rotary wheel. They concluded that the skulls from the Smithsonian and the British Museum were modern fakes. However, all they had to say about Max and Sha Na Ra was "no comment" (*MCS*, 222). Walsh and her team did not explain their reluctance to comment on these two skulls. It is not likely that they found tool marks on these two skulls, as it should have been easy to share these kinds of results. However, if there were no tool marks, they faced a new dilemma. Museums prefer digs that are supervised by a museum. Sha Na Ra is excavated from a private dig in the fifties, which was legal at that time (*MCS*, 224). The museums may not have wished to confirm that a genuine artifact was held in a private collection while the fakes were in the museums.

Whatever the case, the museum confirmed that the Redo crystal skull, which also was in private hands, was an ancient skull — a point forgotten by Walsh in her later publications.

Walsh's perspective suggests that "science" may not provide accurate information on the subject of crystal skulls. It seems that many scientists hold the belief that all the ancient crystal skulls are fakes. It also seems that at least some of the presented information is strongly biased and that information has been omitted to prove the researchers' point of view, making it difficult to trust science. Consequently, we have to go back to a metaphysical approach. Can we use the energy patterns of crystal skulls to place them in groups and indicate which group may be older? In order to do so, we need to discuss some energetic qualities of crystal skulls that have not been mentioned yet.

Additional Crystal Skull Energies

Learning to understand the energies of crystals and crystal skulls is like learning a new language. Initially we cannot understand anything — it is just a mass of sounds. The crystalline energies initially feel like an undifferentiated field of energies. Beginning to recognize aspects of them is like being able to define words; in the mass of sounds, we begin to suddenly recognize certain words and are able to give them meaning. Slowly we can make an increasing amount of sense out of what used to be an undifferentiated mass of sounds. The same thing happens when we begin to recognize frequencies and are able to define them. When you learn a language, there are people who speak that language. But with learning the language of crystalline energies, we do not have that luxury. Working together and sharing our experiences helps us to increasingly understand this language.

In this learning process, I came to an important conclusion: Whenever I think that I begin to understand the energies of crystal skulls, something new comes up, letting me know that there is more to learn. This means that whatever is presented here is only my current state of understanding. Hopefully it stimulates others to contribute to the understanding of this interesting subject of crystalline energies.

In the previous chapter I mentioned two types of harmonic frequencies: crystal harmonic frequencies and crystal skull harmonic frequencies. Once I began to understand the language better, it was possible to define several more frequencies (image 6.1).

Atlantis Harmonic Frequencies

The first frequency system I recognized came from my work with Earth energy grids. In *Gifts of Mother Earth*, a certain type of line called a communication line is described extensively (123-154). The creation of these lines happens spontaneously when two places with similar energies have enough of that energy to create such a connection. Initially these lines were discovered in connection with churches and were therefore called church lines[8].

Early in the research of communication lines, I found lines that connected places that sensitive/psychic people described as "Atlantis sites." Despite not knowing whether that was true, I began to use the term to label a certain type of energy held in these places and in their respective communication

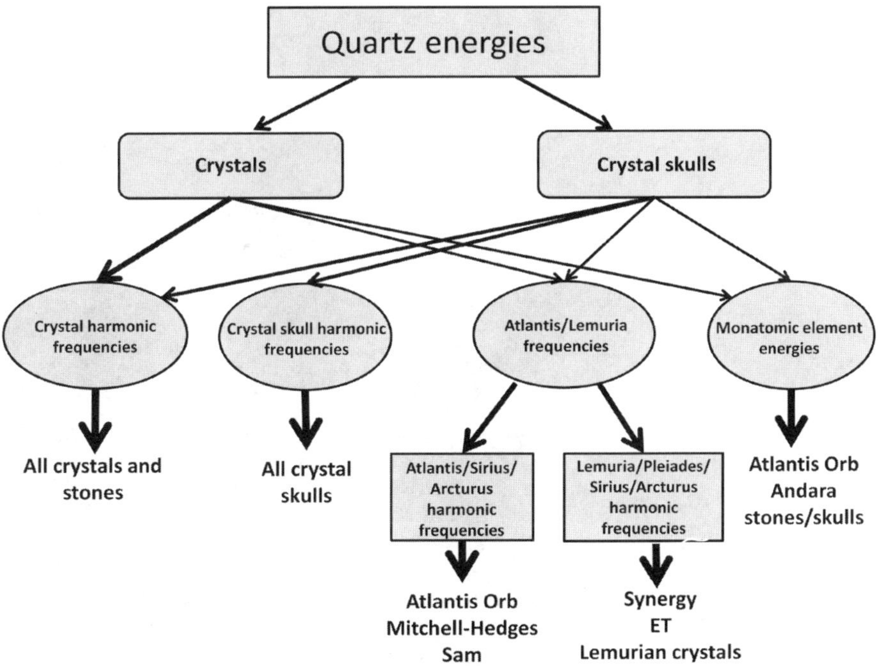

6.1 The five harmonic frequencies connected with quartz crystals and crystal skulls

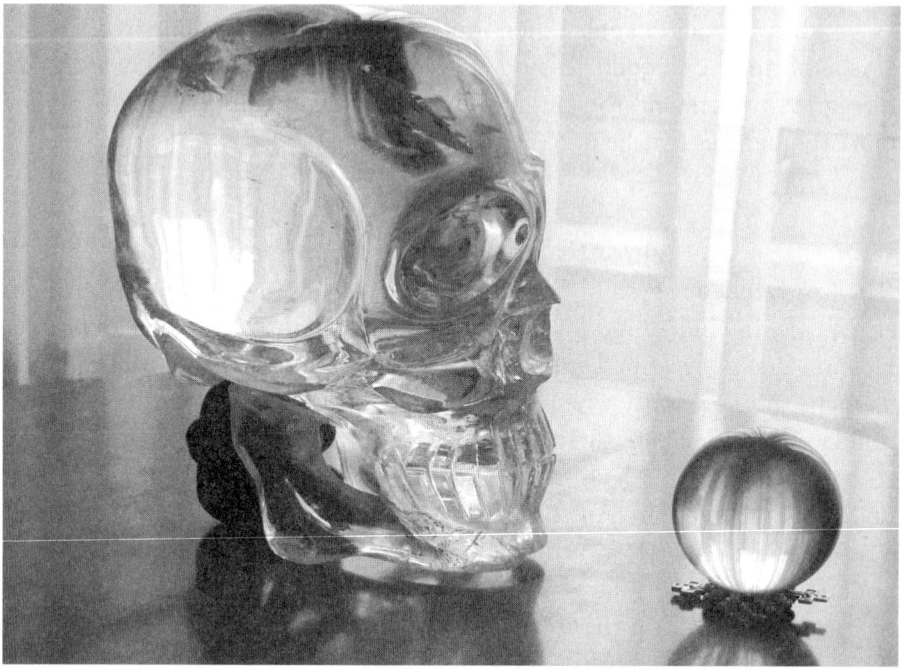

6.2 (Top) The Atlantean sphere and Sam

6.3 Sam and the Atlantean sphere with three "pyramids" inside

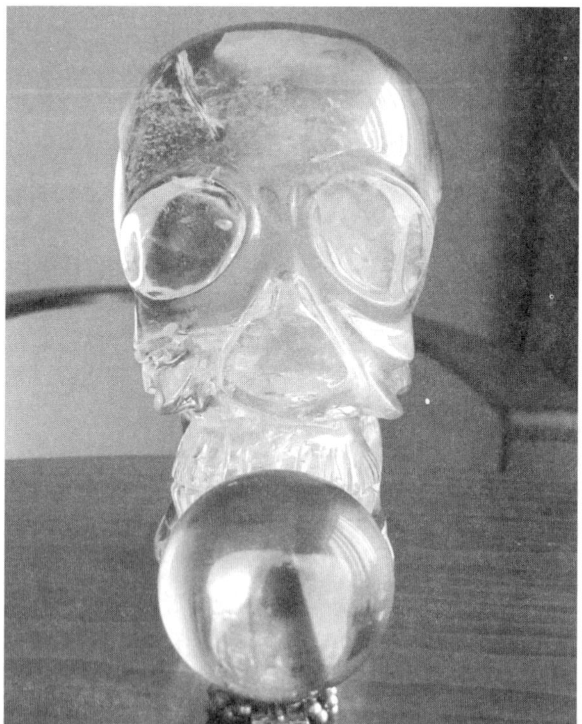

lines. I was surprised to find the same type of energy when I connected with the small crystal sphere called the Atlantis Orb or Atlantean sphere (images 6.2 and 6.3). This sphere was found in 1968 in a pyramid underwater outside of Bimini by Dr. Ray Brown, a naturopath from Arizona. The story is available at several places on the Internet[9].

I found it both fascinating and important that the energies considered Atlantean were in both the communication lines and the sphere. These Atlantean energies could be an integrated part of the overall energy system of a crystal. However, in the case of the crystal sphere, these energies were similar to the crystal skull energies: They had their own harmonic frequencies, hence the name "Atlantis harmonic frequencies." Over time these energies were found in other quartz crystal skulls, like the Mitchell-Hedges crystal skull, and also in contemporary crystal skulls like Sam (images 6.2 and 6.3).

That Sam had these Atlantis harmonic energies was a surprise to me. Originally these energies were not found in Sam, and I do not have the ability to induce such energies in a crystal skull. Does that mean that sources other than crystal skulls' caretakers can download energies into them? It was suggested that the Atlantis energies were downloaded when Sam and the Atlantean sphere were brought together during a symposium in Amsterdam in 2009. However, if downloading is so easy, why don't more crystals and crystal skulls have that energy? It seems that these frequencies are connected only to quartz, as I have not found them in any other type of crystal or stone.

The function of the Atlantis harmonic frequencies is to help us master the crystalline energies from a masculine and mental perspective. They help us to understand how to "work" with crystalline energies. That may be the reason why so many people are so fascinated with Atlantean energies. Our society has a tendency to apply what we know, and that is in alignment with Atlantean energies.

Lemuria Harmonic Frequencies

The fact that there are Atlantean harmonic frequencies brings the possibility that there are also Lemurian harmonic frequencies. We found communication lines that connected places with an energy that is defined as Lemurian. This has been described in *Gifts of Mother Earth* in the same chapter as the Atlantis lines (123-154).

For Sherry Whitfield, it is obvious that these energies are also present in the ancient crystal skull Synergy, of which she is the caretaker (image 6.4).

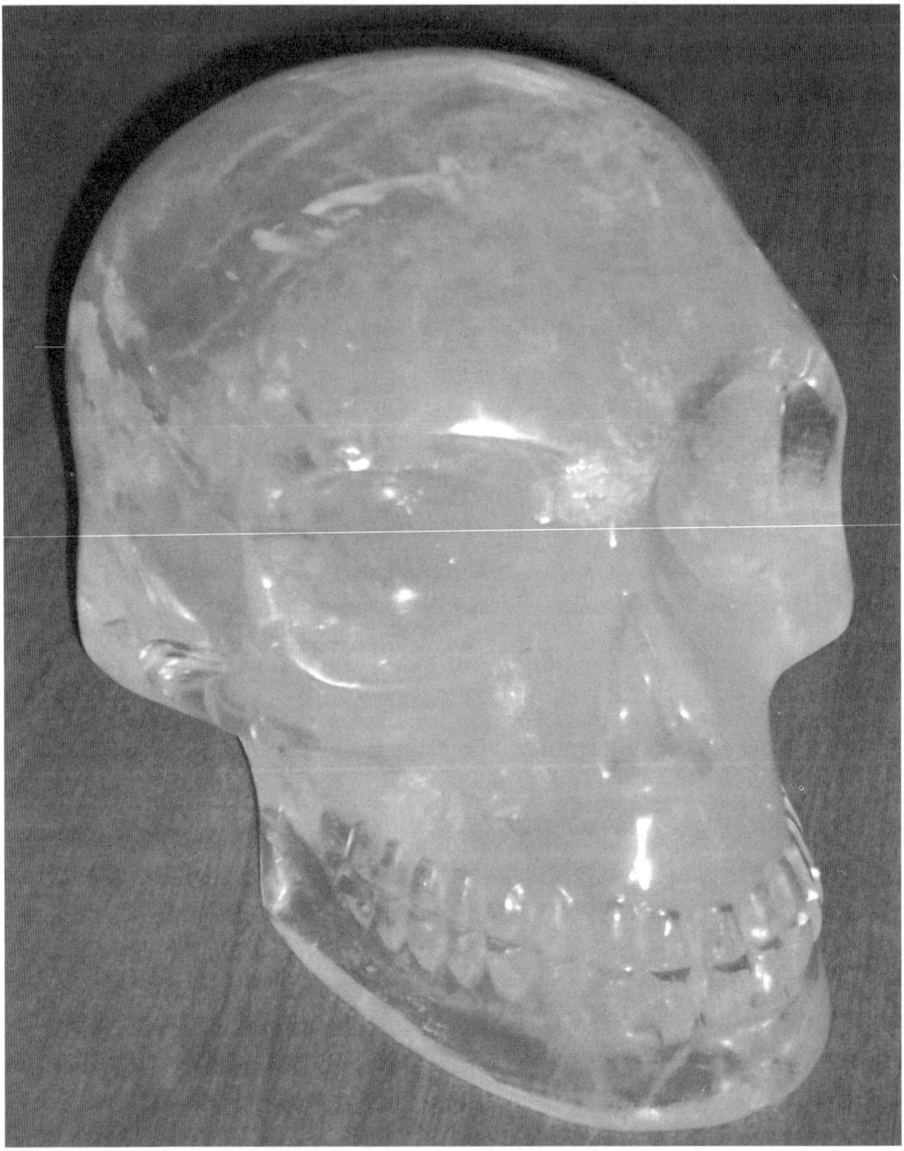

6.4 The Lemurian crystal skull Synergy

I agree completely. Like the Atlantis energies, Lemurian energies form their own harmonic frequencies. These Lemurian harmonic frequencies are also found in crystals that are called Lemurian seed crystals. Unfortunately, many crystals that are called and sold as "Lemurian seed crystals" are not really Lemurian seed crystals, as they do not have the Lemurian harmonic frequencies.

Lemurian crystals were discovered late in the 1990s in Brazil. They were not found in clusters but lying separately in the sand. They received attention because they were found in such a strange place. They are also different from any other quartz crystals because it is said that they look different — they have horizontal striations that run up one or more of the sides. This characteristic, however, is not restricted to Lemurian crystals alone, so using it as a way to define Lemurian crystals easily leads to mistakes. When looking at thirty-one crystals being sold in a store as "Lemurian seed crystals," I found only four crystals that actually had Lemurian harmonic frequencies. Almost all crystals sold on Ebay (an online auction website) are not really Lemurian seed crystals, so be very careful when you buy them. If you cannot sense the Lemurian harmonic frequencies, you at least can dowse whether or not these frequencies are present. The fact that a crystal has striations is absolutely not a correct way to determine whether it is a Lemurian seed crystal or not. The truth may be that these crystals are rarer than sellers want you to believe. Maybe the Lemurian seed crystals have been dug up to such a degree that they are becoming very rare? That is what a dealer in Lemurian seed crystals from Brazil believes and shared[10].

One of the first people to describe Lemurian seed crystals was Katrina Raphael, a well-known specialist in crystals and crystal energies. She described them in 2000 in her newsletter[11]. Since then they have gained a lot of popularity.

The Lemurian harmonic frequencies help us to understand crystalline wisdom in a feminine way. The feminine way invites us to connect with crystalline energies from the point of love and wisdom instead of understanding, mastering, and applying, which is more the Atlantean way. The feminine way is to experience these energies and ultimately to become these energies. The masculine way is to work with them. Ultimately these two ways need to be integrated so we can use the energies in harmony with All That Is.

Monatomic Elements Harmonic Frequencies

The last group of frequencies I am able to recognize is the monatomic elements' harmonic frequencies. These frequencies are connected with monatomic elements. There is a lot of information on monatomic elements available on the Internet; however, the study of monatomic elements is not mainstream science, although some scientific research has been done. There are a lot of websites that either promote products containing monatomic elements (unfortunately they are not always reliable) or share only limited information based on limited understanding.

The best information I have found comes from David Hudson, a person who financed scientific research on this subject and has given many lectures[12]. Some pages on the Internet say that Hudson invented monatomic elements. That is incorrect, but he came up with the term ORMEs, which stands for orbitally rearranged monatomic elements.

To understand the harmonic frequencies of monatomic elements, we first need to understand what monatomic elements are. The three traditional forms in which matter can appear are solid, fluid, and gaseous. Monatomic elements can be seen as another form in which matter can appear. The term already reveals the characteristics: Instead of bonding with other atoms to create a solid metal, monatomic elements cannot bond because the electrons are rearranged in such a way that bonding is no longer possible. Therefore, they can no longer form metals. Monatomic elements have the ability to cluster into small groups, which allows them to form very fine, often whitish powders. There are twelve metals that have the ability to exhibit these characteristics, the most generally known of which is gold. Monatomic gold is sold as having very special qualities and is available in health food stores and on the Internet. I would like to give a word of warning here: To my knowledge it is not yet possible to create pure monatomic gold or any other element[13]. Therefore, none of the claims that special drinks or supplements contain pure monatomic gold are correct. They may contain monatomic gold, but it is never *pure* — there will always be physical gold in the nonmonatomic state present as well. Often there is no monatomic gold at all but just gold particles in a suspension of which the amount of gold is indicated as parts per millions (ppm). Gold particles most likely will not harm us, although there are many unknown factors. Recent studies show that silver nanoparticles that were believed to be antimicrobial, and thus positive, had an adverse effect on plant growth[14].

Hudson discovered ORMEs when he did an analysis of a whitish powder in the soil that came from his land (he was a cotton farmer in southern Arizona). The analysis came back as it being "nothing." In his lectures, he says he did not understand how something he had in his hands could be "nothing" and therefore embarked on a journey of discovery. He hired a chemist, and it turned out that standard analytical methods indeed said that this powder is "nothing." But through intense research that cost Hudson millions of dollars, they found monatomic elements[15]. Once Hudson began to understand that these monatomic elements were known by alchemists and the ancient Egyptians, he realized that they are gifts that he believes need to be made available to people. He collected money and built a plant to produce monatomic elements on a large scale. When the construction was about to open, there was an accident that led to the closure of the plant by the government. He could have rebuilt it further away from populated areas, but he had no funds to do so, and thus his plans were brought to an end.

Monatomic elements are very important. We are beginning to recognize their unique qualities. These qualities were known to the ancient alchemists and are connected with the search for the philosopher's stone and the elixir of immortality[16]. When you work with products or objects that contain monatomic elements, it will become increasingly easy to experience and recognize their specific frequencies. A good way to start is by working with Andara stones. These stones have been found in northern California and look like glass that comes in different colors[17]. They are often found in or close to a whitish powder described as volcanic ash. Heating such ash creates a glass-like material that is sometimes inaccurately called obsidian or obsidianite. An example of glass created in this way is the much sought-after helenite[18]. The technique of heating volcanic ash was discovered when workers were recovering equipment after the eruption of Mount St. Helens. When their torches hit the volcanic ash, it changed into green or ruby-colored glass-like material[19].

The ash from Mount St. Helens does not contain monatomic elements. However, there is ash from other places that does contain monatomic elements, as Hudson discovered. Besides the Andara stones, I also have found a glass-like material made in Mexico that contains monatomic elements. The exact location of this material has not been revealed to me. Crystal skulls made from this material are very powerful. However, not all material that comes from that Mexican source contains monatomic elements. Apparently the ash from that source is not homogenous; in some places it contains monatomic elements and in others it does not. This is also true of a lot of Andara stones. So to know whether your Andara stone, glass from Mexico, or any other material you find contains monatomic elements, you must be sensitive enough to discern their energies or dowse.

Materials containing monatomic harmonic frequencies help us to activate our lightbodies, which leads to enlightenment and ascension. In other words, these frequencies are helping us in the final phase of our journey in mastering physical reality: the journey to oneness.

Crystal Skulls Separated into Energy Groups

Separating crystal skulls into energy groups is tricky. It took many years of trial and error before I came to the insights that I will present here. One of the reasons that it took so long is the complexity of the energies and the fact that they continuously change when we work with them. An important factor that determines the energetic condition of a crystal skull is its level of activation. Therefore I needed to find characteristics that are constant and go beyond the continuously experienced variations. The definition of groups is based on the characteristics that are known at this moment. Over time more characteristics may be discovered that can help us to define even more groups. Therefore what I present in this chapter is the "state of the art" at this moment, without claiming that this is a complete overview.

The definition of the groups is based on the presence of the different harmonic frequencies and on the level of activation. Often only limited material from each group is available because some of the harmonic frequencies are quite rare. I will describe each of the groups that can be recognized and, if possible, give examples. In Addendum I, I have summarized some basic information on crystal skulls from each of the following groups (excluding the contemporary crystal skulls) or I have made references to places where more information can be found. So far I have defined the following groups: original crystal skulls, Atlantean crystal skulls, crystal skulls with Atlantean harmonic frequencies, crystal skulls with Lemurian harmonic frequencies, the skulls with thirty-six layers (with a bluish shimmer at the thirty-sixth layer), the thirty-layer skulls (with bluish shimmer), the skulls with twenty-four layers (also with a bluish shimmer at the twenty-fourth layer), skulls with less than twenty-four layers (without a bluish shimmer), and contemporary crystal skulls.

There are some confusing elements in differentiating energy groups easily. Contemporary crystal skulls can have up to 36 energy layers and can contain Atlantean or Lemurian harmonic frequencies. There are, however, ways to differentiate them from crystal skulls that were carved in earlier phases of history.

The Original Skulls

The term "original skull" is confusing. It suggests that there were crystal skulls that were the very first group of skulls and that they were functioning as a kind of model for all future crystal skulls. It may be that such crystal skulls exist, but if so, I am not aware of any. I use the term to refer to the information fields that, I believe, came from twelve star nations. These star nations provided us with information that, when brought together in an integrated way, will lead to wisdom and understanding of who we are, helping us to shift to higher levels of consciousness. The idea that star nations are supporting humankind on our collective spiritual journey has gained support over time, even though we cannot prove that it is true. It is a "truth" with which people resonate increasingly.

According to indigenous people, there are many star nations[20]. The knowledge and understanding of star nations and the idea that our ancestors came from the stars is a long-held secret oral tradition of indigenous people[21]. One of the people who has come forward with information about star people is Chief Golden Light Eagle/Standing Elk, who mentions the names of different star nations[22]. During the Star Knowledge Conference in Sedona in 1998, a great deal of information about star nations and contact with them was shared[23].

There is generally not much information available about the relationship between star nations and crystal skulls, but there is information in *Crystal Skulls: Interacting with a Phenomenon* (123-140), and we will look at star nations in more detail in chapter 9.

I believe that the original gift of the star nations was information. Initially people could tap into this information without difficulties. When the connections weakened, it was decided to store information, and the form that was chosen was the crystal skull. Therefore, I believe that the original crystal skulls were not physical crystal skulls but twelve information systems that human beings were supposed to integrate with a deeper understanding of themselves and the role they fulfilled in the cosmic whole. It is my opinion that we, the human race, are the thirteenth star nation, represented by the thirteenth crystal skull. Once we function as the thirteenth crystal skull, we will bring the twelve information systems together into oneness. Some believe that this is the moment we will be contacted more directly by representatives of the star nations and may become part of the federation of the star people/star nations (Galactic Federation). For me this is less relevant. What is relevant is the shift in consciousness that will help humankind to survive in this physical reality.

Atlantean Crystal Skulls

It is fascinating to hear and read so many references to the idea that crystal skulls may have come from Atlantis. Some of these references are intended to ridicule the crystal skulls (by those who do not believe in Atlantis or in crystal skulls) while other references are intended to raise the importance of the crystal skulls (by those who believe in both Atlantis and crystal skulls). Edgar Cayce's readings mention that Atlanteans had great knowledge of crystals and stones[24]. This may have contributed to the ideas that crystal skulls originally came from Atlantis, even though Edgar Cayce never mentioned crystal skulls.

We do not know the nature of the characteristics of Atlantean crystals or Atlantean crystal skulls. I have used the characteristics of the energies that are called Atlantean and are in Earth's grids and lines. I also used the characteristics of the energies found in the Atlantis orb, which is very unique in its energies. It has the crystal harmonic frequencies, the Atlantis harmonic frequencies, and the monatomic element harmonic frequencies. Although the assumption based on one object is rather risky, I assume that crystal skulls made in Atlantis had the crystal harmonic frequencies, the crystal skull harmonic frequencies, the Atlantis harmonic frequencies, and the monatomic harmonic frequencies. It seems that no such crystal skull exists or has yet been found. So far the only crystalline structure with such characteristics — excluding the crystal skull harmonic frequencies — is the Atlantean orb. However, I will not be surprised if more crystals and maybe even more crystal skulls appear.

Crystal Skulls with Atlantean Harmonic Frequencies

These types of crystal skulls are defined as having three harmonic frequencies: those of crystals, crystal skulls, and Atlantis. Of all known ("famous") crystal skulls, only one has all these characteristics, and that is the Mitchell-Hedges crystal skull. This crystal skull has stirred up emotions and reactions for as long as people have been aware of its existence. It is most likely that this will continue. Some of these controversies are summarized in Addendum I, skull 1. The Mitchell-Hedges crystal skull has the wide thirty-sixth layer with a bluish shimmer. I have not seen this characteristic with any contemporary crystal skull. As I mentioned in the previous chapter, it seems to belong to a rather unique group of crystal skulls that are generally considered ancient.

There are also a few contemporary crystal skulls that have the Atlantean harmonic frequencies. One of these is Sam, my and my wife's contemporary crystal skull. How these contemporary crystal skulls acquired Atlantean harmonic frequencies is unknown to me. It may be possible that their overall energetic conditions are such that when they come in contact with a place or with a crystal like the Atlantis orb, they begin to resonate with these frequencies and become their carriers. Therefore, having these particular frequencies does not mean the skulls originated in Atlantis. This may also be true for the Mitchell-Hedges crystal skull. It is possible to read energies from a photograph, even though it can be more confusing than having the actual object in hand. When this technique is used with pictures of the Mitchell-Hedges crystal skull, all pictures, independent of their age, show that this skull has the Atlantean harmonic frequencies. It truly is an enigmatic crystal skull (image 6.5).

Crystal Skulls with Lemurian Harmonic Frequencies

There are crystal skulls that in addition to having crystal and crystal skull harmonic frequencies also have Lemurian harmonic frequencies. At this moment I am aware of two crystal skulls that have these characteristics, and both belong to the group of crystal skulls accepted as ancient. These crystal

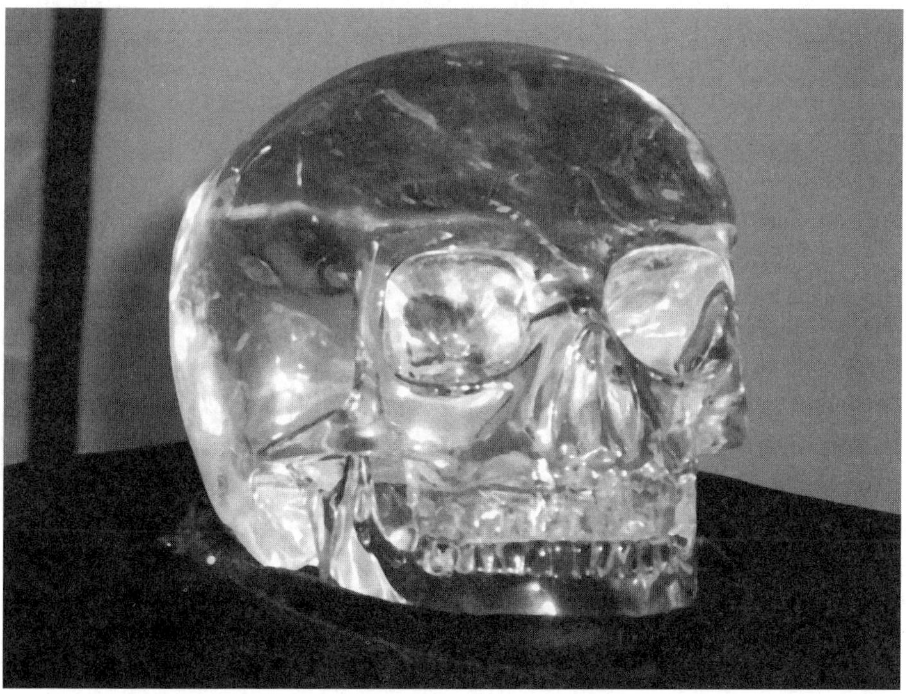

6.5 The Mitchell-Hedges crystal skull

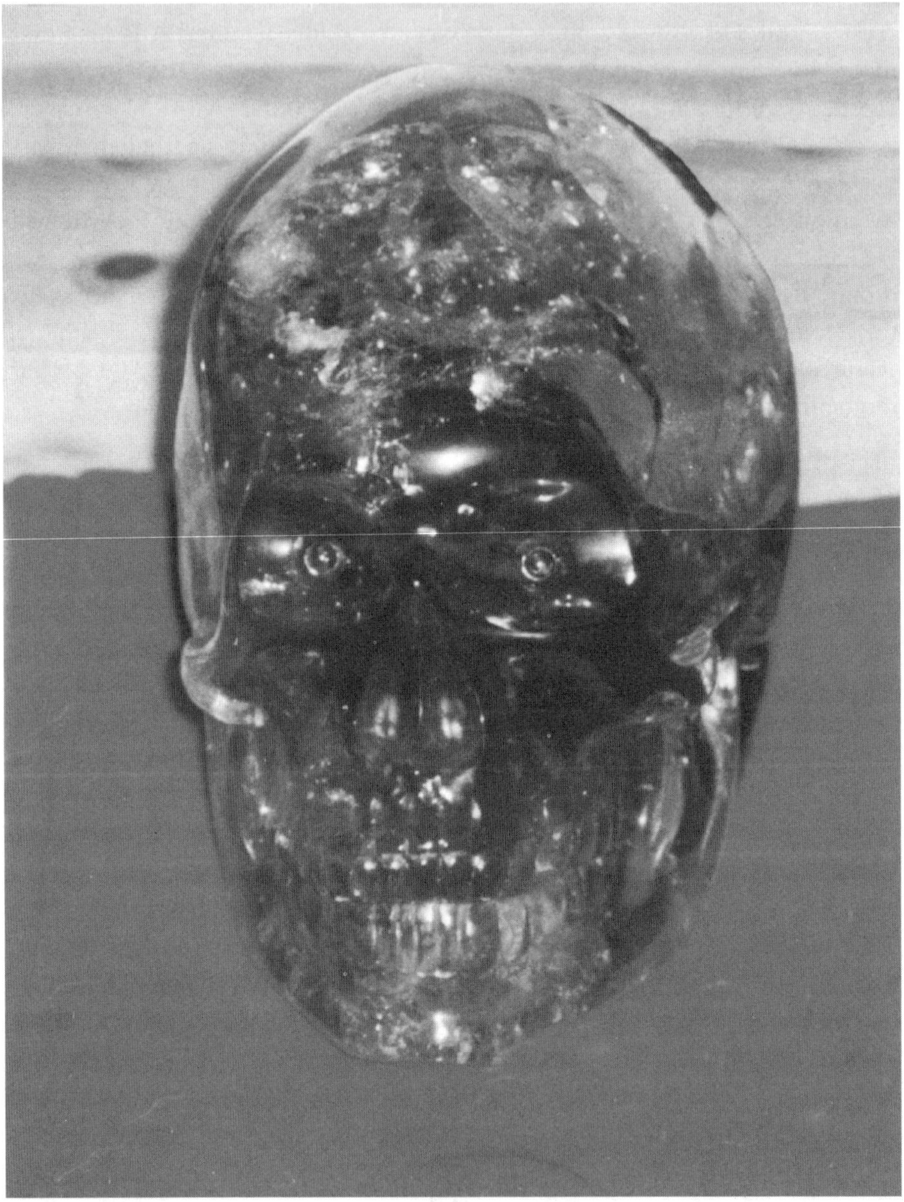

6.6 The crystal skull ET

skulls are Synergy (image 6.4) and ET (image 6.6). Those who can dowse energies, or sense or feel energies, can check for a particular characteristic that is only found in these two of the famous ancient crystal skulls: a barrier at the twenty-fourth energy layer placed there by those who created and worked with these crystal skulls in the past. It is called a barrier because it holds energies that make it more difficult to go beyond this layer to higher energy layers. Because this type of barrier is never found in contemporary crystal skulls, it seems that it was programmed purposely into these crystal skulls. Based on the function of the energy layers discussed in the previous chapter, it seems that the ancient people were inviting those who worked with the crystal skulls to first master the third-dimensional physical reality and the phase in between before moving more fully into the fourth-dimensional reality. The "barrier" is like a warning: Do not move too fast because it will not benefit you. It seems that the ancient people wanted to give a clear and powerful message. However, for most people who work with crystal skulls nowadays, this signal will be in vain and unnecessary because of the lack of sensitivity and understanding. A barrier at the twenty-fourth energy layer has so far only been found in these two crystal skulls.

Of these two crystal skulls, only Synergy has a clear bluish shimmer at the widened thirty-sixth layer. This shimmer is only vaguely present at the slightly wider thirty-sixth layer of ET, which is also less wide than Synergy's and those of other ancient skulls. It seems that ET's activation has not gone as far as the other ancient crystal skulls.

There is not much controversy around these two skulls. ET is one of the ten crystal skulls of which Joky van Dieten is the caretaker. Although it is claimed that nine of them are ancient or old, only ET is generally mentioned as one of the ancient skulls. Unfortunately, due to Joky's health conditions, ET has not been around as much as people would have liked. ET is a good example of a crystal skull that has lost a significant amount of its activity due to the lack of focused connections with it. (For more information, see Addendum I, skull 2.)

Since Sherry Whitfield has become the caretaker of Synergy, the "Lemurian" crystal skull, Synergy has become a very important part of the crystal skull energy field. It also has become an important part of the many activities involving crystal skulls. Since Sherry committed to be Synergy's caretaker in 2001, the crystal skull has been part of many events all over the world. It has visited many sacred places and crop circles, all of which contributed to the powerful energies connected with this crystal skull. It also is called a Lemurian crystal skull because its origin is an island north of Australia that is considered to hold Lemurian energies[25]. Of all the older crystal skulls, Synergy has the most detailed history (see Addendum I, item 3).

The fact that these two crystal skulls hold the Lemurian harmonic frequencies is not proof that they originated in Lemuria. There is at least one contemporary crystal skull (image 6.7) that also has these Lemurian harmonic frequencies. The Lemurian harmonic frequencies may have been introduced into these skulls when they were present during ceremonies that were performed in areas with Lemurian energies holding Lemurian consciousness. It is not known when or how the Lemurian harmonic frequencies were downloaded into the contemporary skull AhBeSo. Initially these energies were not present in the skull, but at a certain moment, after an intensive search for understanding Lemurian energies, it was discovered that this skull was a carrier of these energies. How this happened, I do not know. Obviously we still have a lot to learn.

Crystal Skulls with 36 Activated Layers

The group of crystal skulls with thirty-six layers that will be described here all have been activated in the past and are generally accepted as being ancient. In the process of activation, the ancients created a barrier. That barrier and a bluish shimmer at a widened thirty-sixth layer make these ancient skulls different from the small group of contemporary crystal skulls with thirty-six energy layers. We saw the phenomenon of a barrier with the two crystal skulls that have Lemurian harmonic energies — Synergy and ET — which both have a barrier at the twenty-fourth layer. The crystal skulls in this group have a barrier located at the eighteenth energy layer instead. This suggests that those who activated these crystal skulls felt that people needed to first master physical reality before moving into Oneness consciousness. Their message is to first learn to feel that you are an integrated part of the world you live in, learning to love and respect all your relations. Once you are able to do that, you may be ready to move on. Most of the crystal skulls that are considered "ancient" belong to this group, such as Sha Na Ra, Einstein, Max, the Mayan skull, the amethyst skull often nicknamed Ami, and the amethyst crystal skull from San Jose, Mexico. There are other skulls belonging to this group, but they are not included here because there is insufficient knowledge about their whereabouts and no pictures are available.

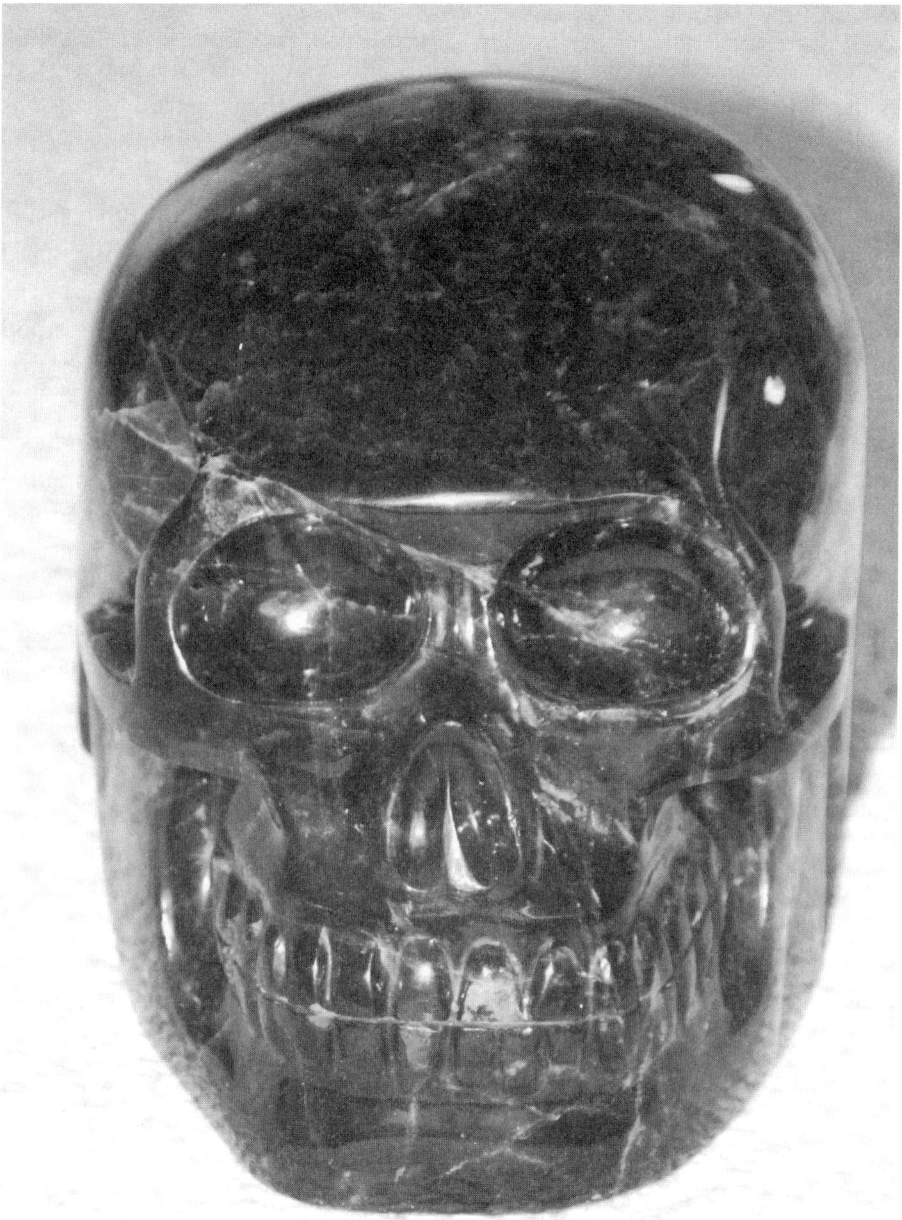

6.7 AhBeSo, a contemporary crystal skull belonging to the author and his wife that holds Lemurian harmonic frequencies

All the mentioned crystal skulls — with the exception of the Mayan skull — have a widened thirty-sixth layer with a bluish shimmer. The Mayan skull is like ET — its bluish shimmer is weaker and its thirty-sixth layer not as wide. So again, this could mean that the Mayan skull has not completed the journey of activation to its optimal potential.

Together with the Lemurian skulls, the crystal skulls with thirty-six layers form a group that without doubt can be placed in the "ancient" category. Based on their energies, there is little doubt that these crystal skulls belong to the group of skulls that were carved at a time when people still fully understood crystal skull energies and the awakening of the skulls' potential. The fact that ET and the Mayan skull only have a faint bluish shimmer at the thirty-sixth layer may indicate that they were carved later, although it also could indicate that their activation was never completed, given that the skulls mentioned in the group of skulls with thirty-six layers do not have the Atlantean harmonic frequencies, which seems to suggest that they are post-Atlantean.

There is another crystal skull with thirty-six energy layers that should be placed in this group. This skull is named Lucy, and Kirk Landauer is its caretaker. He bought this skull from an antique dealer. He bought another skull — Ixchel — from the same person, and that skull will be described in the next group. The only information Kirk has about Lucy is that it was with Ixchel, which he bought first, and that he wished to keep the two together. The skull was bought about twenty-five years ago. It is unusual because it has more of a Simian (monkey) shape than a human shape (image 6.8). However, it has all the usual "real" crystal skull characteristics, which means it has the crystal skull harmonic frequencies. This skull has thirty-six activated layers, but it does not have a barrier. However, it does have the widened thirty-sixth layer with the bluish shimmer. For me, it is a riddle how this skull acquired such a high activation without the barrier at either layer eighteen or twenty-four that other similar crystal skulls have. The person or persons who were caretakers of Lucy in the past had knowledge of activating a crystal skull beyond what is known and even possible today. This is one of the many riddles you come across when studying the energies of crystal skulls. (For more information about Lucy, see Addendum I, skull 10.)

The known crystal skulls that belong to this group show many differences. Max and Sha Na Ra have unique shapes, while the shapes of the Mayan skull and Einstein are similar, Einstein being the larger of the two. Stephen Mehler has studied both Einstein and the Mayan Skull. He came to the conclusion that Einstein is a master crystal skull that was the center skull of a

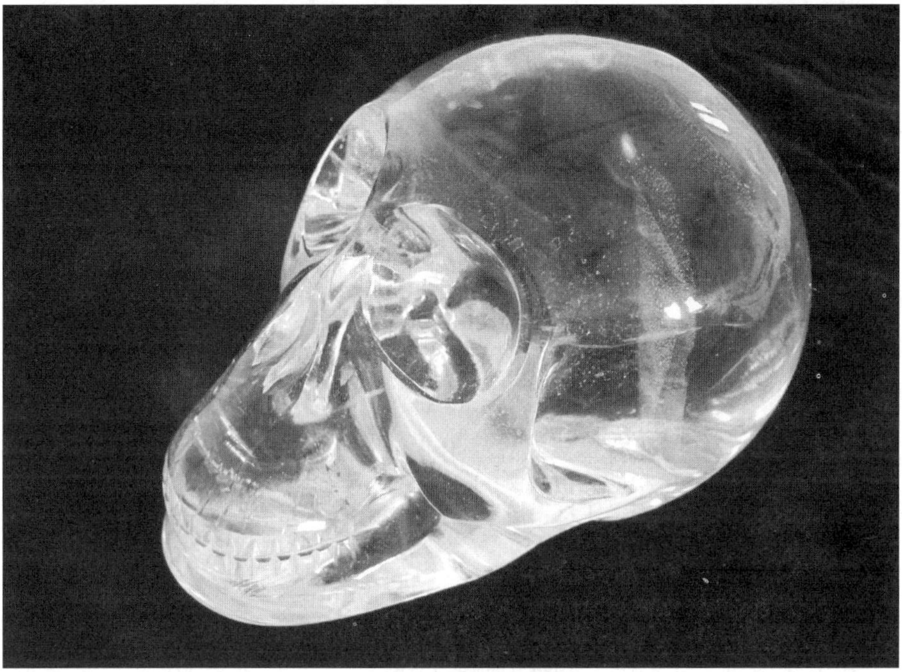

6.8 Lucy, a crystal skull with Simian characteristics and special energies

group of thirteen. The Mayan skull could have been one of the twelve around Einstein[26]. Both of these two crystal skulls have a particular indentation at the temple area, which the amethyst skull Ami also has. This may mean that this skull might originate from the same area or from the same time frame. However, this is quite speculative. The same could be said of the amethyst skull from San Jose, Mexico. Also this skull has a similar indentation[27] (see Addendum I, skull 8).

Einstein came into the public view during the 10–10–10 event in New York[28]. Unfortunately, the Mayan skull has been missing for quite a while. At this moment, the current whereabouts of the Mayan crystal skull are unknown.

The amethyst crystal skull Ami was in a vault for around fifteen years but was bought in 2009 by an unknown buyer. It was hoped that the new caretaker would be willing to allow people to connect again with this special crystal skull, but so far that has not happened. For more information on Einstein, Ami, and the Mayan skull, see Addendum I, skulls 6, 7, and 9.

The crystal skull Max, also called the Texas crystal skull, travels the most frequently. JoAnn Parks, the caretaker of Max, has contributed to the possibility for people to connect with crystal skulls more than anyone else. For more than twenty years she has traveled with Max all over the United States and even abroad. Max is a unique crystal skull that will be described in more detail in Addendum I, skull 5.

Last but not least in this group is Sha Na Ra. This skull has a shape that has been called "primitive" and differs from all other known crystal skulls. It was found in a rather unique way. The skull was discovered in a private dig that was guided by Nick Nocerino through what was called psycho-archaeology. Nick was the caretaker of the skull until his passing, at which time Kirby Seid helped the Nocerino family by bringing Sha Na Ra to events. In 2009, Michele Nocerino brought Sha Na Ra to the 9–9–9 event[29], which marked the beginning of her taking on the responsibilities of caretaker of this special skull. (For more information on Sha Na Ra, see Addendum I, skull 4.)

The crystal skulls of this and the previous group are important as beacons on the path of understanding crystal skulls. They are far ahead on this path in the sense that those who created them understood crystal skulls and their energies at a level we are now slowly beginning to remember. We are beginning once more to develop the skills to work with contemporary crystal skulls at levels that come increasingly close to the level of these fully activated crystal skulls. However, there still is much to learn.

Crystal Skulls with 30 Layers Activated

I have encountered only two crystal skulls that have this characteristic. They have thirty layers activated, and the thirtieth layer is wider with a bluish shimmer. The skulls are rather small; they are about 3½ inches long.

I am not sure what to think of these crystal skulls. They do not seem to be "real" skulls in the sense that the material does not seem natural. This material occurs in nature but is rare. These skulls are carved from a dark-green material that looks like glass. However, they have both the crystal and crystal skull harmonic frequencies, and they also contain the monatomic element harmonic frequencies. Although the material looks like helenite, a material created by heating volcanic dust from Mount St. Helens[30], they are energetically completely different. Helenite has a maximum of twelve energy layers while these two skulls have thirty energy layers. Both skulls are in my and my wife's possession. (More information is given in Addendum I, skull 11.)

The understanding of the purpose of these skulls is minimal. In many ways, they are unique, and more study is needed to understand them and their different energies. The fact that they have a widened thirtieth layer with a bluish shimmer suggests that they are not contemporary crystal skulls. And given the material they are made of, they may have been created by people with an expansive knowledge of crystalline energies and how to activate them to such a high level.

Crystal Skulls with 24 Layers Activated: Ceremonial Skulls

The name of this group may be confusing and therefore needs clarification. While this group of quartz crystal skulls has only twenty-four layers fully activated, they are "fully activated." Looking at their energetic qualities, it seems that these crystal skulls were activated to twenty-four layers on purpose. This is based on the fact that the twenty-fourth layer is wider and stronger than those twenty-fourth layers that form a barrier in the crystal skulls with Lemurian harmonic frequencies. It feels as if an intentional block was placed to limit activation to this level, which is reflected by the bluish shimmer at the twenty-fourth layer. The motivation to place this block at layer twenty-four seems to be similar to that of the barriers placed at layers twenty-four and eighteen that we saw in previous groups: to master the third-dimensional reality and the in-between phase from the third to the fourth dimension. The shamans and medicine people from the times when these crystal skulls were created believed that there was no need to go beyond the energies of the twenty-four layers. With some training, it is possible to continue the activation of these crystal skulls, but it almost feels unnatural to do so. The fact that these crystal skulls have a very broad twenty-fourth layer with a bluish shimmer indicates that these twenty-four layers have been activated to their optimal state.

Many people who have worked with the crystal skulls in this group feel that these skulls have been used for ceremonial purposes. There may be many crystal skulls that belong to this group, but there are only a few that are "around." There are stories of more crystal skulls held privately in Mexico and that some of these crystal skulls might belong to this group. The ones that are available to various degrees are Ixchel, Madre (of which the caretaker is Laurie Walker), Pancho, and Paco. Ichabod and the Redo family skull with the cross are held privately and also belong to this group.

Pancho differs from the other skulls because it is hollow. Pancho's caretaker was Mario Bojorquez, but unfortunately Mario left Pancho in a taxi cab in New York and has not been able to locate it since.

Ixchel was the mystery skull during the 11–11–11 crystal skull event in Los Angeles[31], where its caretaker, Kirk Landauer, showed it for the first time to a large gathering. In many ways, the shape of this skull is different, and it is a wonderful addition to the crystal skull family. Paco was at the first crystal skull conference in Mexico City in 2009[32] and is also in a private collection.

In many ways, these crystal skulls are fascinating. While the crystal skulls from the previous groups are activated to the optimal state of thirty-six layers, these crystal skulls were prepared purposely for specific functions. It seems likely that this type of crystal skull is from a more recent time period than those in the groups mentioned earlier, although it is possible that the time periods of the creation of these different groups overlapped each other. Because there are several crystal skulls with the same characteristics, it seems likely that these crystal skulls were created and activated in the same way during the same time period.

Activation to twenty-four layers does not reflect an inability to activate to a higher level, since creating these energetic states still requires mastery of the crystal skull energies. (More information on each of the crystal skulls mentioned in this group is given in Addendum I, skulls 12–17.)

Crystal Skulls with Less Than 24 Layers but Most Likely Not Contemporary

This group of crystals skulls reflects a time period during which the ability to activate crystal skulls optimally or to a specific state seems to have been absent. It is difficult to ascertain the function of these crystal skulls. They were most likely considered to be important tools supporting people on their spiritual paths. Their function may have been to keep the legend of the crystal skulls alive, even though the mastery of the energies of the crystal skulls seems to have been lost. I believe that these crystal skulls are from a more recent time period than the previous groups.

All crystal skulls in the previous groups are quartz crystal skulls. Quartz is a unique material and is the best material to hold all of the crystal skull energies necessary for the journey to oneness. Each type of crystal skull supports this journey, but not to the same extent as the quartz crystal skulls.

Here we find crystal skulls made from crystals other than quartz. All crystal skulls, independent of their material, are important because they help us on the journey of remembering who we are. People lost the ability to use all of the aspects of quartz crystal skulls; therefore, the specific material of the crystal skulls became less important. In addition, it is possible that there were other reasons to make crystal skulls from different materials — for example, because the specific material, like jade, had a certain value[33].

The crystal skulls in this group range from being very powerful to being hardly activated. It is likely that more crystal skulls from this group will be found or are already in private collections. I know of several crystal skulls from this group that are in Mexico — often held privately. Unfortunately, the caretakers prefer to remain anonymous.

Crystal skulls in this group are not less important; their potential has been activated to a lesser degree. Because most people of our time period are not able to connect fully and utilize all levels of the crystal skulls with thirty-six layers and a bluish shimmer, these skulls have much to offer us. Several crystal skulls of this group can be met and seen, because their caretakers make them available. Examples are Rainbow, Zar, and Nefertiti (all three belonging to DaEl Walker); the Jesuit, Janus, Baby Luv, and Shui Ting Er from Joky van Dieten; Amar from Grace and Maurice Dunner; the British Museum skull; and the Paris skull. I have included the Smithsonian skull, although I believe that it is a contemporary crystal that may not be much older that sixty years (see Addendum I, skull 28).

There also are smaller skulls that fall in this category, like Ti and Bet that originate in Tibet along with some small skulls coming from Nepal, of which my wife and I are the caretakers. Skulls that belong to this category also appeared during the first crystal skull event in Mexico City in 2009[34].

It is not easy to separate this group energetically from contemporary crystal skulls. Some crystal skulls, like the Smithsonian skull and the Nepalese skulls, are placed arbitrarily in this group because they seem to be outside of the flow of real contemporary crystal skulls (crystal skulls that were carved over the past forty to fifty years). To place crystal skulls in this category, additional information has to be used, such as history, place of discovery, and metaphysical information. (For more information on these skulls, see Addendum I, skulls 18–30.)

Crystal Skulls Considered Ancient but Not Mentioned in Any of the Groups

To disagree with caretakers about the age of ancient or old crystal skulls may be downright dangerous, especially with crystal skulls that are called "ancient" by their caretakers even though their energetic characteristics and sometimes the sources they come from indicate clearly that they are not. This is a highly sensitive subject that most people do not wish to discuss — to the extent that it has become a "no-zone." As I have mentioned, it is not easy to define with certainty which crystal skulls have been carved in which time period. However, the increasing understanding of energies and how people have worked with them in the past helps to determine in which of the defined groups an old or ancient crystal skull most likely belongs.

I consider all crystal skulls to be contemporary if they are not mentioned in one of the above groups. This is especially true for the quartz crystal skulls. Many that are presented as ancient do not have any of the discussed characteristics. Of course, only those crystal skulls presented publicly can be evaluated. There are many crystal skulls hidden in private collections — including possibly ancient skulls.

When crystal skulls are sold as ancient, it is almost always a money-making scheme. Some Chinese carvers have the ability to make crystal skulls look ancient, and when crystal skulls are placed next to ancient objects, they sometimes take on energies of those objects and therefore may feel old themselves. Many people have bought these "ancient" skulls in good faith but unfortunately have been cheated. It is sad that with a growing interest in crystal skulls the desire to be a caretaker of an ancient crystal skull increases, creating opportunities for those who wish to take advantage of others.

In no way are my statements intended to accuse anyone. Crystal skulls amplify, creating all kinds of actions, reactions, feelings, and situations. If you follow your heart, you will always choose wisely.

We can apply the energetic characteristics of crystal skulls to skulls that some people consider ancient but are not mentioned in the previous groups. This leads to some surprising discoveries. Let us start with the Mongolian crystal skulls that started to appear about five to six years ago. These skulls have a different shape than almost all other crystal skulls and have large eye sockets. They were not found by archaeologists or anyone else but suddenly started to appear in increasing numbers, all from the same source. These Mongolian skulls can be separated into three types. The most common type is the orange Mongolian skull that many claim to be made of orange calcite. However, when I look at the energies of these skulls, I cannot detect any energy layers. These skulls have neither crystal harmonic frequency layers nor crystal skull harmonic frequency layers, which means that they are not made from natural material and, from an energy point of view, cannot be called "crystal skulls." This does not mean that these skulls do not have energies connected with them; they are able to form energy fields, and these fields can sometimes feel quite strong, especially when a caretaker works with them with love. However, they do not have the energies that characterize crystal skulls, so from an energy point of view, they are not crystal skulls.

The second type of Mongolian skull is made of tabular coral. Because tabular coral is a natural material, you might expect these skulls to have the crystal layers — and that is indeed the case. These skulls hold a potential of eighteen energy layers. However, they do not have the crystal skull harmonic frequencies and the connected layers. Could it be that the shape or the intent prevents the appearance of the crystal skull harmonic frequencies?

The third type of Mongolian skull is made from fossilized wood. Of all three groups of Mongolian skulls, these are the only "true" crystal skulls, having both the harmonic crystal and crystal skull frequencies. However, the layers do not indicate an optimal activation, making it unlikely that they are ancient.

There is another group of skulls labeled as Mongolian that comes through a different person. Again, there is a suggestion or even a statement that they are ancient skulls. Many of them are similar to Hongshan-style crystal skulls on Ebay.

There are two types in this group. One group is the jade skulls, which often look old. These skulls have both the crystal and crystal skull harmonic frequencies. However, all the ones that I have looked at physically or through pictures reveal the same thing: They are hardly or not at all activated, which suggests that they are contemporary. The large number of identical or similar skulls suggests that many copies have been made. Image 6.9 shows an example of such a skull that is in my collection.

The second type in this group, which is a large number of the crystal skulls sold under the "Mongolian Hongshan-style" label, is made of artificial material — resin — that is often mixed with quartz powder to make it possible for the skull to hold energy. But that does not create the natural crystal harmonic frequencies. The fakeness of these skulls is so obvious that I am truly surprised that they are purchased as crystal skulls. Again, this type of crystal skull does not have any energy layers. Some of them, sold as red obsidian, are actually red-dyed resin. When I checked one day on Ebay, of the 141 skulls sold under the descriptor "Hongshan skull," 39 were made of resin[35].

There is a third group of crystal skulls that are sold as ancient Mongolian skulls. These skulls are larger than the average human's and are made of a dark material that sellers claim is jade. They have symbols on top of the cranium that help to give the impression that they are ancient. Several of

6.9 A recently carved jade skull that is sold as coming from the Chinese Hongshan culture (5,000-6,000 years old). From the author's collection.

these skulls have been sold for high prices. Unfortunately, these skulls are also fakes — they also are made of artificial materials. These skulls have been worked with energetically to make them feel old, but the truth is that they hold unpleasant low-vibrational energy.

Another group of crystal skulls from the same source as the first group of Mongolian skulls is the Himalayan skulls. I always have had difficulty with this group. I tried to feel whether they were old/ancient and kept being confused. However, if I look at them from an energetic point of view, it becomes much easier to understand what they are. There are two groups: the eight small Himalayan skulls and the fourteen large ones (not thirteen, as many people believe).

Seven of the small Himalayan skulls seem to be made from quartz and are therefore true crystal skulls. However, I have seen six of them and not even one has twenty-four or thirty-six layers activated; they have the energies of contemporary crystal skulls. Several of them now are wonderful tools, having been activated through the activities and love of their caretakers. None of them have barriers or a widened layer with a bluish shimmer.

The large Himalayan skulls, however, are a different story. None of them have energy layers. Again, having quartz powder mixed in with the resin makes it possible for them to hold at least some energy, which is sometimes pleasant and even powerful, reflecting the connection with their caretakers. Of course, they do not have the qualities of "real" crystal skulls.

Sharing this information is in no way intended as judgment. It is not known how aware those who sell such skulls actually are. Resin skulls are energetically not the same as crystal skulls of natural materials, and they do not have the qualities and characteristics of real crystal skulls. But I feel that it is important to bring these facts about resin skulls into awareness for those who are interested in crystal skulls, thereby increasing their discernment when buying from Ebay or other places that make claims or suggestions about the age of a skull.

Contemporary Crystal Skulls

All crystal skulls, other than those that are mentioned explicitly as being "different," belong to the group of contemporary crystal skulls. The majority of these crystal skulls have been carved in the past fifteen to twenty years. As I mentioned earlier, most contemporary crystal skulls are carved in Brazil and China, with small groups being carved in Mexico, Nepal, Germany, and the United States. China, especially, has become an important source of new crystal skulls for caretakers all over the world.

Because it is recognized that different carvers create different qualities of crystal skulls, it is dangerous to generalize. Every crystal skull, with few exceptions, can become a beautiful skull when its potential has been fully realized. All it takes is love, connection, dedication, and persistence. Dark energies are very rarely connected with contemporary crystal skulls.

Over time, the needs of clients have changed carving styles. Some of these changes are a consequence of artistic expression, but some are based on market competition. Initially, people wanted to have a crystal skull to understand the offerings of a crystal skull. Now, the joy of buying crystal skulls of different materials and of different forms also determines people's choices. The increasing expense of quartz is also a reason people buy crystal skulls of other materials that tend to be less expensive.

Making changes to carving style and form can be wonderful as long as the shape stays close enough to that of the human skull. Unfortunately, that is not always the case. Even carvers with a strong reputation create skulls with shapes that no longer have the crystal skull harmonic frequencies. It appears that the art is more important than the essence of the true nature of a crystal skull — especially in China, where the crystal skull face has become a part of beautiful carvings. Unfortunately, many of these carvings move so far away from the human skull shape that, despite their beauty, they are of no interest to those working with the gifts of crystal skulls to support their spiritual journeys.

By now it must have become clear that working with crystal skulls is a journey. Caretakers of crystal skulls are at different points on that journey. No point is better than any other — it just is where a person is and that is always exactly the right place to be. It is not about getting a crystal skull to the highest level of activation as quickly as possible; it is about the journey of remembering who we are and expressing our true selves. Crystal skulls help us on this journey, and they always reflect where we are.

Summary

Through the study of energies that are connected with crystal skulls, it is possible to define different groups of crystal skulls. These different groups reflect how people have worked with crystal skulls in the past and how well they understood the crystal skull energies. Based on these energies, it seems likely that none of the crystal skulls were made in Atlantean times and they were instead made after the disappearance of Atlantis. Over time, the ability to work with crystal skulls was lost in such a way that their potential could no longer be awakened to a high degree.

We are now in a phase in which we are remembering how to work with crystal skulls. This is part of remembering who we are and is a process. Contemporary crystal skulls help us on this journey because we need to discover every aspect of crystal skulls step by step in the process of awakening their full potential. In that process, we begin to understand who we are, what our motivations are, what our beliefs are, and whether we are guided by love or by fear and neediness. The ancient and old crystal skulls help us by showing us what we can do with crystal skulls. They are like beacons on the path of our pilgrimage that show us that it is all about the journey and never about the goal.

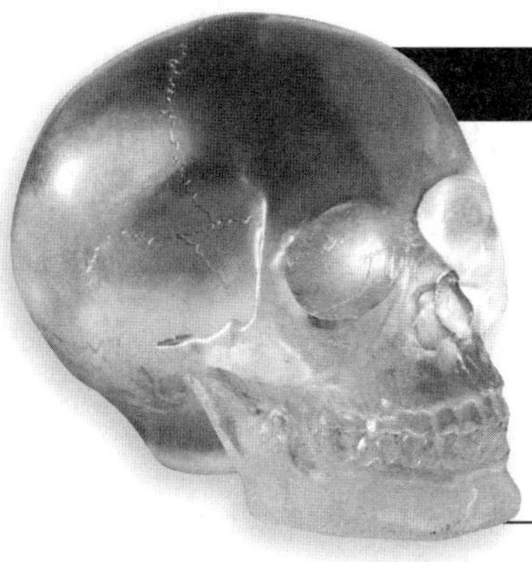

CHAPTER SEVEN

Processing Information Connected with Crystal Skulls

One of the characteristics of crystal skulls is their ability to store information. This quality fascinates many people. What secrets did the ancients program into crystal skulls? Do they indeed hold information that can help humankind change course and live in love, sharing the abundance of Earth? If there is information, how do we access it? How is information deposited into contemporary crystal skulls? These questions seem to be particularly important for those who work with crystal skulls.

Many people have attempted to access the information stored in crystal skulls. One of the best-known and published examples of this attempt is spoken of in *The Skull Speaks*[1]. The cover of the book reads, "The Mitchell-Hedges Crystal Skull — an ancient information source — has been accessed — and a new hope for mankind revealed." This suggests that the information presented in the book comes from within the Mitchell-Hedges skull. Also, the text on the back cover suggests that the information is locked inside the crystal skull. However, in the book itself, the editor, Brian Hadley-James, mentions that it is not certain that the information is actually in the skull. For him, it is about knowledge, wherever that knowledge comes from[2].

In his follow-up book, *Beyond the Veil of Time*, Brian Hadley-James is much clearer. He describes and discusses the channeling from Carole Davis-Wilson and states that the information was channeled from the same beings they encountered when she channeled with the Mitchell-Hedges crystal skull. Hadley-James is now convinced that the information did not come from the Mitchell-Hedges skull[3].

I agree with what Bradley-James says, and I even go a step further: I believe that most of the information that is said to come from a crystal skull actually comes from the channels themselves or is channeled from other sources. Whenever people channel with a crystal skull, they often mention that the skull is speaking to them. However, I believe what actually happens is that they awaken the "transmitter" characteristic in their crystal skull. In doing so, any being can come through the crystal skull and present itself as the skull. To be sure that the information comes from a higher source, it is important to activate the crystal skull to a sufficiently high level so that it can function as a higher-frequency transmission station.

In every channeling, it is important to allow yourself to feel whether you resonate with any of the information presented. Never give your power away to any source, and be careful with any information that starts with, "My skull says ..." Whenever that happens, it may be possible that the person gives away his or her power to the crystal skull. We need to take responsibility for everything we say, wherever the information comes from. Only in a channeling situation can we allow a consciousness to speak through us. In that case, the content can be seen as coming from a different source than the channel. Outside the situation of channeling, everything we say and share is our responsibility. I am aware of people who share information that they say came to them through channeling so that they cannot be held responsible for what they share.

Whenever you listen to a channeling, always be aware that channeled information needs to go through the channel, who needs to process the information into words they speak. In that process, information and energy is always lost or changed to some degree. There are only a few channels who can get out of the way to such a degree that they come close to being pure-trance channels. Even then, in almost all cases most words and information can only be passed on when they are already available in that person. When I was in training to channel, I was told by my mentor that my "keyboard was too small" to allow the information to flow through me uninterrupted and pure. There is no doubt that there are more channels whose "keyboards" are too small.

Caretakers of crystal skulls, especially those of ancient crystal skulls, use channeling to various degrees to pass on information. By now it may be clear that this information is not necessarily found within the crystal skull itself but may come from another source and be supported by the qualities and characteristics of the crystal skull. So where is the information that is connected with a crystal skull located, and how do we access that information?

Storage of Information in Crystal Skulls

When we want to access information, we need to know where and how it is stored. In many ways we can compare a crystal skull with a computer: When we work with a computer, we use certain programs to store information, and if you don't know or have the program, you will be unable to access the information. It is as if that information does not exist. The same is true for crystal skulls. Information was brought in a certain way (a program) into a crystal skull, and we need to understand this "way" (need this program) to be able to access that information.

Before we look at the "program," the first question is whether the information actually exists inside the crystal skull. This is a key question. People talk about information in crystal skulls both in general terms and also in relationship to a particular skull. Every crystal skull may have its own information. In addition, I believe that every crystal skull enables us to connect with the collective crystal skull field. We will look at both aspects, but let us start with information within a crystal skull.

Although it is generally accepted that there is information held within crystal skulls, there are only a few theories that try to describe how and where the implanting of this information occurs. I have mentioned one method earlier: holographic imaging. From a technological point of view, lasers are needed to bring information through holography into a crystal skull, and lasers of the same frequency are needed to retrieve the information. Those studying and working with crystal skulls believe that thoughts can also bring information into crystal skulls. I believe that the electromagnetic frequencies of our thoughts may have a function similar to the lasers in holographic imaging. This means that if you want to retrieve information, you need thoughts of a similar vibration. If we do not know the level of consciousness from which a person was thinking when information was brought into a crystal skull, it may be very difficult to retrieve that information. This is a relatively unexplored area, even though many people use the principle of thought (intent) to program their crystals and crystal skulls.

Marcel Vogel described a theory that defines the place where the information is stored in a crystal or crystal skull. This theory is called the Lattice Defect Theory. Stephen Mehler supports this theory in his book[4]. There are four types of defects that can be found in a crystal lattice: point, line, planar, and bulk[5]. Vogel focuses on the point defects. There are several types of point defects, but in his theory, Vogel seems to focus on the vacancy point defects, which are caused by a missing atom in the crystal structure. Vogel focuses on quartz in particular, as it seems that this defect occurs in quartz quite often. Mehler mentions that in the case of quartz, the importance is in missing silicon atoms. According to Vogel, information can be stored in the holes caused by these missing atoms.

As logical as this theory sounds, it is not likely that this is the way information is stored in crystal skulls. Information needs a carrier — unless it exists in a coherent field, like the collective consciousness field of humans.

We are familiar with the principle of carriers of information and work with this principle every day many times. Whether we talk about the radio, television, telephone, or computer, the information that moves from one place to another is carried by a certain frequency of electromagnetic energies. In this way, we find our radio and TV stations — we dial (or nowadays "zap") through frequencies to get the channel or station we want.

Although this common technology is applied everywhere, there are controversial ideas about how it works. To explain this technology, Maxwell's four equations are used. Maxwell's equations are a set of partial differential equations that, together with the Lorentz force law, form the foundation of classical electrodynamics, classical optics, and electric circuits. These fields in turn underlie modern electrical and communications technologies[6].

After having worked with the principles for a long time, Maxwell's four equations have again attracted the interests of physicists. People now say that these equations are not only for traverse waves (what are known as Hertzian waves, connected with electromagnetic energies) but also for longitudinal waves, which also are called scalar waves[7]. There is a lot of discussion about the function of these scalar waves, especially since they cannot be measured with standard equipment. Nevertheless, it is increasingly believed that these scalar waves hold the information that is carried (and transported) by electromagnetic energies[8]. When electromagnetic waves are canceled out through destructive interference between two electromagnetic waves, scalar waves remain (are created)[9].

How does this relate to crystal skulls? There are many different electromagnetic energies connected with crystal skulls. These energies are a consequence of the atomic structure — and in the case of quartz, also of the piezoelectric qualities. As we saw earlier, crystal skulls take on the electromagnetic frequencies of their environment. All these frequencies carry information. From my perspective, not only electromagnetic frequencies but all frequencies carry information, which suggests that all the frequencies of the energy layers of crystal skulls may carry information. Because these energy layers are activated through our consciousness, we increasingly add potential for more information to the crystal skulls as we continue to activate them.

Increasingly, results from physics research demonstrate that information is also held in atoms and in quantum particles such as photons. According to an article on physicsworld.com, research now shows that both atoms and photons can teleport information over long distances[10]. This may suggest that once we have a deep connection with our crystal skulls, we may connect with them even over a long distance. Many caretakers will confirm this idea without any hesitation.

When quartz receives an impulse, it will change. It will go back to its original state when the impulse stops, and in the process, it will send out electricity/light. This is a consequence of the piezoelectric qualities of quartz. Light contains photons, and photons contain information. Every thought will induce the release of photons from quartz, making the information available for us to receive. We still need to deal with the challenge of how to translate this information into awareness.

Another important conclusion that can be drawn from the article on physicsworld.com is that information is found inside an atom. This makes it unlikely that information is stored in the space of a missing atom, as was suggested by Marcel Vogel and supported by Stephen Mehler[11].

Retrieving Information

The real challenge in the retrieval of information from crystal skulls is a combination of actual retrieval of the information (reception) and becoming aware of it (perception). It is possible that we access information partly without being aware of it. Whether we receive information consciously or subconsciously, we need to translate it into a perception in order to understand it, work with it, and share it. The first question is whether we are able to access information consciously in crystal skulls.

Assuming that information is connected with the different frequencies that are part of the energy system of a crystal skull, we still have to find a way to access it. Knowing that information may be programmed in an unknown way, it may be quite a process to learn to recognize the unique frequencies and then to access them. Such a process may appeal only to certain people. Personally, I do not know how to consciously access the information in a crystal skull yet. I always trust that when I need to know something, I will receive it in one way or another.

While we may not yet be able to consciously access the information in a crystal skull, we may pick up pieces of information spontaneously. Through sharing such pieces of information with others, we might be able to coalesce the pieces in a pattern that offers deeper understanding. This approach represents a reflection of the realization that we are all connected — that we are all one.

The key point remains how to perceive or be aware of such information. We may spontaneously receive more information than we think we do. We often translate that experience by saying, "There was a lot of energy." All energy contains information. To move from an experience of energy to a perception of the related information is difficult for most people. We need a "translation" from the experience of feeling a lot of energy into something we can express in words so that we can understand it, work with it, and share it. Everyone who meditates knows that it is not always easy to express in words what has been experienced during a meditation, even when we know that we have received energy and information.

In chapter 4, I described the different activity levels of the brain, which are defined as frequency bands. These different activity levels help to translate energy and information into awareness — reception into perception. Therefore, training the brain is important in the retrieval process of information from crystal skulls. Meditation and sharing are important tools in this process. Ultimately, it is not important where or how information is received. The information always needs to involve the brain enabling us to work with it, share it, or write it down.

Brain and Heart

The role of the heart and the relationship between the heart and the brain in the process of becoming aware of something have been described in *Gifts of Mother Earth* (10-12). This process is also important for understanding how we perceive information from crystal skulls. Therefore, I will summarize the main points.

The Institute of HeartMath has done research to understand how information flows through our system. In order to study this, they connected test subjects with electrodes to monitor the reactions from the brain, the heart, and the nervous system and placed them in front of a computer screen. The subjects were shown two types of images, either extremely wonderful or extremely awful or scary. Neither the subject nor the researchers knew which of the two types of pictures would appear on the screen. The results were quite remarkable.

The most important aspect of the institute's discoveries was that the heart was the first to react to the picture. Even more striking was the fact that the heart reacted even before the image was shown. This was true for all subjects tested. This clearly indicates that the heart is the key organ in receiving information. The heart passes it on to the brain, and the brain passes it on to the body, which reacts in alignment with the quality of the picture. That message is sent to the brain, and the brain concludes that the picture is either nice or terrible. This means that the information received by the heart goes quite a long way before it becomes a perception. During each of these different steps, information may get lost.

In this process, another factor plays a role: the mind. The mind may be the most challenging aspect of being human. It can be defined as the total sum of experiences in our lives. The mind is also connected with the collective mind — or collective human consciousness — and therefore is influenced by it. In turn, each mind brings information into the collective. The mind lives either in the past (beliefs, frustration, pain, and so forth) or in the future (fears).

The heart is connected with feelings and with the spiritual aspects of ourselves. It has a direct connection with the soul. The brain is the system that is connected to our physical life and is our information-processing and survival system. The mind is in between the heart and the brain. Both the mind and the heart use the brain to bring things into awareness. Unfortunately, in most situations the mind wins and therefore will determine most of the choices we make in our lives.

When we meditate with crystal skulls, our hearts receive a lot of information. What does reach the brain goes through the filter of the mind. Most of what our hearts try to tell us will never reach us in a way that helps us to expand our understanding of ourselves.

Based on this discussion, it should be clear that it is important to train the mind to quiet down. A quiet mind will help you hear the signals from your heart, and that will amplify your perception of information. It also may be clear that the phrase "live from your heart" is not only wise but essential on our spiritual journey.

Scrying and Psychometry

Nick Nocerino and those who studied with him used a method called scrying to obtain information from crystal skulls. Stephen Mehler defined scrying as a method in which a person, through his or her own consciousness, interacts with a crystal skull to "see" images in the skull[12]. According to Wikipedia, scrying is "magic" that involves seeing things psychically in any substance that is reflective, translucent, or luminescent — such as crystals, stones, glass, mirrors, water, fire, or smoke[13]. Scrying has been used in many cultures as a means of divining the past, present, or future. It is a visual form of obtaining metaphysical information and as such is not the best method for everyone to obtain information. Some people may just know or hear the information. Therefore, psychometry often works better for certain people. Psychometry is a form of extrasensory perception and is characterized by the ability to make relevant associations from an object of unknown history through making physical contact with that object[14]. Psychometry seems to be used more frequently than scrying. Of course, it is possible to use these two methods in combination.

Based on the earlier discussion about the brain and the mind, it may be obvious that both scrying and psychometry are "tricky" methods. Because these methods can be influenced easily by the mind, a clear perception may be challenging. Nevertheless, these methods are used to obtain information from crystal skulls, often with interesting and confusing results. Scrying and psychometry do not always work, as demonstrated most clearly with the Mitchell-Hedges crystal skull. Using the methods of scrying and psychometry, it was initially called a "very special" crystal skull with interesting images, and it was seen as the oldest crystal skull[15]. Later it was considered a modern fake that had been carved in recent times[16]. What is the truth?

Another challenge, particularly with psychometry, is that when a person with a strong belief holds an object, that belief actually becomes part of that object, and it will be picked up by psychics as truth. Whenever we receive information from an object, it may be either something that the object witnessed or something that comes from those who held the object. This, of course, is particularly true for crystal skulls, given their characteristics.

Information in the Crystal Skull Field and Crystalline Grids

Information can be attached to an object or connected to the energy layers and energy field (aura) around an object, and there is yet another system that holds information: a coherent field. A generally known example of such a

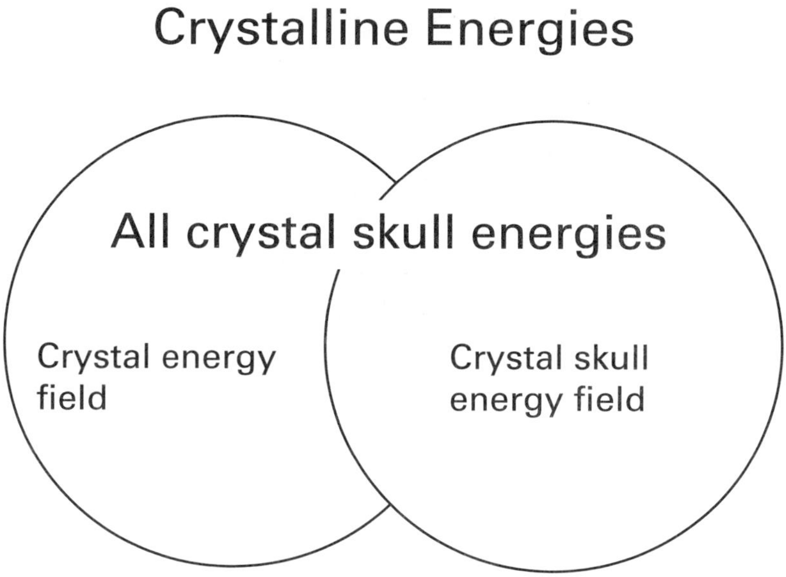

7.1 The crystalline field with subfields such as the crystal skull collective field

field is the human collective consciousness. There are many coherent fields, such as the collective crystal skull field, which is an aspect of the crystalline field. The crystalline field holds information about crystalline energies and systems — like stones, crystals, and crystal skulls. Within the crystalline field are other fields, like the crystal skull field (image 7.1).

Fields form layers of energy around the Earth similar to the energy layers surrounding crystal skulls. However, the layers around the Earth are not as regular and may overlap and vary greatly in width and intensity. The crystal skull field is a coherent energy field that also forms a layer around the Earth. This field holds all the information that is connected with crystal skulls for as long as they are in existence. We use only a limited part of this information, which is held in the crystalline grid system — a system of lines that is connected with the surface of Earth (image 7.2).

There is a connection between the field around the Earth and the grids on Earth. This connection is called a vortex (image 7.2). This energetic connection between the two systems spirals in either a clockwise, or a counterclockwise direction. If it spirals clockwise, information/energy comes from the field into the grids on Earth. If the vortex spins counterclockwise, it brings information/energy from the grid into the field. Most vortexes have a combination of both spinning directions with one direction being dominant.

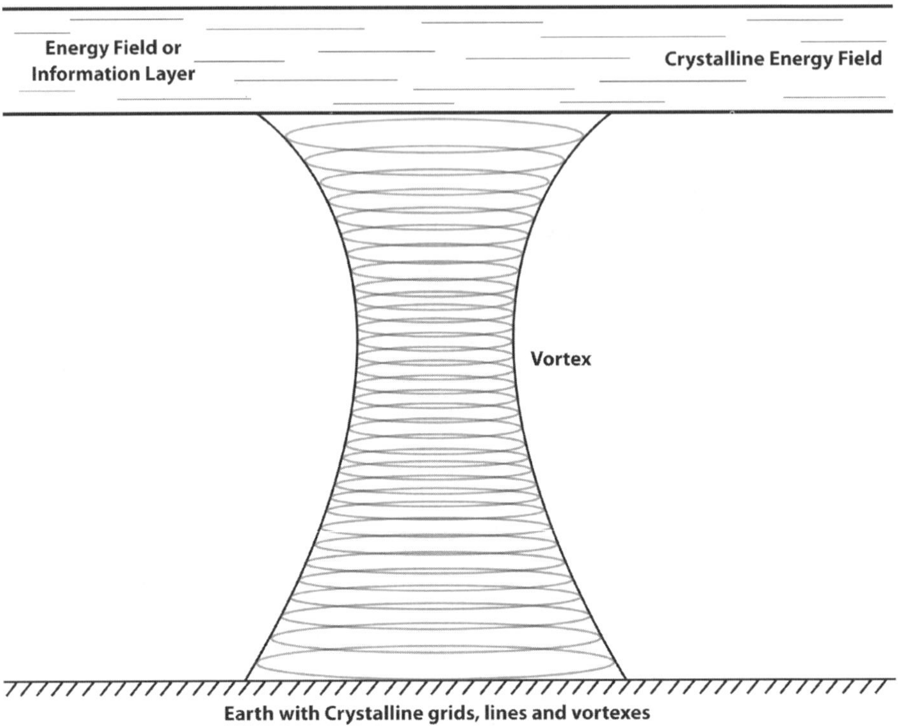

7.2 A representation of the crystalline field, crystalline grids, and the connecting vortex (not to scale). Created by Evita de Vos.

Humans are creative and have the ability to create information that is new — that is not yet in the field (see next subsection: Crystal Skulls and Scalar Waves). Through vortexes, new information can be added to the field as part of the total knowledge of that field. This process explains how information expands, which is an integral part of our evolutionary process.

Every time a person connects with a crystal skull, that person works with either the crystal aspects or the crystal skull aspects of it — or both. Whatever happens, there is always a connection with an aspect of the grid (and often also with the field). Those people who, often subconsciously, explore new aspects of a crystal skull tap into the crystal skull field and bring this new information into the grids. This means that there is constant movement and dynamic interaction.

The grid system, especially, is changing continuously due to all of the work that people do with their crystal skulls. We do not have to be conscious of our connection with the field; often we connect spontaneously with it and, without knowing, bring information into the grid system. This happens especially when we meditate. We rarely fully know what happens during meditation. However, meditation is important, independent of the amount of information we actually perceive. Meditating with a crystal skull is your greatest contribution to the increase in information in systems connected with crystal skulls. That is more important than the information that you are actually aware of. Once information is in your crystal skull or in the grids, other people may be able to be aware of it. In that way, we all contribute in our unique ways to the deeper understanding of the gifts of the crystal skulls.

It was already mentioned that crystal skulls are transmission stations. This means that another consciousness can work through a crystal skull. When that consciousness is of a higher level, it will always respect the free will of people. Any being who does not respect our free will or tells us what we should do is of a lower vibration, and we should avoid connections with such beings. In such a case, go to your heart, and with love and respect, command the being to leave. Consciously ask for and invite only beings of light and love — higher consciousness — to connect with you and your crystal skull.

When we focus on our crystal skulls, we awaken aspects of the skulls' potential. Which of these aspects will be awakened depends on both our conscious and subconscious intentions and even those of our higher consciousness — our souls. What occurs is always far more than we are aware of. The beauty of this process is that our level of awareness does not limit the amount of information we bring into the grids and vortexes. The fact that we are willing to meditate with our crystal skull(s) is the greatest contribution to the expansion of information in grids and fields.

You may wonder whether you need to sit on a crystalline grid vortex for optimal effects. In a sense, you are always sitting within a vortex. Each vortex covers a certain surface, and the energy of all the vortexes together covers the whole Earth. That is how Earth was created. To a large degree, this still is true for vortexes in nature. However, in cities, towns, and other developed areas, several of the grids and vortexes are either disturbed or diminished. Many examples have been given in *Gifts of Mother Earth* (165-173).

Recent unpublished research has demonstrated that the crystalline grid has twelve frequency levels. Of these, the first five levels are natural to Earth and are always present. They are supposed to cover the whole Earth. However, it was found that in developed areas like cities, towns, and communities, these grid lines begin to disappear. In a large city, crystalline grid levels one through five are missing. These levels are the foundation of all other grid systems, and therefore missing a system that forms the basis of all other grid systems will have an effect on life as a whole[17].

Fortunately, crystalline grid lines of levels six through nine can be created by working with crystals, and levels six through twelve can be created with crystal skulls[18]. Therefore, especially in areas of cities, towns, and other developed areas working with crystal skulls, it is very important to compensate for all that we have destroyed and help to rebalance the energy system of Earth.

Crystal Skulls and Scalar Waves

Some people may find the subject of scalar waves challenging to understand. Although it may seem to be complex, the role of scalar waves in the process of interacting with crystal skulls is fascinating. For those with psychic abilities, it is interesting to observe this phenomenon. Scalar waves are not always part of the energies that are generated when people work with crystal skulls; they are more often present when people with experience work with crystal skulls, although they may appear when people sit with a crystal skull for the first time.

It is easiest to share what happens with an image (image 7.3). When we place a crystal skull on the ground and focus on it with the intent to optimally activate it for a given situation, several things happen. Because it all appears to happen simultaneously, it is difficult to say what happens first, but the key point is the scalar waves. We defined them earlier as standing longitudinal waves that carry information. As soon as there is intent to activate a crystal skull, there may be a scalar wave system containing different frequencies. These frequencies change dynamically during the period of connection.

The scalar connection is between the infinite consciousness — also called the zero-point field or quantum field — and the crystal skull. This means that, depending on the person(s) who activate the crystal skull, new information from the field of infinite possibilities will be added to the energy system of the crystal skull. During the activation, the crystal skull also creates a vortex. This means that the scalar information will be distributed to both the grids and the field. In addition, the crystal skull will send out target waves of energy, much like the ripples on a pond after you have thrown a stone into it. Connection with a crystal skull truly is a dynamic and powerful phenomenon.

Is this far-fetched? There are scientists who support what I just described. The most important of these scientists are Konstatin Meyl and Thomas Bearden. Meyl is a German professor of electrical engineering who has given

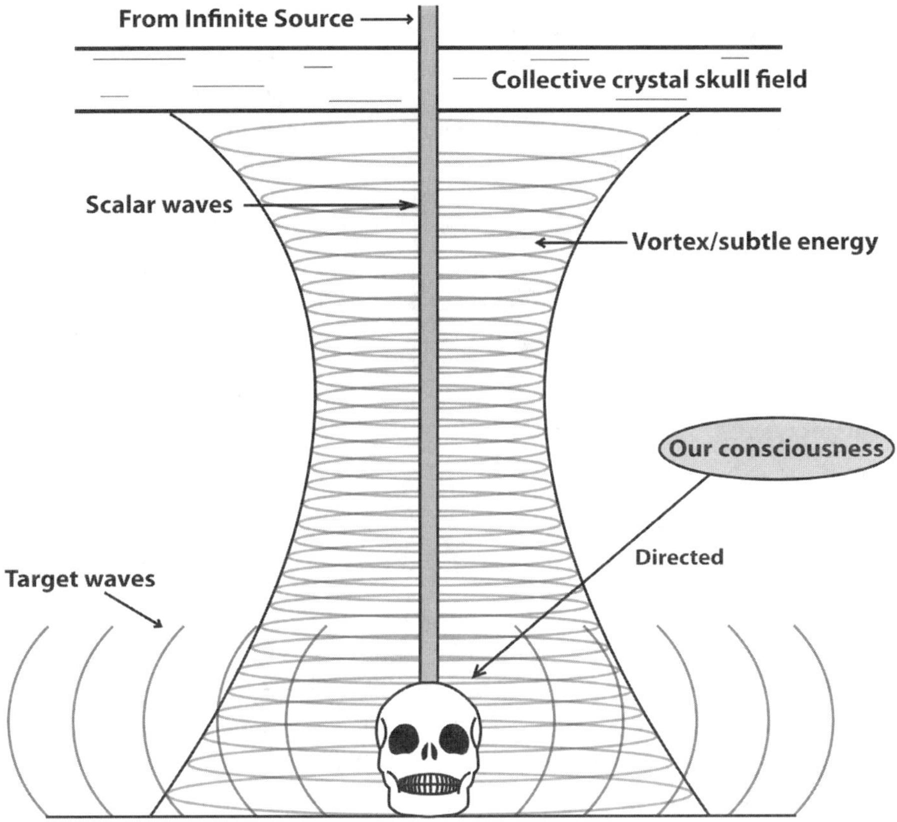

7.3 A representation of the energies connected with a crystal skull when it is activated from a distance (not to scale). Created by Evita de Vos.

detailed mathematical reasoning for the existence of scalar waves[19]. Bearden is a retired American Lieutenant Colonel and a nuclear physicist. During the Cold War, Bearden became aware of Russian scientific work that was based on the work of Nikola Tesla. This brought Bearden to the conclusion that scalar waves were the result of human interaction with the electromagnetic potentials of the zero-point field[20]. This is in alignment with what has been described through image 7.3. However, I would not call the potential of the zero-point field electromagnetic in nature but rather a form of subtle energy, like Glen Rein does.

Glen Rein is another researcher who works with scalar waves. He proposed a theory, a healing model, that describes the bio-energy field as a composition of different types of energies: two types of electromagnetic

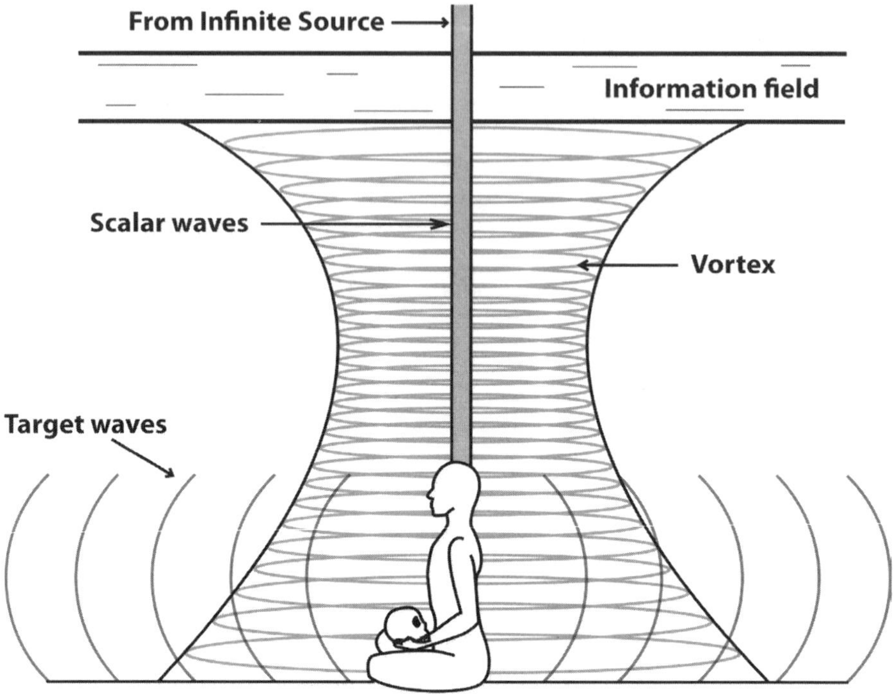

7.4 A representation of the energies connected with a person holding a crystal skull during meditation (not to scale). Created by Evita de Vos.

energies and one type of subtle energies. These energies are non-Hertzian energies, like longitudinal waves, scalar waves, and tachyon energy[21]. In his model, Rein proposes that the healing information originates in the higher-dimensional level of Spirit, which the quantum physicist David Bohm calls the implicate order[22]. The implicate order is the quantum field, infinite consciousness, the zero-point field, or the Infinite Source. This is the field we connect with when we activate our crystal skulls to a sufficiently high level. From the implicate order, the energies are brought down through the different systems as described earlier. Rein proposes that the scalar waves form the bridge between the implicate order and the explicate order (i.e. the physical reality, the manifested reality[23]). This is what I observe when looking at activated crystal skulls.

Since the model shown in image 7.3 seems to be in alignment with models of other people, let us expand this model a bit further. Let us look at what happens when a person holds a crystal skull in their hands during a meditation (image 7.4). The same basic energies are present, but now the scalar waves enter the person holding the crystal skull. Due to the dynamic movement of the energies, it is not clear whether scalar waves also enter into the crystal skull, but I feel that this is not the case. The energy that comes in is translated by the person and brought into the vortex that will bring the energy/information into both the field and the grids.

The target waves are coming from the person holding the crystal skull. In this process, the person may be aware of some of the information that comes through, but most of the information will simply pass through. In this approach, the person may be a limiting factor. The person, based on where she or he is on the journey, may not be a pure channel and therefore may deform the information from the scalar waves as they pass through. Therefore, it is important to be connected with the heart and always work with the purest of intentions.

Another way to meditate with a crystal skull is to sit in front of it. Image 7.5 shows what happens when a person sits in front of a crystal skull that faces him or her. This creates a different flow. The scalar beam activated through the intent now splits up into two beams: one going to the person and one to the crystal skull. A new and additional flow can be observed. This is a circular energy flow that moves between the person and the crystal skull that the person is connected with. There are now two types of target waves: one connected to the skull and one to the person. Although there are different energies involved, it may not feel different to the person meditating. People often like to hold a crystal skull because it feels like the effects are stronger. Whether this is true energetically is doubtful, but it may easily be perceived as such. There are many possible scenarios, but by now the principles should be clear.

I would like to present one other situation. In image 7.6, a person is sitting in front of a crystal skull that is facing him and another person is sitting in front of a crystal skull that is facing away. For the sake of clarity, the vortex, the field, and the target waves have not been included in this image — only the scalar waves and the circular flows. It shows that the direction of the circular flow depends on whether the crystal skull faces you or faces away.

When we place a crystal skull in front of us, the way it faces makes a difference. Does this difference also exist when we hold a skull in our hands? Many people will tell you that this is the case. From an energy aspect, however, it does not make a difference. The skull as a whole is within the aura and reflects that. However, if a person believes that it makes a difference, the crystal skull will reflect and amplify that difference and the person will receive conformation that they are "right."

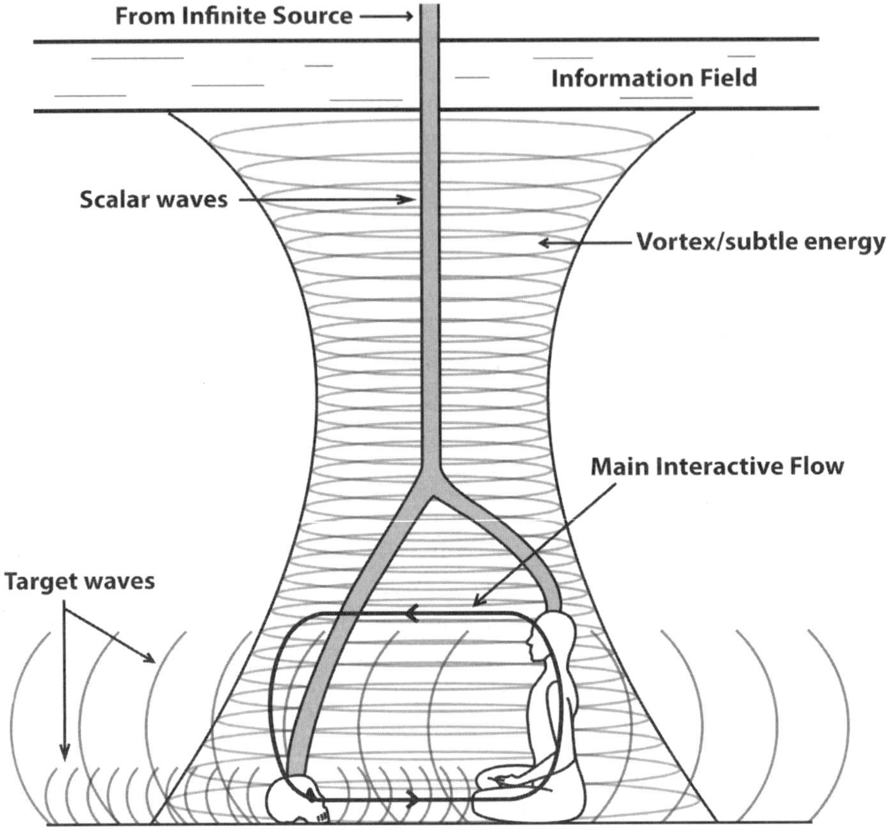

7.5 A representation of the energies connected with a person and a crystal skull when the person is facing a crystal skull during a meditation (not to scale). Created by Evita de Vos.

Image 7.6 is an oversimplified presentation. Besides being connected to the main scalar waves, each person can also separately tap into the Infinite Source and create a direct personal link through scalar waves. Some people do not connect at all with the collective scalar beam and only have a personal connection. Some do not have a scalar connection at all.

The purpose of sharing this information is to help you understand that there are many ways information can come to you when you meditate with a crystal skull. That is why it is so difficult to interpret the information that people give when they connect with crystal skulls. This also plays a role when we try to understand a crystal skull through psychic means. We can get infor-

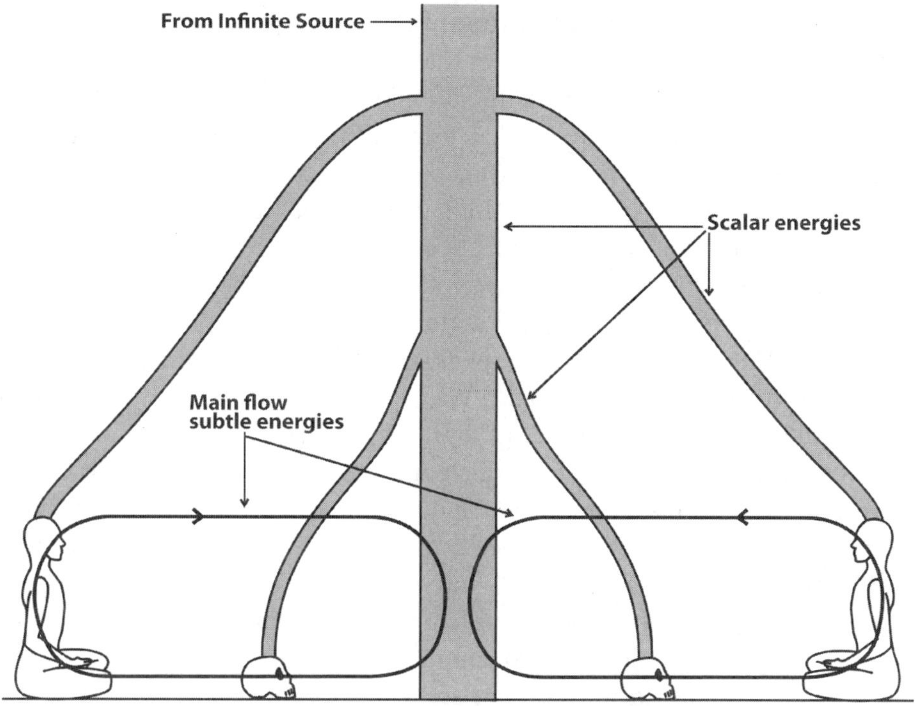

7.6 A representation of the main energy flows when a person is looking at the front and at the back of a crystal skull during meditation (not to scale). Created by Evita de Vos.

mation from the crystal skull field or from the quantum field that has nothing to do with the skull that we hold, and learning to discern requires training. Therefore, it would be wise to be careful to see information that we receive while sitting with crystal skulls as facts.

The implications of the presence of scalar waves are significant — we can bring new information into a crystal skull, into the collective crystal skull field, and into the crystalline grids. This indicates that information connected with crystal skulls is not a fixed phenomenon. It is interesting that this new information can be brought in without those who do so being aware of it. We can only conclude that crystal skulls and the connected energy field are dynamic systems. It is important to realize that we may contribute to this dynamic when we work with crystal skulls. Therefore, we are again reminded to always work from the heart.

Training Our Awareness: Processing Information

Although we have mentioned several aspects of how to train the ability to process information, it is good to summarize some key points. When we talk about scalar waves and subtle energies, the organ that initially receives information is the heart. The heart is our access into the spiritual realms. It receives information from every thinkable source. This means that it is important to train ourselves to live from our hearts to the best of our abilities. The basic meditation given in chapter 4 will help us to do that.

When we live more from our hearts, we will be less in our minds and less in survival mode. When that happens, we will begin to develop the ability to use a wider range of our brains. We can train this ability with the "Crystal Skull Brainwave Training and Programming" meditation from chapter 4. That meditation helps us to train the brain to go to any or all of the brain frequencies at will. This improves our ability to process the information that the heart receives into a perception we can work with. In this process, we have to be aware that our minds tend to interfere with the translation into awareness. The mind wants the awareness to be in alignment with its existing belief structures, but if we allow that to happen, we will be stuck in our minds and our ability to move forward on our spiritual journey will be limited. When we are in such a process, crystal skulls with their ability to amplify can become a problem: They may reinforce our being stuck in the mind. Through meditation, we can more easily move from the mind to the heart and free ourselves from our programmed beliefs. The importance of this cannot be stressed enough.

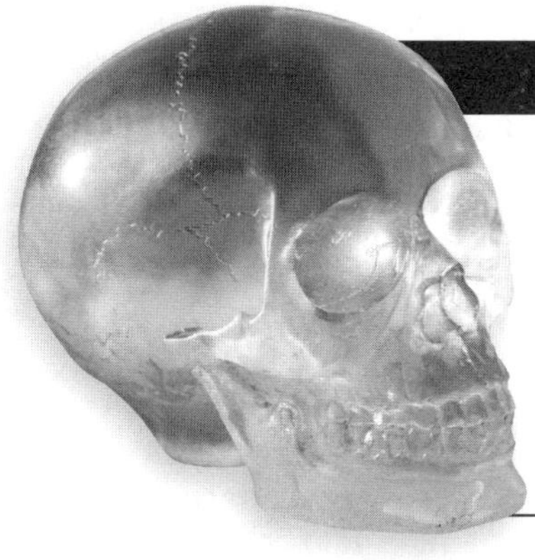

CHAPTER EIGHT

Crystal Skulls and Creating Your Reality

Crystal skulls are powerful tools to help us on our spiritual journey. They help us to see ourselves (reflection and refraction), they help us to connect with other consciousness and energy fields (they are transmitters and help us to attune), they store information that we can learn to access, they expand our awareness, they help us to focus and amplify our experiences, and they support us on the journey from duality to oneness. With all of these qualities, crystal skulls can help us in so many ways that sometimes people become scattered and lost. As we work more with crystal skulls, we need to stay focused and clear about our desires. Of course, these desires are not supposed to come from our minds but from our hearts. When we make a choice we wish for that choice to become reality; therefore, we need to be clear about our choices and the intent that reflects what we desire. Without a clear intent, we cannot expect to see a creation being manifested in the way we wish, emphasizing the importance of intent.

Many books have been written about creating your reality and the intent that makes that possible. Some of the most popular examples are *The Secret*[1] and *The Law of Attraction*[2]. These books try to explain how attraction works and what we need to do to create what we want. These books are no doubt positive contributions to helping us understand more of how attraction and creation work; however, many of those who work with these books are not as successful as they would like to be. Because crystal skulls are such powerful amplifiers, it becomes even more important to understand how we can create the reality we want — we do not want to amplify something that does not work optimally. When people have difficulties creating the reality they desire, working with crystal skulls can magnify these difficulties. I have mentioned several ways to prepare yourself to work with crystal skulls, and these preparations also apply to working with intent. Good preparation is very important, and the basic meditation given in chapter 4 definitely helps. We will discuss in greater detail a number of aspects that are relevant to setting intent.

Intent

There are many ways to illustrate the process that takes place from the moment of setting intent to the realization of it. Let us use a symbol that has been used through eons of time: a circle with a cross that divides it into four quadrants. For American indigenous people, this symbol is the basis of the medicine wheel with the four directions. The following discussion is not based on the medicine wheel traditions but is an integration of many traditions, adapted to help explain the process of creation. Sometimes people see a symbol only from their specific tradition, focusing on details rather than understanding the principle. A circle with a cross is definitely one such universal symbol.

In image 8.1 we see a circle with two axes: the left-right or west-east axis and the up-down or north-south axis. The circle indicates that each point of the circle is equally important, even though we can choose to give importance to certain points. In this circle we define four points that we will call "directions." In doing so, we give these four points on the circle a certain value. The point at the right is defined as the east, the point where the sun comes up that is therefore the point of all beginning. It also is considered to be the place of the spiritual aspect of our being. This point is the source of intent — the place where the creation cycle begins. Every intent and creation needs to come from a spiritual perspective, from the divine, to be for the highest good of all; otherwise, it can be distorted by ego.

At the opposite side is the west, the place of manifestation of intent and of the physical aspect of our being. It is here that we can see whether intent has manifested as intended; and if not, then something is out of alignment. Most likely the lack of alignment is a consequence of the aspects on the north-south axis.

At the lower part of the cross is the south, the place of creativity and the important emotional aspect of the system. The quality of our emotions has a strong impact on the process of manifesting or realizing an intent. This aspect is often the most challenging because most people have not mastered

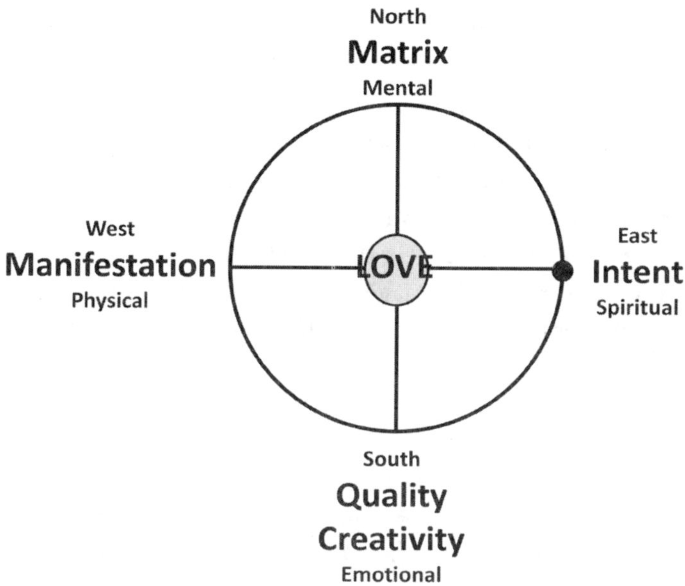

8.1 A circle with four basic principles that define the unfolding of intent into manifestation

their emotions, thereby unpredictably impacting the creation process. The emotions determine the true feeling about intent, being impacted by worries, insecurities, and fears, as well as joy, happiness, and gratitude.

The final point at the upper point, the north, reflects the mental aspect of our being where the blueprints and plans of creation take form. Belief structures are located here. Conscious and subconscious beliefs will have quite an impact on the formation of plans and consequent actions. If there is doubt, manifestation will fail.

While the east-west axis helps to make the difference between intent and the result of intent apparent, the north-south axis makes apparent the effects of emotions and beliefs, the emotional and mental states. These two conditions determine to a large degree the success of the manifestation of the intent.

In the center where the two axes cross, everything is in balance. It is balanced through a key state of human life: love! Without love, there will never be balance. Intentions and the related outcome inform whether we are in a state of love, because when we live in love, manifestations will be in alignment with intent.

The Creation Cycle

We are used to thinking in opposites — good versus bad, positive versus negative, masculine versus feminine, and so on. We always compare, thereby holding ourselves in the third-dimensional consciousness of duality. Since crystal skulls invite us to move to oneness, we need to find a way to overcome duality. This happens when we add a third element, creating a triangle — a symbol of oneness. The third aspect that exists (in addition to the masculine and feminine) is the child (see image 8.2), the energy of innocence, joy, and exploration. This triangle is known in Christianity as the Father, Son, and Holy Spirit.

These three aspects are part of the essence of every human being. They can also be described by their key qualities: femininity holds the quality of wisdom, masculinity holds that of power, and the child holds that of love. A child represents love, radiates love when it is born, and therefore needs love in order to thrive. Image 8.2 also lists the three elements that are connected with these three aspects and qualities. (I will expand on these three elements in chapter 9).

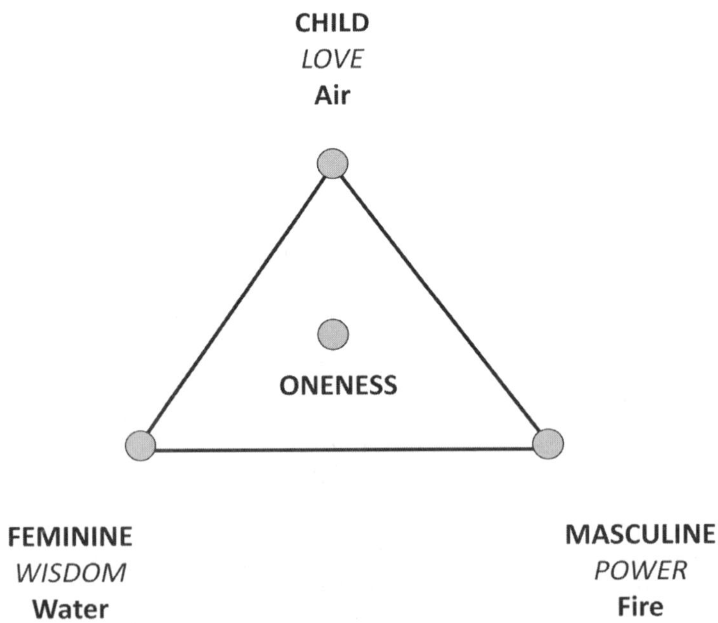

8.2 The triangle of oneness showing three universal principles defined in three different ways

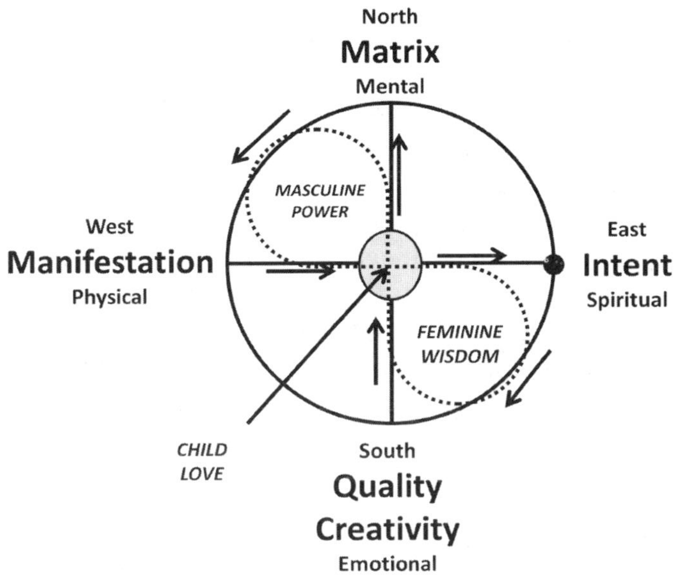

8.3 The flow within a creation cycle creates an infinity symbol. The three parts of the infinity symbol represent the three divine aspects of the oneness triangle.

The balance of these three components within us is necessary in order to experience oneness, so it may be no surprise that all three components are part of the creation cycle (see image 8.3).

The creation cycle has an optimal flow. Without this flow and direction, the results will not be optimal. First a clear intent is set. Then the emotional qualities are added. The emotional qualities determine the nature of the creativity, either by the mind or by the heart. When emotions are determined by the mind, they are colored by fear — at least to a certain degree. When determined by the heart, emotions such as joy, happiness, and gratitude will be experienced and these emotions will fully support the creative process, so that our intent can be realized in an optimal way. From a place of joy, happiness, and gratitude, we can feel our intent becoming a reality, and we are already celebrating!

Next we bring in the mental qualities, which are also determined either by the mind or the heart. The mind will offer beliefs based on past experiences and fear of the future. Questions like, "Can I do this?" and "Do I have what it takes?" will arise. The heart will tell us to trust that we will always receive the signals that will guide to all that we need to complete the cycle and produce the results aligned with intent. In this phase, we can imagine how the intent has manifested and imagine all aspects we need to create the intended reality.

Finally, the results are manifested in the west, where action is needed to bring all into form, into reality. Based on the results that are experienced, the next intent will be set. This cycle will be repeated over and over, because we are creating continuously through conscious and subconscious intents. When the result of a cycle is disappointing in any way, it can influence our emotional and mental conditions, which may disrupt the energy flow of the next creation cycle and thus increase the probability of another disappointment.

Image 8.3 reveals that the flow in a creation cycle holds the form of an infinity symbol. In the first half of the infinity symbol, the energy flows clockwise, reflecting the feminine wisdom aspect of the cycle. Wisdom is required in order to create the desired outcome. The second part of the infinity symbol flows counterclockwise, reflecting the masculine aspect: the power to create upon the foundation laid down by wisdom. The two powers are balanced at the center, at the cross point, by the energy of the child, the energy of love.

If we keep in mind the process of the creation cycle, we can avoid frustration when the desired outcomes do not manifest. The creation cycle helps us to reflect, inviting necessary changes. Crystal skulls, when used in connection with the heart, are the perfect tools to help create a life that will align intent and manifestation.

We are continuously creating our reality. It is important to create without attachment. When you are attached to the outcome, you are not in your heart, because all attachments come from the mind. When we are attached, we create an emotional and mental state that is bound to jeopardize the intended creation. Attachment is a way for the mind to control our lives. It always reflects fear and a lack of trust. The mind wants to control in order to prevent repetition of past negative experiences. Consequently, we are stuck in the past repeating similar patterns. The heart has no attachments because it is always in the "now" moment and has the child's qualities of innocence, exploration, and total joy — qualities that the minds of most people miss. Therefore, by being in a state of nonattachment, we will always experience the optimal state of what is possible in each moment. The experience helps us to see where we are in our process, invites us to make changes where needed, and increasingly helps us to understand who we are.

Brain States and Intent

It is important to prepare before setting intent so as to avoid the mind. When we lower the vibrations of the brain into theta — or, more ideally, into delta — we move more easily from the mind to the heart. As this requires training, I gave a meditation in chapter 4 to help you recognize the different states of the brain and how a crystal skull can be programmed to help you move into these states. Training the brain to go to these states diminishes the chance that the mind will dominate.

The process of creation is in every way a process of self-reflection. Because crystal skulls are such powerful reflectors, they are ideal tools to support the process of understanding where we are on our journey and make changes where needed to be able to create the life we choose.

Meditation to Set Intent

Understanding how a creation cycle works helps to prepare us to meditate to set a clear intent. It also helps to go through the creation cycle using our imagination. Imagination is a key element that has not yet been mentioned. Although setting intent from the heart is enough to learn how the system works, if we really want to manifest something, it is helpful to use imagination. In the presented meditation, imagination has been built in (see also the meditation CD).

Select a crystal skull you would like to use as an amplifier and transmission station to call in guides, angels, or other helpers you are connected with. Sit in a quiet and comfortable place and prepare this place in a way that feels right for you.

Start with the basic meditation in chapter 4, which will bring you into a state of love and feeling connected with the universe. All the needed energies will then be available for your direction.

> *From this loving place of love, set your intent. Make it simple, and formulate it so as to avoid any misunderstanding. Realize that when you are in a meditative state, the subconscious is active and interprets everything literally. Because we have to go through the subconscious to get to higher consciousness, we need to make sure that the message is clear and cannot be misunderstood. This is a pitfall many people fall into by setting a vague intent — one that has multiple possible interpretations — or by assuming that what is missed in clarity will be filled in automatically.*

Feel how the setting of this intent is affecting you emotionally. Be aware of the thoughts that surface. Allow them to surface. Do not push them away.

From the awareness of your emotions and thoughts, feel whether you are still in your heart. If not, go back to your heart. Look again at your emotions and the thoughts that come up. Then look again at whether you are still in your heart. If you are again out of your heart, it may not be the right time to set this intent. It is important to work with these emotions and thoughts in order to transform them before setting the same intent again.

When you feel that you are able to stay in your heart, imagine how you would like your intent to be manifested. Feel the quality of what you would like to create. How would you feel if your intent became reality?

Once you have felt the quality, imagine the details of how you want it to look and how that is in alignment with the quality you desire. This is the moment of connecting with seeing the desired form, seeing it as an actual reality.

In your imagination, your intent has now been realized. How does that make you feel? Again, become aware of whether you are still in your heart and whether your heart sings. If that is the case, let go of any attachment. You know that you have sent out a clear intent, and now it is time to allow the universe to support you in the final manifestation.

If you are not in your heart and do not have the feeling that your heart sings, you know that the intent is bringing up issues. See if you can feel what these issues are. It is important to work on these issues first before releasing your intent to the universe and allowing things to unfold. However, you also can choose to send your intent out anyway and learn from the experience. That will always help you to better understand your mind so you can make future changes, and it will make the next step easier.

Thank yourself and all those who guided you for the experience, and go on with life.

Do not set too many intents at the same time, especially concerning important aspects of your life — it may create too many signals for the universe to follow, and some of these signals may even contradict each other. When intent does not manifest after a while, meditate and feel whether you still are connected with your intent. Adjust if necessary by going through the visualization/meditation just described.

Cocreating Energy Fields

One of the fascinating things you can do with intent and crystal skulls is create different kinds of energy fields. These energy fields can create an environment that helps in meditation, the process of transformation and transmutation, and in training awareness. In addition, it is wonderful to explore different energies that are part of our lives and connect more deeply with them. After all, we are one and separation is an illusion. Crystal skulls help us to understand and experience the diversity in oneness. They help us to see that every field is an aspect of a larger whole. Every exploration of energy fields also reflects to us to help us see more of who we are. Crystal skulls will amplify experiences and intensify the reflection of each field to us.

When I talk about fields, I'm talking about coherent fields of energy and information. I mentioned that the collective crystal skull field is such a field, and so is the human collective consciousness. Every animal and plant creates a coherent field that holds the information of its species and their experiences. There are coherent fields connected to families, tribes, cities, countries, continents, the world, the solar system, stars, galaxies, universes, and so on. There also are collective fields for atoms, metals, stones, and crystals. When similar systems are active, coherent energies will be created. Even when a field is coherent, there may be incoherent aspects within that field. In the human collective field, we see coherent energies as well as chaos and incoherence.

When we want to experience certain energy fields, it is wise to connect with fields that can help us on our journey and to raise our vibrations. Be clear about the field you would like to connect with. Once you are connected, you will (co)create a kind of subfield in which the interaction between you (or the group you are part of) and the field itself takes place. The use of crystal skulls helps to amplify the intent and helps you become more attuned and more focused. Through reflection, crystal skulls also help us to become aware of the field and the effects it has on us.

Over time, Jeanne and I have created many different fields with crystal skulls during the meditations in our house. We noted that different people resonate with fields in different ways. They always experience something, but the intensity varies greatly depending how easy it is for a person to connect with that particular field and how well he or she resonates with it. Some of the popular fields are those of dolphins, whales, angels (in particular, archangels like Michael, Raphael, Gabriel, and Uriel), devas or a particular deva, elementals, Mother Earth, the solar system, and many more. We can connect with the different extraterrestrial consciousness groups like the Sirians,

Arcturians, Pleiadeans, Orions, and others and explore how these fields of consciousness help us on our journey. The importance of exploring extraterrestrial consciousness will become clear in the next chapter.

Meditation to Cocreate an Energy Field

The following meditation helps create energy fields (see also the meditation CD). Start by creating an optimal environment. Select the crystal skull or skulls that you would like to use for the creation of the field. During group meditations in our house, we use all the crystal skulls we have in the circle. You can also choose to hold a crystal skull in your hands. As always, feel what works best for you. Follow with the basic meditation from chapter 4.

> *From this loving place and connection, bring your awareness to the crystal skull(s). Set the intent to activate all crystal skulls present to the optimal level for all present at that moment. Feel the change in energy.*
>
> *In your imagination, make contact with the being or beings you want to connect with. For example, if you want to connect with dolphins, see yourself making contact with them and call them into the space you are sitting in.*
>
> *Invite them to cocreate an energy field that is optimal for all who are present, including the dolphins.*
>
> *Then sit in this cocreated field for as long as it feels comfortable, trusting that you will receive all energies and information that is optimal for you in this meditation.*

There are a few things that may help you to focus or intensify the experience. It may be helpful to have objects that can help you make the connections and contribute positively to the field. For example, if you choose to cocreate with dolphins and you have bones, fossilized ear bones, or dolphin pictures or statues, you can place them around the crystal skull or skulls — or within a circle of crystal skulls and/or crystals.

When you have more crystal skulls, every crystal skull that you take in your hands while the field is created will reflect this field. Every crystal skull, being unique in its energies, will help you in different ways to connect more deeply with aspects of the created field. This is always a wonderful journey with the possibility of many gifts.

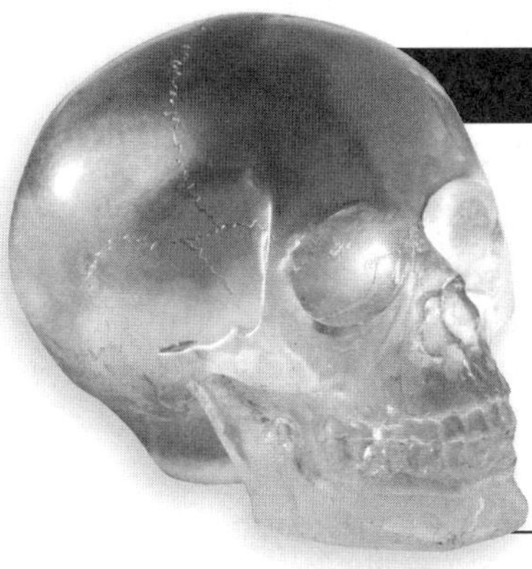

CHAPTER NINE

Legend of the 13 Crystal Skulls and Star Nations

Belief in the legend of the thirteen crystal skulls has grown over time. Although the details may vary depending on the source, the general principle remains more or less the same. In *Crystal Skulls: Interacting with a Phenomenon*, the subject has been given considerable attention (121-166). Some of that information will be included in this chapter to enable the understanding of new insights and discoveries.

The essence of the legend/myth is that star nations have gifted the people of Earth with information that will help them to shift into a new state of consciousness. This information is present in the form of thirteen crystal skulls. The time that this shift into a new state of consciousness may occur is around the end of the Mayan calendar, which is believed to be December, 21 2012, the time we live in now [when I'm writing this book]. A part of the legend is that the crystal skulls need to come together in order to help with this shift. However, it is not clear whether this means a coming together of all crystal skulls or just some specific ones. Of course, many people believe that it needs to be the ancient ones.

There is no proof for the existence of this legend. Some argue no such legend exists among the indigenous peoples, while others disagree. Indigenous people only release information when they feel it is the right time. Nevertheless, some have spoken out on the subject, and some of the stories have been summarized in my first book (*CS,* 141-145).

The most important aspect of the story of the thirteen crystal skulls is that it resonates strongly with many people, as well as with many of those who work with crystal skulls, including Nick Nocerino[1]. The popularity of the legend of the thirteen crystal skulls was demonstrated in November

2011. Hunbatz Men, a Mayan daykeeper of the Itza Mayans, made a pilgrimage with crystal skulls — supposedly thirteen ancient skulls — across the United States, visiting a number of sacred sites. The intent was to "download" information from these sites into the crystal skulls and to transfer this information later to the thirteen members of the Itza Mayan Council during the 11–11–11 crystal skull event in Los Angeles (not San Francisco, as the article mentioned)[2]. The journey received much attention, and many people gathered at the sites visited, even though there were neither thirteen ancient crystal skulls nor thirteen Mayan Elders present as suggested[3]. According to the stories, the mentioning of thirteen crystal skulls was enough to attract more people than the sacred sites could handle.

In the legend, the thirteen crystal skulls are generally described as being in a circle of twelve with the thirteenth skull in the center. Twelve is a number included in many systems — such as number of months, the number of hours, the signs of the Zodiac, and the disciples of Jesus. This number is related to one of the five Platonic solids: the dodecahedron (*CS*, 152-154). According to Plato, this solid is connected to the universe.

In *Crystal Skulls: Interacting with a Phenomenon*, I stated my belief that crystal skulls were made in a phase when people found it increasingly difficult to tap directly into the information fields gifted to us by the star nations and therefore needed a storage device. I also stated that these star nations are extraterrestrial consciousness from different star systems who have given information to Earth in support of transformation and a shift to higher consciousness (*CS*, 161-162). I believe that this contributes to the reason that crystal skulls are often linked to 2012. This is the year is that it is believed the Mayan calendar will end and that a shift to higher consciousness may occur. Both the end of the Mayan calendar and the gathering of the twelve or thirteen crystal skulls are believed to induce a shift in consciousness. Therefore it is not surprising that they are linked, especially because the Mayan people believe that they are the ones who have to bring the crystal skulls together.

In this chapter, we will look at the meaning of the number twelve in relationship to crystal skulls and at the significance of the number thirteen in relationship to the journey to oneness.

The Significance of the Number 12

In the previous chapter, the triangle of oneness was shown. This triangle represents three universal aspects/energies: the feminine (wisdom), the masculine (power), and the child (love) (see image 8.2). In that image in the previous chapter, three elements are also mentioned: water connected with feminine, fire with masculine, and air with child.

When four of these triangles are connected at the points with each other, we produce image 9.1. Now there are twelve elements — four of each of the three elements. The number four is also represented by the square in the center. The number four represents earth — the fourth element. This image is telling us that the fourth element, earth, comes forth out of the other three elements: water, air, and fire.

This story is not as strange as it may seem. *The Sefer Yetzirah, the Book of Creation*, a Kabbalistic book more than 3,000 years old, has the same story. According to this book, there are three elements called the three mothers. These elements are water, fire, and air. The book says that earth is not a basic element but a confluence of the other three[4]. This means that systems beyond

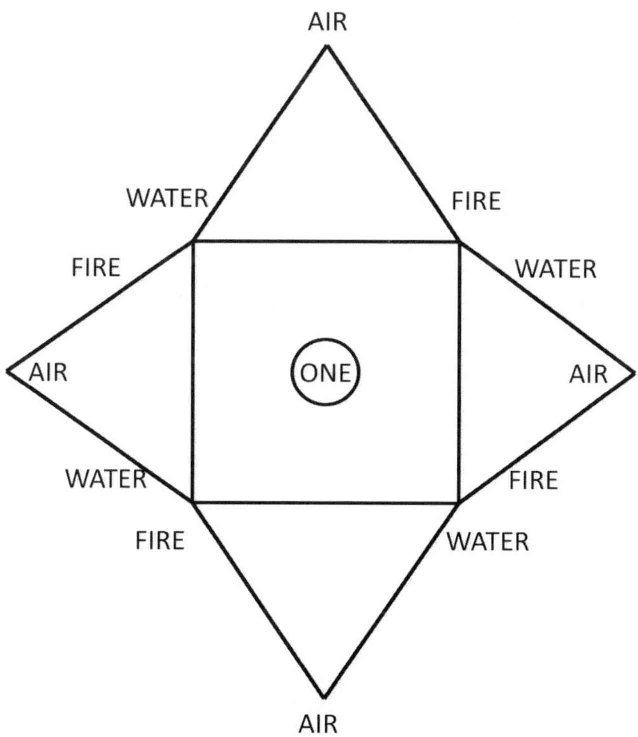

9.1 Four oneness triangles connected by the points form a square, creating four groups of three elements. The fourth element, earth, is symbolized by the square.

the physical only work with the three elements while the physical works with four. This explains the reason why information from the star nations (beyond Earth) and from a higher consciousness (which is beyond the physical) will be connected with only three elements.

The four triangles are a tool to illustrate information discovered through meditation and other techniques. The twelve star nations form four groups of three in which each group of three represents each of the three elements and thus also the triangle (see image 9.1). Therefore, there are four star nations connected to each element. The ones that are connected to the element of water are Arcturus, Cygnus, Sirius, and the Pleiades. The group that is connected to the element of air includes Ursa Major, Alpha Centauri, Cassiopeia, and Andromeda. The group connected to the element of fire includes Zeta Reticuli, Dragon, Orion, and Taurus.

In the center, we have the place of the thirteenth skull or thirteenth consciousness. This is the consciousness that will bring the consciousness of the twelve together into one, the place of oneness. What is missing in the list is the thirteenth star nation. I believe human beings from planet Earth represent the thirteenth consciousness. We human beings are being asked to integrate the consciousness of the twelve star nations, the twelve aspects of consciousness, into oneness. This is our task, and this will lead to the shift in consciousness so many people talk about.

The 12 Star Nations

In image 9.2, the names of seven star nations are in bold, while the other five are in normal letters. This is done on purpose. During studies with crystal skulls, portals, and indigenous stories, a pattern began to emerge. This pattern revealed that certain names were mentioned more often than others. This is also true when we look at books and channeled information from or about extraterrestrial consciousness.

Chief Golden Light Eagle, also called Standing Elk, has shared a lot of information about the star nations. This is available on YouTube[5]. In this video, he shares that the most important star nations are from the Pleiades, Sirius, Arcturus, Orion, Alpha Centauri, and Andromeda.

After *Gifts of Mother Earth* was published, I continued to study portals. A portal is a doorway between two or more dimensions, places, or realities. Portals are similar to vortexes but exist beyond Earth's reality (*GME,* 191-199). Dowsing shows that some portals are connected through lines with similar

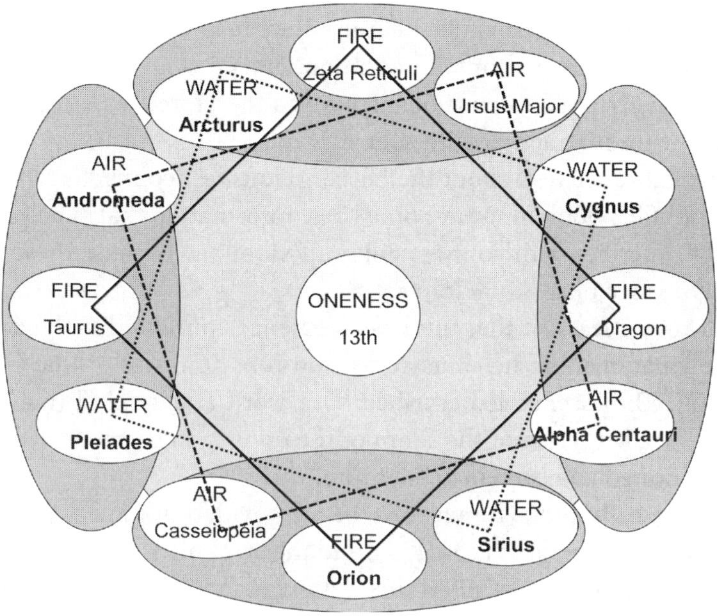

9.2 Twelve star nations grouped into four groups based on the elements they are connected with. Connecting the elements creates three squares.

portals and form grids while others do not form grids in such a way. The ones that form grids may have grids that extend worldwide and are either continuous or in clusters. These portals seem to connect with ETs who are more directly connected with us and seem to interact more frequently with us.

The portals that are connected with each other through lines and form grids belong to the seven star nations whose names are written in bold in image 9.2. The six star nations that are mentioned by Chief Golden Light Eagle all belong to this same group.

The study of portals and the extraterrestrial energies and consciousness that connect with them is similar to learning a language. In the beginning, only energies are detected, but after a while, differences in these energies can be discerned. After a much longer time, definitions that others can resonate with take form. While learning the language of portals and the consciousness, energy, and information connected with them, patterns begin to emerge.

The portals help us to recognize the energies of the different consciousness expressions that we call ETs. Once we begin to recognize these energies, we become aware of their presence any time we choose to attune to them.

Here is where our crystal skulls help us: They help us to attune to the consciousness of the star nations. In addition, crystal skulls hold energies that resonate with certain ET consciousnesses and therefore are perfect transmission stations for interacting with them.

Sharing information about the ET consciousness connected with crystal skulls could fill a book in itself. Some basic information that is helpful to explore these energies with your crystal skull(s) follows because these energies are so supportive of spiritual journeys.

Over time I learned that there is an essence connected with each of the twelve star nations that helps us access the consciousness of that particular star nation. The essence is described by a word and symbol that function together like a key. It is not the room or the door to the room — it is a key to open the door so you can enter the room.

The keywords and symbols have been provided in *Crystal Skulls: Interacting with a Phenomenon* (130-131), and the symbols are presented again in Addendum II. Also, at the end of this chapter is a meditation to connect with any of the twelve star nations (ET consciousnesses) using the symbols.

I also learned that every crystal skull has a key vibration that resonates with one of the twelve star nations. In other words, you may be subconsciously attracted to a certain crystal skull not only because of the crystal that it is made from or the vibrations that it holds but also because it helps you to connect with a certain star nation.

Meditating with crystal skulls connected with the different star nations and meditating at portals made it clear that the beings of the twelve mentioned star nations truly want to help us. They leave us many signals to help us understand that they are connected to Earth and support us individually and as a collective. An example illustrating some of their signs follows.

One of the Portal Systems of Arcturus

One of the star nations I feel strongly connected with is Arcturus. While studying portals that are connected with Arcturus, I learned to differentiate them and found that there are several types of portals. I decided to map the portals of a certain type, and I called it "level 1" because it felt like it was the lowest in vibration of the ones I had found. Mapping is an adventure, especially in the Sedona area with its beautiful red rocks, and it is also a wonderful and rewarding journey. The purpose of the energies of this type of portal is to stimulate us to allow our higher self to teach the self (personality, mind).

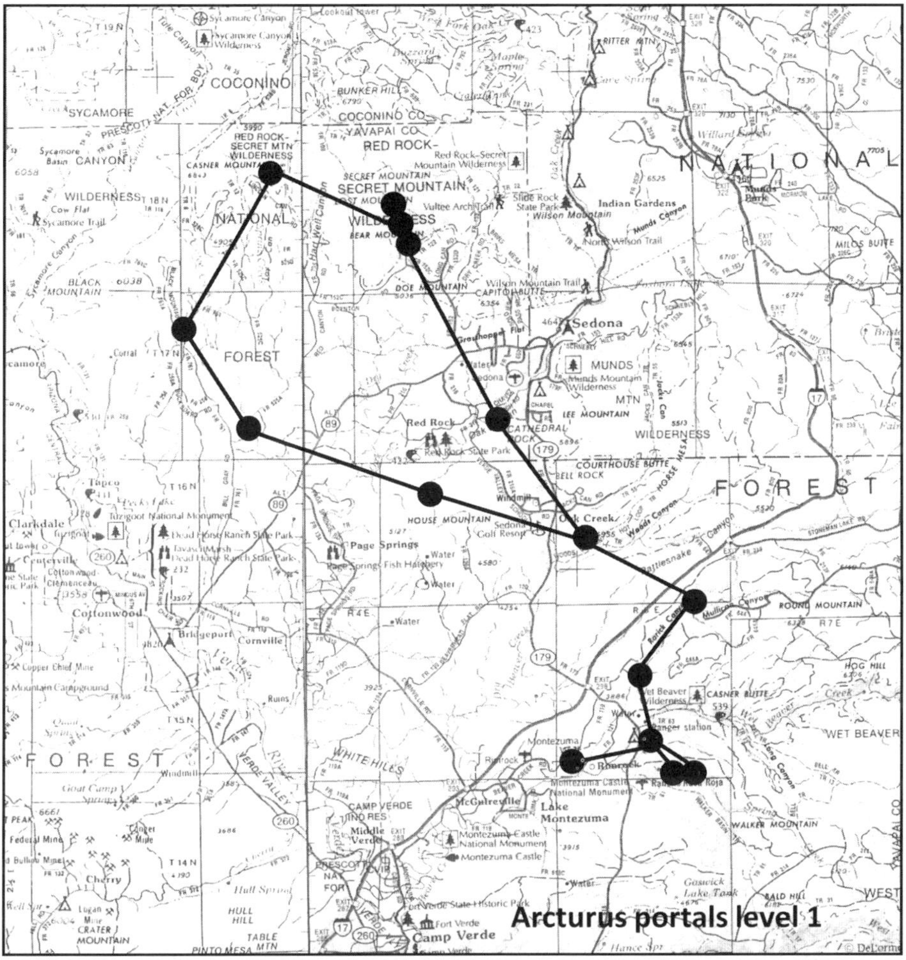

9.3 Locations of Arcturus portals and their connecting lines in the Sedona area (Arizona), forming the constellation of Boötes (the Herdsman)

These energies are very important for everyone because they will strongly support our spiritual evolution.

The result of mapping these portals was surprising. It showed a star constellation that is known as Boötes, the Herdsman, in a rather extensive way (image 9.3). The placement of the stars is not exactly like most books and websites that portray this constellation, but it is close enough (image 9.4), especially since there is variation in shapes among those books and websites[6]. In addition, the shape may change when you look at it from different angles in space. Since the major star of Boötes is Arcturus, it seems that the Arcturi-

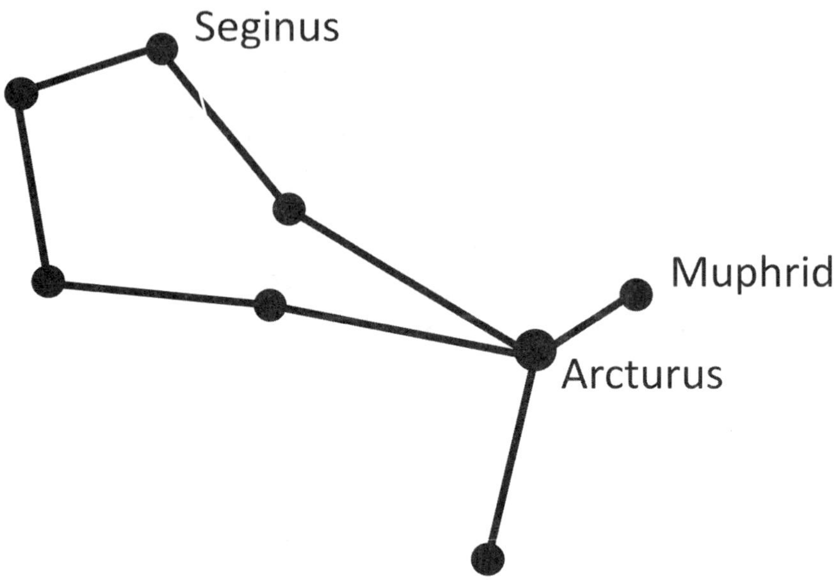

9.4 The Boötes constellation. This image is based on the most common representations of this constellation on the Internet.

ans wish to explain their origin and thus who they are through the layout of the portals in the landscape.

There is no doubt that the indigenous people were aware of the energies of the star people they considered their ancestors. There is a beautiful example how the Sinagua people, who lived in the Sedona area from around 700 to 1425 AD (*GME*, 150-151), used an Arcturus portal (image 9.5) to connect with their ancestors.

When you approach the area, you will see two slabs of sandstone that have many petroglyphs. Unfortunately, the glyphs have been eroded away to a large degree (images 9.6 and 9.7). It appears that these petroglyphs supported the preparation to connect with the ancestors. There are similar arrangements in other parts of the area. Symbols work with the heart, with the "real consciousness," instead of with the brain consciousness, the mind. So the symbols, the petroglyphs, are meant to help you to connect or reconnect with your soul, which is the proper place to connect from when you want to connect with the ancestors.

When this first step was completed, the next step was to prepare the offering. There may have been many different offerings, but one of the important ones was cornmeal. Corn was ground on the spot to make fresh corn-

9.5 (Top) A crystal skull at the location of an Arcturus portal in a canyon south of Sedona (Arizona)

9.6 Two red rock slabs with petroglyphs (quite eroded) as part of the access to a sacred site: an Arcturus portal (south of Sedona, Arizona)

9.7 (Right) Detail of a petroglyph of the red rock slabs of image 9.6

9.8 A matate — a rock on which corn has been grinded to prepare for a ceremony (offerings)

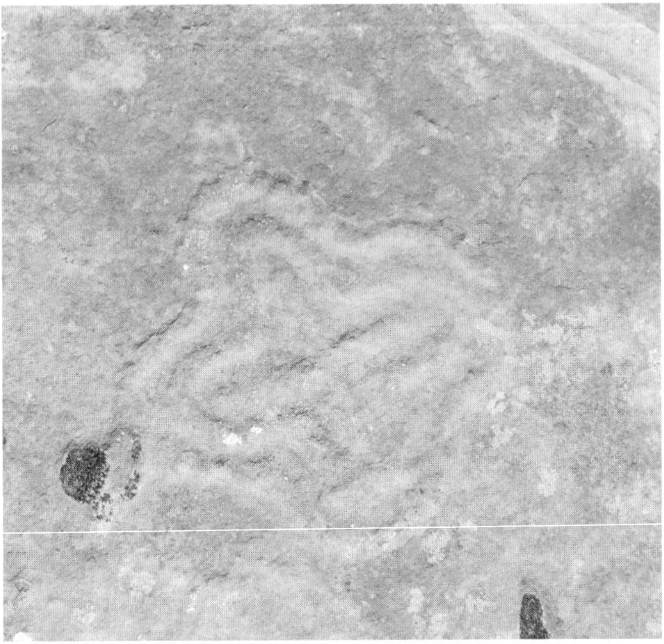

meal. Grinding was also part of the ceremony that prepared the person for the connection. The grinding was done on stones, and over time this made deep holes. A stone with grinding holes is called a matate (image 9.8). The stone with which you do the grinding is called a mano. [Note: The manos in the picture are not the original ones — they were placed there recently, and because I did not know by whom and under what condition, I did not want to remove them for the picture.]

Once all preparations were completed, it was time for the connection (image 9.9). Sitting in the Arcturus portals is a very powerful experience. I have brought many people to this place to let them have this experience. They all had powerful experiences. It seems that the Sinagua people wanted to express their experience with an image or images. They made many petroglyphs on the wall at the right side of the portal. You can see them to some degree in image 9.9. Because of lichen and other growth, most of the petroglyphs are barely visible. Only the petroglyphs at the lower left corner of the wall are clear and undamaged.

9.9 Connecting with the ancestors at the Arcturus portal after preparation

9.10 The crystal skull Sam marks the center of an Arcturus portal in a Sinagua ruin in the Sedona area (Arizona)

Most places that have been used in the past to connect with the ancestors are less clearly marked. The Sinagua people must have had a very deep connection with the ancestors through using these portals. They have built rooms or houses at places where portals are located. There are too many rooms on portals to accept that this is a coincidence. The smaller ruins especially are all built at places where portals can be found. An example is given in image 9.10. Although this example is an Arcturus portal, there are ruins where Sirius and Pleiades portals have also been found. Within the Sedona area, the Sinagua ruins and petroglyph sites seem to be mainly connected with these three types of portals. Does that mean that the Pleiadeans, Sirians, and Arcturians are the key players in the interactions between Earth and ET consciousness?

The Key Players

The seven star nations that have portals that are connected with grid lines have their names in bold in Image 9.2. It seems that these seven nations are the key players. However, in a sense all twelve star nations are key players, because we need information from all twelve star nations to create an understanding that forms the basis for the shift in consciousness. Therefore, the importance of a particular star nation depends on your perspective. Nonetheless, certain energies are more commonly found and experienced on Earth.

Many indigenous traditions involve stories about contact with star people, which suggests that their role may be far greater than we generally tend to think. Our "thinking" about star nations is changing. There is more openness, although it's in a limited way. Television programs like *Ancient Aliens* contribute to more openness to the possibility that we have had — and still have — contact with star people in many different ways.

From my perspective, it is impossible to indicate which of the seven star nations whose names are in bold in image 9.2 is the most important. Therefore, it is better to ask whether there are star people we have more contact with. Of course, I restrict my discussion to those star nations that support the spiritual evolution of humankind and do not include abduction or other physical experiences with UFOs and ETs. Again, I refer to the consciousness of beings from star nations who live in a higher-dimensional reality than our physical third-dimensional one, and I restrict our discussion to those who have a direct connection with crystal skulls.

There seem to be three star nations that have the most direct connection with Earth. This is reflected in stories and traditions of indigenous people and in channelings. These three star nations are the Pleiades, Sirius, and Arcturus. It is interesting to note that all three star nations have a connection with the element of water (see image 9.2). Although Orion is mentioned frequently, there are fewer stories of connections with beings from Orion than with the other three star peoples.

The Pleiades

I will not give an extensive overview of books on the Pleiades, Sirius, and Arcturus within the context of this book. The Pleiades, especially, seem to be a source of many channelings, and consequently many books have been written about them. Some of the books have become well known, like those of Barbara Marciniak, Amorah Quan Yin, and Barbara Hand Clow[7]. These books may have contributed to people's claims that they feel a connection with the Pleiadeans.

A very unusual book about human beings and the Pleiades is *Lemurian Scrolls*. It is written by a Hindu teacher who is called a living legend. The book is based on ancient texts that describe how man journeyed from the Pleiades millions of years ago. It also describes the struggles faced through the eras as souls matured into their ultimate destiny and divinity[8].

There are many stories about indigenous people holding the belief that their ancestors came from the Pleiades. These stories are difficult to verify, especially because there are not many references. In addition, extensive research is beyond the scope of this book. The main point is that when a subject gets a lot of attention, it is important and most likely holds at least some truth. A few tribes that are associated with this story are the Maya[9], Inca, Iroquois, Lakotas, Cherokees, Navajos, and Hopi[10]. There are also reports that this belief exists in Asia. For example, the Balinese and the Tana Toraja (in Indonesia) both believe that they originally came from the Pleiades[11].

While studying Earth energies in Taiwan, I heard that the indigenous people — who have disappeared completely — held the belief that their ancestors came from the Pleiades. At a certain location, I was asked what kind of energies were present. They had brought me to a Pleiadean portal, and I replied: "If I were in the United States with an indigenous person, I would say that this is a place that helps them to connect with their ancestors." The man became very excited and shared that there was an interview from around 1925 with the last shaman of Taiwan's indigenous tribe in which the place where we stood was described as the place where they connected with their ancestors who came from the star group that was identified as the Pleiades.

We may find a similar situation in Sedona, Arizona. The Sinagua Indians used to live in this area from around 700 AD to 1425 AD. Although it is unknown whether the Sinagua called the Pleiades the home of their ancestors, it *is* known that they connected with them, because at different locations they built rooms around Pleiadean portals — for example, in a cave in a wall of a canyon (image 9.11).

The Pleiadean portals do not form a homogenous group of portals. Their energies are recognizably different, although recognizing these differences took me quite some time. Research so far has shown at least seven types of Pleiadean portals. The energy connected with the Pleiadean crystal skull portal in Fyrkat, Denmark, is a mixture of these different types of energies and may even encompass more energies than I have been able to recognize so far. The Pleiadeans have given us as part of the collective crystal skull field those energies and information that the Pleiadean Council believed to be essential for human spiritual evolution. Our ancestors have been connecting with

9.11 A Pleiadean portal in a Sinagua ruin, found in a canyon cave in the Sedona area (Arizona)

aspects of these energies via the different portals. We now are beginning to rediscover these energies, allowing them to help us on our spiritual journey.

The keyword of the Pleiadean energies is "healing." These energies help us to bring everything back into balance to allow our system to move into higher vibrations as a part of the shift to higher consciousness.

Sirius

Besides the Pleiades, Sirius may be the star system that is most often mentioned. One of the persistent New Age beliefs is that the souls who are connected with dolphins and whales originate from Sirius. When you connect with the energies and consciousness of dolphins, and when you begin to recognize different aspects of Sirian energies through a connection with their portals, this statement feels increasingly true.

The Dogon tribe in Africa has a strong connection with Sirius. This became well known through Robert Temple's book *The Sirius Mystery*[12]. In this book, he described that the Dogon and three other related tribes possess knowledge about the existence of Sirius B, a white dwarf star located next to the very bright Sirius A that science has discovered recently. These tribes claim that their knowledge came from star people from Sirius who they call Nommos. The Nommos live in water[13]. However, there is a lot of doubt whether Robert Temple's conclusions are correct[14].

An interesting book on Sirius, its energies, and its influence comes from M. Temple Richmond[15], who believes that Sirius is the great star of initiation. I believe that the keyword for Sirius is "knowledge." Temple Richmond seems to confirm that in his book, which describes Sirius as a source for wisdom and love[16]. As we mentioned earlier, love transmutes knowledge into wisdom.

The Hopi people know Sirius as the Blue Star Kachina. An old Hopi prophecy says that when the Blue Star Kachina appears in the heavens, the fifth world will emerge[17]. According to the Hopi, we now live in the fourth world. They believe that all previous worlds have been destroyed and this one will also be destroyed. This is interesting because Sirius, which is the star of Isis for the Egyptians, also symbolizes rebirth. There will be a rebirth of *true* knowledge — not what is fed to us through schools, religion, and governments — that will emerge when we increasingly come from a place of love.

When we look at the meanings of the different star systems in relation to our spiritual evolution, it is less important to look at scientific facts than to look at metaphysical and esoteric meanings.

Sirius is very important for the Masons, who base their traditions and esoteric knowledge to some degree on Egyptian knowledge. In their traditions, Sirius is seen as representing knowledge. Sirius is also represented as a triad, as is demonstrated in the Egyptian hieroglyph for Sirius (image 9.12). This hieroglyph consists of a phallus symbol (the pyramid) which stands for Osiris; the dome, which stands for Isis, his wife; and the five-pointed star, which stands for Horus, their child. Horus also has the eye as his symbol. The all-seeing eye, which appears in many esoteric traditions, including the Masons', is also used as a symbol for Sirius. Additionally, we see the all-seeing eye on the American one-dollar bill. A great overview of the importance of Sirius is given on the website SecretArcana.com[18].

In summary, we can say that Sirius seems to have played and still plays an important role in human consciousness. From a metaphysical point of view, Sirius has been and still is important in many traditions.

Channeling has contributed to an increasing acceptance of Sirius as an energy system that has had a significant effect on Earth. People like Murry

9.12 The Egyptian Sirius hieroglyph consisting of a pyramid (Osiris), dome (Isis), and five-pointed star (Horus)

Hope[19] provide information on Sirius that may have some basis of truth. At least the channelings give us the opportunity to learn to discern what we can and cannot resonate with. This has helped me to begin to discover different types of Sirian energies. However, there is still a long way to go before we will understand more fully the diversity of the Sirian energies.

Arcturus

Arcturus does not get the same type of attention as the Pleiades and Sirius. Edgar Cayce, the sleeping prophet, mentioned the radiant golden-orange star Arcturus over thirty times in his readings and regarded it as the "stargate" — an entranceway to other parts of the universe or to other realms of consciousness[20]. In many website articles, it is said that Edgar Cayce called Arcturus one of the most highly developed civilizations in our galaxy. However, I have not been able to find a source that can identify the reading this statement comes from.

One of the few books that summarizes channeled messages from the Arcturians mentions that they make contact to help when Earth enters a new age of spirituality[21]. This seems to be the basic message from most channelings.

Channeled material often mentions that there is collaboration between Arcturians and Sirians. According to Lyssa Royal, the combined energies of Arcturus and Sirius provide a balance of physical, emotional, and spiritual healing[22]. This matrix has been tapped into by humanity since its inception and has been known through many archetypal ideas. According to Lyssa, the Arcturians take care of emotional and spiritual healing while the Sirians relate more to physical healing.

Although I am not sure that this is true, I have noticed that there are places where portals to Arcturus and Sirius are connected to the same energetic systems. My experiences suggest that there is more collaboration between star nations than we are aware of. After all, we are only at the beginning of gathering information about and from these star nations.

Studies of Arcturian portal energies indicate that the portals hold different types of energies. Three types of Arcturian portals seem to hold different frequency levels of a particular system that refer to different aspects of "teaching." The first level reflects the energy that supports the process of teaching the self, the personality, about the higher self/soul. This is the phase of reconnecting to the soul and learning to listen to the messages it gives us. The second level is the teaching of others. This is not from a place of "I know" but from a place of humility, a place of sharing. It comes from the realization that, through sharing, we teach ourselves and others. In sharing, we are both student and teacher. The third level — that of being a master — seems quite far away for most of us. It fully supports mastery of self and living in connection and harmony with All That Is.

The energies of these three levels are intense and stimulating. I believe that we have only touched the surface of the Arcturian energies. These energies can help us significantly in expressing who we are fully and in living in alignment with our true selves.

Orion

Of the several books that have been written about Orion, the best known may be *The Orion Mystery* from Robert Bauval and Adrian Gilbert[23]. The most interesting concept addressed in this book is the alignment of the three pyramids of Giza and the stars of Orion's belt. Although the alignment is not perfect, the book made a deep impact, and the idea that the three pyramids represent the stars of the belt of Orion has become accepted almost a fact. A similar relationship has been made between the three pyramids of Teotihuacan in Mexico and the belt of Orion[24].

Gary David's book *The Orion Zone* gives a lot of information about Orion. David found a correlation between the Orion constellation and the ruins of the Anasazi in the American Southwest[25]. Although there are some deviations, the layout of the Anasazi ruins is so close to the Orion constellation that it is unlikely that this is coincidental. The Anasazi used to live in the Southwest from 750 AD to around 1540 AD and built their different villages in such a way that they have laid out the constellation of Orion on the floor of the desert.

As David explains, the Anasazi are the ancestors of the Hopi. The Hopi people are strongly oriented to the constellation of Orion. Their god of war and death, Masau'u, is believed to be from Orion[26]. I have done limited research to check whether the ruins that reflect the form of the constellation of Orion may have Orion portals. I have checked three of the southern ruins of the constellation as described by David. All three have an Orion portal. The lines that are connected with these portals seem to confirm that David's assumption is correct: The Anasazi indeed laid out the Orion constellation marked by different structures (which are now ruins).

I have defined the key characteristics of the Orion energies as "duality/oneness." Its energies seem to induce polarity when approached with fear. This seems to be in alignment with equating Orion with the god of war and death, Masu'u. All wars have been fought over differences, fear, and power (duality). However, the energies of Orion also invite us to overcome duality and move into oneness. The energies of Orion are powerful and should be approached from the heart to avoid being caught in the game of opposites.

Alpha Centauri

There is far less information about human connections with the star system of Alpha Centauri and the galaxy of Andromeda. If indigenous people have connections with these systems, the information is shared rarely or not at all.

The fact that there is less information about Alpha Centauri is not so surprising, as this constellation is hardly visible from the northern hemisphere. African myths mention a race of shape-shifting reptilians who came down from Alpha Centauri, intervened in our DNA, and subjugated humankind. These beings are known by many names, including Chitauri (which is similar to "Centaur") and Imanujela (which is similar to the Hebrew "Emmanuel"/"Immanuel")[27].

The energies of Alpha Centauri, as we experience them through the crystal skulls, help with integration. This integration seems to apply to different levels of energy. It is about integrating experiences into our system, be they emotional, mental, or spiritual. After an experience we may be off balance, and the energies that come from Alpha Centuri through crystal skulls help us to bring back this balance through integration.

The Andromeda Galaxy

I am referring to the Andromeda galaxy and not the star system within our galaxy. Most mythological information about Andromeda refers to the star system Andromeda and not to the Andromeda galaxy. There is not much information available that helps us to understand the possible relationships, energies, or beings from the galaxy of Andromeda. I cannot resonate with most of what I find on the Internet. The energy that comes through the crystal skulls that are aligned with what we believe to be the galaxy of Andromeda has a quality that is recognized as love. Based on information that has come through, they resonate with the number thirteen and therefore I call the beings I connect with the Council of 13.

Cygnus

The seventh star nation of those that have grid lines is the least known, Cygnus. I am aware of one book on this subject, *The Cygnus Mystery* by Andrew Collins[28]. He has uncovered astronomy that is about 17,000 years old with standing stones, temples, and monuments across the globe that are oriented toward Cygnus's stars.

According to Collins, modern-day technology has confirmed that high-energy particles come from a binary star known as Cygnus X3. These peculiar, neutrally charged, strongly interacting particles resonate at some of the highest energies detected. They are called "cygnets," which means "children of the swan"[29]. A stream of plasma containing these particles is pointed straight at us. Collins believes that the ancient people were aware of these energies that strongly influence us and that these energies have contributed to our spiritual evolution[30].

While these energies may have a strong effect on us, I believe that Cygnus's strongest influence comes from higher-dimensional consciousness connected with this system. The beings who hold this consciousness have contributed to the collective crystal skull field. Through their knowledge and their energies, they help us change with grace from living in duality to living in oneness. The only thing we need to do is be willing to open ourselves to these energies.

The Remaining Five Star Nations

The five remaining star nations belong to star systems that have portals that do not form grid systems. These portals are less common, and it seems that there are no connecting lines between them. However, sometimes a portal can be at a location that is connected through communication lines (*GME*, 113-154) with other places. In this way, they form an outline of a star system. I am familiar with two examples of such situations, both of Ursa Major — the part that is known as the Big Dipper, in particular. Both examples are in locations that form the outline of the Big Dipper and have a portal to Ursa Major.

The first example is a small Big Dipper laid out in the landscape of the eastern part of Belgium near the town of Wéris. The Big Dipper is laid out by megaliths that are found in that area (image 9.13). [Note: Image 9.13 is part of an unofficial handout that was available from a museum in Wéris.] All the megaliths are standing exactly at the right place to form the layout of the Big Dipper in the landscape, with the exception of one menhir (standing stone). However, it is known that this menhir is not in its original place. One of the

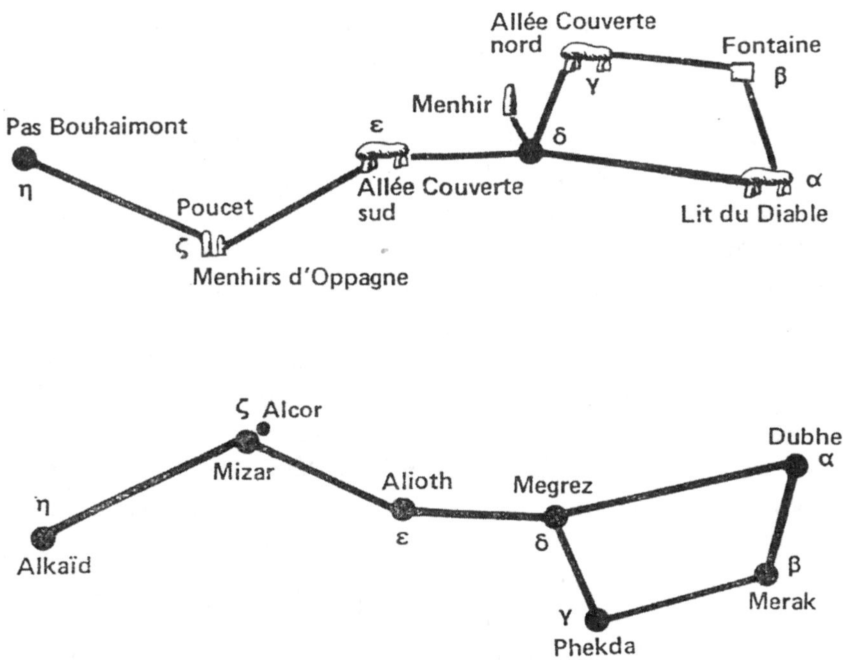

9.13 The Big Dipper laid out in the Weris area in eastern Belgium

9.14 The menhirs of Oppagne that are part of the star system of the Big Dipper in the Weris area in eastern Belgium

megaliths can be seen in image 9.14, which shows the three menhirs from Oppagne, which is also the location of the portal to Ursa Major. All of the megaliths are connected with communication lines outlining the Big Dipper.

The second representation of the Big Dipper is nicknamed the "Cathedral Bear"[31]. "Bear" refers to the fact that Big Dipper is part of the Ursa Major (Big Bear) constellation. The Cathedral Bear is located in northern France and stretches into Germany. This is a larger form stretching over a couple hundred miles and was found by Gregory Rigby. I checked his finding and, as in Belgium, the points are connected with communication lines. Most of the points are cathedrals, such as Chartres, Bonne Mare, Saint Quentin, and Reims — hence the name Cathedral Bear. There are also points at buildings in Verdun and Landonvillers, both in France, and Donnersberg, in Germany, that are not cathedrals. In this setup, the Ursa Major portal is located in the Cathedral of Chartres. Rigby mentioned it is likely that these places are much older than the structures that are now found there, and I fully agree. It seems that these locations have been used as sacred places over long periods of time. Who created these areas in the first place?

Crystal skulls that are connected with or resonate with the energies and information of Ursa Major help us gain insight into ourselves and the environment. We may have information, but without insight, that information is much less impactful.

To complete the descriptions (although limited) of the different star systems connected with crystal skulls, I will present the qualities of the remaining four star nations: Cassiopeia, Zeta Reticuli, Dragon, and Taurus.

The energy of Cassiopeia helps us understand ourselves and the world around us. The star system is named after Queen Cassiopeia in Greek mythology, who boasted about her unrivaled beauty. Like many people, she saw herself as she had chosen to. Our way of seeing ourselves is often an illusion that determines our daily lives. The energy of this star system helps us to see and understand who we truly are.

The energy of Zeta Reticuli helps us during the process of change. For many people, change does not come easily. Often it feels safer to stay where we are, because when we change, we have to be willing to face aspects of the unknown — "shadow" aspects of ourselves. However, everything is changing continuously. Therefore, it is important to accept change as a natural part of our lives and to learn to trust the guidance of our souls and the universe.

Dragon energy, the energy of the Dragon constellation, helps us during the process of transmutation — the letting go of all old behaviors, emotions, and ways of thinking that are no longer needed. This energy also help us on a physical level to let go of all material objects that we no longer need. Clear out your closets!

Finally, the energy of Taurus helps during the process of transformation, helping you to become a different you. The Taurus energies connected with crystal skulls are different from the astrological qualities. Many people are like caterpillars that keep eating and are afraid to go to the next step: the pupation. This is the phase in which we need to let go of our old lives and ways of living. In a sense, the caterpillar (the ego-oriented person) needs to die in order to allow the butterfly (the spiritual person) to emerge.

The 13th Crystal Skull

The twelve crystal skulls that are associated with the twelve star nations help us remember who we are and express more of our true selves. It is possible to try to arrange a certain hierarchy of importance across the twelve energy aspects that they represent, but such efforts will miss the point. The twelve crystal skulls hold the power of the circle, where all points are equally important. It is a mistake to credit one aspect as being more important than another. However, people may feel a stronger attraction to one or a few of the twelve. This attraction is most likely due to greater personal need for specific energies, given the state of an individual's evolution. Always follow your guidance without succumbing to the game of hierarchy, and you will stay in tune with the essence of the journey.

Many people will say that the central skull is most important, as it is the skull that holds the energies to help us to integrate all energies into a general understanding. However, that does not make it the most important one. In the original setup of the information systems given by the star nations, the thirteenth star nation — represented by the thirteenth crystal skull — was defined as the human species on Earth. The energies of the star nations invite us to bring all information together in one consciousness, leading to the experience of oneness inside ourselves. This will be reflected in the gathering of all of the other star nations in oneness as well. This is why the beings of the star nations are supporting us so much — it is as important for us as it is for them.

Connecting with Star Nations

Many people feel some kind of connection with star nations. Often people ask how this connection can be deepened. There are many ways, of course, but within the context of this book we will use symbols and crystal skulls. There is no need to know which star nation your crystal skull is primarily connected with. You can dowse the answer if you would like to know; however, every crystal skull is able to attune you to whatever or whomever you would like to connect with. Once the connection is made, your crystal skull becomes a transmission station you can exchange energy and information with. Mostly you will experience this connection as energy and information coming to you.

We have made connections with most of the twelve star nations during our weekly meditations, and the energies and the experiences people have are very profound. Over time we learned that the symbols connected with the twelve star nations are very helpful to focus our intent and establish a direct and powerful connection. Therefore, these symbols have been included in the book in Addendum II. I invite you to use the symbol of the star nation you feel attracted to and begin to explore your connection with the beings of that nation. Your experiences can be profound and very supportive of your journey to oneness. We are all one — not only with all that exists on Earth but also with all that exists in the universe. The work of Dolores Cannon indicates that we all have connections with the different star systems and truly we are all from one source[32].

To help you with your connection to the star system of your choice, I offer a meditation (see also the meditation CD). I recommend that you use a quartz crystal skull for this meditation, but it is not necessary.

Crystal skulls have such a wide range of vibrations that they are most suitable for these connections. Choose the symbol or star nation you wish to connect with and open Addendum II to the page where that symbol is printed. [Suggestion: Make a copy of that symbol so that you are not distracted by other symbols and do not need to keep the book open.] Create an optimal environment and start the following meditation (or a different version that you prefer and have available).

Start with the basic meditation given in chapter 4.

While staying in that state, open your eyes and look at the symbol. Set a clear intent to use this symbol as a key to enter the consciousness field of the beings of [your selected star nation]. Some people prefer to keep the copy of the symbol in their hands or place their skull on top of it. I also have seen people placing their feet on the symbol.

Trust that you now have made a connection. Never doubt yourself, because then your vibration will go down in frequency and a connection may no longer be possible or will become limited.

Allow whatever happens to happen. Being in a state of love means that you will always encounter beings from the star system you connect with who also live in a place of love.

When you feel complete, express your gratitude for the connection and the gifts you have received. By definition, every connection will bring you gifts in the form of energy, insights, information, or healing, whether or not you are aware of it.

Take a few deep breaths and bring your awareness to your feet and your body. When you feel ready, open your eyes.

Share or write down your experiences in order to follow the development of your deepening connection.

As I mentioned, the connection with star beings is a process that will unfold over time. Every time you connect with these higher vibrations of beings living in a higher-dimensional consciousness, you will expand and grow. Do not be surprised when you experience some discomfort due to cleansing and shifting energies; it is all for the highest good as long as we come from a place of love. Realize that these beings are our relatives and they love to connect with us. As I mentioned, the connection is mutually beneficial, even when that may seem difficult to believe!

The purpose of your connections with the different star nations through your crystal skulls is to speed up your contribution to the collective growth of humankind to oneness so that we can integrate collectively the energies from the star nations to allow the shift in human consciousness to take place. We are all on our way to oneness!

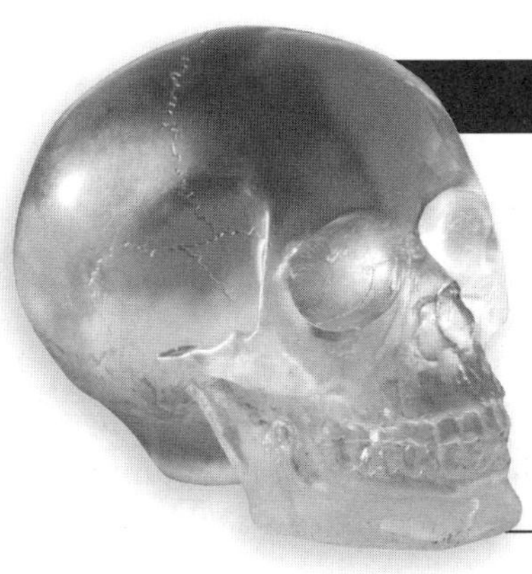

CHAPTER TEN

The Crystal Skull Journey: *a Support for Human Spiritual Evolution*

In the previous chapters, we focused on the nature of crystal skulls as well as what you can do with them, such as how to activate your crystal skull and how to work with it. This has laid a foundation for working optimally with your crystal skull so it can support you on the journey of remembering and understanding who you are. By now it should be clear that crystal skulls are wonderful tools to help you on your journey from duality to oneness.

We have looked at crystal skulls mainly from an individual perspective. However, we also are part of a collective. In this chapter, we will look at how crystal skulls can help the evolution of the human species as a whole. This is particularly important because, as a species, we have a powerful effect on our world, on Earth.

When I talk about having an effect on our world as a species, I do not mean from an ecological perspective. Much has been written about the tendency of the human species to destroy the environment and about the horrible realization that humans are the only species capable of killing large numbers of their own outside of the need to survive (genocide). This does not mean that every person will kill another human being; however, voting for any president willing to go to war — or one who even goes to war — contributes to this strange phenomenon of killing members of our own species. In the twentieth century alone, more than 10 million people were killed through what is called genocide — an intention to destroy, in whole or in part, a national, ethnic, racial, or religious group[1]. These numbers are staggering, and unfortunately, these acts continue — although thankfully on a lesser scale than in the past century.

Genocide, war, and aggression within families are all based on perceived differences. We tend to measure values by comparing things. When we do not like a difference, not only do we judge it, but we may even want to destroy it, especially when we experience this difference as threatening. The only way to break through this seemingly endless pattern is to stop looking at the world from a place of duality in which things are either right or wrong. We need to move to a place of oneness where differences are variations within oneness. We all are unique and therefore different from everyone else, but at the same time we are all interconnected — one consciousness, one big family. From that place, we can see every other human being as family. In a family, all members are different, and often the only place where we can accept and enjoy these differences is within the family.

There is another reason why it is important to resolve conflicts, wars, and aggression: All human energies are part of a collective consciousness, and the energy of our collective consciousness has a tremendous effect on Earth. Though the effect we have on Earth as a collective is not well known, it is of great importance to understand it. Understanding the effects may be the basis for true change and for a spiritual evolution based on the oneness of Earth and all that lives on her.

The Effect of Human Collective Consciousness

Generally, modern people live in their own worlds, disconnected from most other people. They have connections with family, friends, colleagues, and members of the same religious or New Age groups, but most are disconnected from Earth herself. We forget that Earth is a crystalline being that reflects and amplifies energies in the same way as crystals and crystal skulls. In a sense, Earth is a super reflector and amplifier, and she particularly reflects the collective consciousness of humanity. This reflection can be experienced as turmoil in weather as we see nowadays in many places in the world, but it may also be expressed as earthquakes. Much of the anomalous weather we experience is a consequence of the collective consciousness of humankind. We are the ones who create weather changes that are beyond the normal patterns. Earth and the human collective consciousness are two energy systems that interact dynamically.

The fact that Earth is crystalline in nature brings up another important point: Crystalline energies only express their full potential when they are activated, which is also true for Earth. In my opinion, Earth also needs to be activated to its full potential, and humankind as a whole — the collective human species — has been given that responsibility. I do not need to say that we are far from giving form to that responsibility. Earth is an entity who responds to our consciousness. I also believe that this is true for plants and animals. They all reflect the state of our collective consciousness in their own unique way. The importance of this cannot be emphasized enough.

Most people have difficulty believing that we have a responsibility to Earth and everything that lives on it as I just described. I do not often hear similar thoughts about this subject, so it was quite surprising to read a similar belief in a book called *The Camino: a Journey of the Spirit*, written by Shirley MacLaine. In this book, she describes her walk of the Camino, a pilgrimage to Santiago de Compostela in northern Spain. During her journey, she talks in a kind of dream state with a person called John the Scot. In their exchanges about Lemuria, he says: "The Earth was a loving organism responding in direct ratio to the collective consciousness of Mankind - it was not the other way around. The collective spiritual consciousness of mankind actually molded and orchestrated the ecological movements of nature. The spiritual nature of man was more powerful than nature. The Deity made souls to be cocreators in life, with dominion over all life-forms"[2].

This is a powerful statement! Although it was referring to Lemuria and therefore described in past tense, in my opinion it is still true. The problem is that most people are directed by their minds and fears instead of being guided by their hearts and souls. Therefore, they are unable to perform the task for which they were created.

A similar idea was mentioned by the Pleiadeans, channeled through Carole Davis, in the second book written by Brian Hadley-James. In a channeling, they were talking about the pole shift and Monitor, the Pleiadean who shared through Carole Davis-Wilson, said that the duration of the pole shift would be determined by the combined "minds on the Earth" and "that which controls your body also controls what happens to the Earth"[3].

Another example comes from *Transylvanian Moonrise*, by Radu Cinamar and Peter Moon, in which a Tibetan lama answers, a question about the effects of negative emotions on the aura. In his answer, he shares that negative emotions will have an effect on the aura and the corresponding body organs, which can cause psychic disturbances. He then states, "In a similar way, this process happens in the Earth's aura which is deeply influenced by the aura of the human beings that live on it"[4].

One of the most powerful examples comes from the Kogi tribe[5] — a tribe that lives in the Sierra Nevada de Santa Marta in Colombia. The Kogi are seen as the last holders of the ancient wisdom who were able to keep that wisdom because they managed to escape Spanish influence. In their view, all that exists in the physical also exists in "aluna." It is not easy to understand with our Western minds what is meant by "aluna," because it goes beyond physicality. It is the world of thought, consciousness, and spirit. The Kogi maintain balance in the Sierras where they live by working with proper thought (consciousness, awareness) in aluna. From their perspective, this is essential to be able to maintain balance within our world. In their vision, the Sierras are a model of the world, and through this model, they can balance Earth as a whole.

The Kogi experience our destruction of the balance on Earth. They call us the younger brother who does not understand. We, the younger brother, have no awareness that our thoughts create imbalance in aluna, which leads to the destruction of Earth, but this is already visible in the climate changes (*GME*).

All of these examples support the idea that we are all interconnected as one. It also tells us that the state of our collective consciousness determines the overall condition of Earth and all that is connected to her. Therefore, it is important to create a collective consciousness that reflects this soul responsibility and shifts from disrupting the functioning of the Earth to supporting her. Crystal skulls seem to be a wonderful — if not the best — tool to support that process.

Crystal Skulls and Individuals

If we want to induce change in our collective consciousness, we need to change first. There are many books, DVDs, CDs, workshops, seminars, teleseminars, and training programs to help us change and find our true selves. It is a challenging process, because even people who work hard to change complain that either change moves slowly or they are stuck regularly. People find it difficult to free themselves from the collective influence and therefore are caught in the collective patterns. However, it is important to be diligent and to persevere. It may help to find tools and groups to support you in this process.

In the previous chapters, we have seen that crystal skulls stimulate the process of change and healing. They help us to move to higher vibrations and higher levels of consciousness. An increase in vibration helps us move from the lower fear-based frequencies to the higher love-based frequencies. It also helps to stimulate our brain to become more active in all frequency ranges, thus allowing us to process more of what we receive into perceptions. We can then use the perceived information for our growth and expanding awareness.

We have also seen that working with crystal skulls is a journey. Through our choices and intents, we give direction to this journey. These choices are supposed to be conscious; however, most people make regular choices without awareness. Or, as many people say, they "don't know where that came from." Because crystal skulls are such powerful amplifiers, we have to be very careful when we work with them. Our subconscious issues may be amplified and create new patterns that may jeopardize our spiritual journeys.

Before discussing the human collective consciousness more deeply, I would like to mention an issue connected with crystal skulls that affects both individuals and collective energy systems. This issue is the phenomenon of the creation of ancient crystal skulls, either by carvers and business people or by people who desperately want to have an ancient crystal skull. Some may think that I give far too much attention to this subject, considering it is a subject that most people avoid. However, I consider this issue important and would like to share why this is so.

When crystal skulls are carved, any thought and intent the carver has about the purpose of the skull will be put into the skull. This means that when a crystal skull is made to be sold as ancient even though it is not, the crystal skull will hold the carver's thoughts and energies in its field. People who purposely make fake ancient skulls work from ego, and that energy comes with the crystal skull. Naturally, that energy will be amplified through the caretaker working with this skull. If a skull is made from natural material, it will amplify these thoughts and energies even more. Most of the influence and effects will be subconscious.

Humans have definitions for what is "positive" versus "negative." However, a crystal skull amplifies any type of energy and will not differentiate the energies, as humans do. They simply amplify what is — independent of the quality.

It is interesting to note that once a person has convinced him- or herself that they have an ancient crystal skull, it seems to be very difficult to change this belief, even when the person knows that the crystal skull is not really ancient. Once the amplification of desire has occurred, it becomes truth, making it difficult to change. The amplified belief is stronger than the real truth that the belief is incorrect.

Because everybody is on a journey and each journey should be honored, it may seem that a belief whether a crystal skull is ancient or not is irrelevant. It may seem that the energies connected with that skull will affect that person only. Unfortunately, that is not true. The energies of caretakers who hold incorrect beliefs have a significant effect from the collective perspective.

When you work with a crystal skull, every thought and belief has an effect on the collective crystal skull field. As I mentioned earlier, crystal skulls have a collective energy field similar to the human collective consciousness field. The aspects of the collective energy field of crystal skulls we work with actively are held in the crystalline grids. These crystalline grids, especially the levels connected with crystal skulls, are in a development phase. We are only beginning to remember. As a consequence, the energies in the grids are weak and every belief amplified through crystal skulls will have a strong effect on the energy and information held in the grids. This is the reason the ego energy around "wanting an ancient crystal skull" has a significant impact on the energies held in the grid system. Crystalline grids induced through work with crystal skulls are compensating for the loss of the first five crystalline grid levels in developed areas like cities and towns. Therefore, the quality of the energies in the grids that we create through our work with crystal skulls is of utmost importance. My invitation to every caretaker is to ask yourself what you would like to bring into these crystalline grids. Would you like to bring in love, truth, and empowerment, or ego, power games, and deception?

The collective crystal skull energies in the grid system in turn have an effect on the collective human consciousness. That means that every caretaker has taken on quite a responsibility. Always be aware of your intent, thoughts, and emotions. When you work with your crystal skull, ask yourself with every thought and emotion whether you want that thought or emotion to be amplified and brought into the crystalline grids and the collective human consciousness. Ask whether it really contributes to a shift to higher vibrations. Asking these simple questions may help you to change your life and truly fulfill your soul purpose, contributing to the shift in human consciousness.

Crystal Skulls and the Collective

The effect of crystal skulls on an individual person is of prime importance. After all, we are primarily responsible for ourselves. By expressing who we truly are to the best of our ability, we fulfill our role in the whole and contribute optimally to the collective human consciousness. We do not have to do more than that. Guided by heart and soul, we express naturally who we are and do exactly what we are supposed to do. This all sounds easy, but most people experience this process as challenging. One of the reasons that life is challenging, besides our own internal emotions and beliefs, is the collective consciousness.

Every vibration we send out — whether it is emotional, mental, or experiential — will have an effect on the collective consciousness, and the collective consciousness also has an effect on us. The collective consciousness contains every thought and emotion that has ever been experienced by any human being throughout time. Many of these experiences can be helpful on our journey as well as many experiences we would not wish to connect with.

Everything is vibration. The law connected with vibration is the law of resonance, which states that we resonate only with a small part of the collective and the resonating energies may strengthen our experiences. Depending on our vibrational state, these experiences will be positive or negative. That is the reason why it is so important to work with crystal skulls from our hearts so as to create a vibration as high as possible. The energies of love, joy, and happiness will then resonate with similar aspects in the collective, increasing our wonderful energies even more.

We always receive from the collective that which resonates with our vibrational state. When we are in a high-vibrational state, we will experience situations that reflect this state, and this will contribute to the increase of higher vibrations in the collective. This is the process of evolution. This happens in addition to other processes that we have described earlier in the book, like the addition of energy and information through tapping into the Infinite and creating new experiences through scalar energies.

In a sense, the word evolution is incorrect. We are actually remembering who we are. This allows us to reawaken consciousness that was always present but was inaccessible for most people. I have heard people say that we cannot talk about spiritual evolution because many past civilizations were more advanced spiritually and technologically than we are. They refer to Atlantis, Lemuria, and to civilizations like the Egyptians, the Maya, and the ones from Tiahuanacu and Puma Punku in Bolivia. However, there is an important difference. In past times, the spiritual and technological knowledge was held by a few people who were mainly the leaders, such as pharaohs and priests. Higher knowledge was not meant for everyone. Today we see this phenomenon in secret esoteric societies where membership is only for the chosen few.

The uniqueness of modern times is that spiritual evolution is for everyone. Of course there is free will — giving people the right to choose to be part of this evolution or not. There are clear signs that many people have chosen the spiritual path and are searching for meaning.

There are many energy systems available on Earth that support the personal and collective spiritual journey (see *Gifts of Mother Earth*). Some of these different systems are important for the evolution of the human species. The two main systems are the human collective consciousness field and grids and the morphogenetic fields and grids.

The Collective Human Consciousness

We already mentioned that the collective human consciousness is found in fields and grids. There are two collective human consciousness systems: the third-dimensional collective consciousness with its field and grids and the fourth-dimensional or Christ consciousness with its field and grids. Both have been described extensively in *Gifts of Mother Earth* (89-110).

These systems are always set up in the same way. There is a field that holds all information of a particular system, and there are grids that hold information that is actively being worked with on Earth. The field and the grids are connected through vortexes (*GME*, 111-120).

Every time a person works and connects with their crystal skull, an energy field will form around this person. This field will always have an effect on the crystal skull field and grids, on the third-dimensional collective consciousness, and perhaps even on the fourth-dimensional collective consciousness. Every conscious or subconscious act will become part of the collective consciousness grid. If it is a new experience, it may even become part of the field, causing this field to expand. When we meditate with our crystal skulls, the opposite may also happen: We take information from the grids or the field. This whole process will be amplified by the crystal skulls, giving us the opportunity to expand, change, and obtain insights. At the same time, we will have an impact on the whole and therefore contribute to the whole.

In *Crystal Skulls: Interacting with a Phenomenon*, I described the effect crystal skull meditations have on vortexes of different grids (85-88). These are grids other than those of the human collective consciousness. Regular meditation will expand all vortexes within the area. As we have seen, the size of the area that will be affected depends on the number, size, and activity level of your crystal skulls. The energy of this field activates the vortexes within its field but the energy also spreads through the lines of the grids to other places. This means that meditation helps to expand grid systems to an optimal level.

Crystal skulls are such effective tools because of their ability to tap into the infinite consciousness — the implicate order, as David Bohm calls it (this was described in chapter 7). I mentioned that scalar waves bring in information from the Infinite Source. Through our work with crystal skulls, this information/energy is spread through grid lines and vortexes into the collective consciousness field. This allows new information to be brought into the collective consciousness field. This is an exciting realization — we are expanding the potential of human beings by working with our crystal skulls. This adds to the overall importance of working with crystal skulls.

When activated sufficiently, crystal skulls will also help us to connect more deeply with oneness consciousness. This contributes to the expansion of the collective Christ consciousness field and grids. When the grids and field become stronger, it will become easier for people to have fourth-dimensional oneness experiences.

Consciousness is never static; it is a highly dynamic process. This dynamic can take place within the consciousness that is located in the grids or within the consciousness that is located in the field. We can even expand beyond the grids and the field and tap into the Infinite. In each moment, the choice is ours, and crystal skulls will amplify whatever we choose.

Morphogenetic Fields and Grids

Other information systems that are important for our spiritual evolution are the morphogenetic grids and fields. This information relates to our planet Earth as a whole. This system has been more extensively described in *Gifts of Mother Earth* (175-190). This system is responsible for providing the matrix for Earth and everything that lives on her. In addition, each species has its own morphogenetic field and grid. Without such a field, a species cannot exist. Our human morphogenetic grids and fields are described as the third- and fourth-dimensional consciousness grids and fields.

The morphogenetic grid system on Earth can also be called "the matrix." This matrix determines the physical state, form, behavior, and aspects of consciousness for Earth and all that lives on her.

In the beginning of this chapter, I mentioned that human consciousness determines what happens on Earth to a large degree. This is reflected in our ability to change the morphogenetic grids and fields. Although we have this ability, please do not meddle with these grids. Governments and all kinds of societies in the past and present have had great interest in these grids, knowing that through them one can "rule" Earth (*GME*, 178). It is important not to interfere with this system because we do not (fully) understand how it works. Our task is to create interconnectedness through love and oneness. This interconnectedness will allow all morphogenetic grids to align naturally and optimally with the morphogenetic field — the potential of all species and of Gaia as a whole. Our task is not to direct but to allow the system to unfold. Our task is to support the unfolding through love and feeling one with all our relatives — the stones, crystals, plants, and animals.

To increase the vibrations everywhere on Earth, all we need to do is create a field of love that will be amplified by our crystal skulls. That will stimulate all morphogenetic grids to move closer to their optimal state because that is how love functions. Love always creates the optimal state of everything and helps to increase the vibration that will lead us closer to oneness.

Supporting the Development of Crystalline Grids

Crystalline grids are an important part of Earth and of all the different stones, crystal, and crystal skulls. As I mentioned earlier, there are three groups of crystalline grids. The first group consists of the five basic crystalline frequencies. This group is important because it is the foundation for all other grids. They are the grids that bring in the (new) information that is needed for the dynamic of the whole system of grids so they can unfold and expand.

In chapter 7, I explained that the lowest five levels (the first group) of the twelve that exist disappear when we, human beings, create our modern structures with their artificial electromagnetic systems. These lower five grids have disappeared in developed areas, even within small communities. Because the five lower crystalline grids are the basis for all other grid systems, their disappearance throws other systems off balance.

The only way to create a crystalline grid in cities and towns is by working with crystals and crystal skulls. When we work regularly at a specific spot with our crystals and crystal skulls, we create crystalline vortexes that become permanent. They link into the grids, creating crystalline grid lines having levels six to nine (when we work with crystals) or levels six to twelve (when we work with crystal skulls). Initial research showed that when there are enough new crystalline vortexes and lines, the lines of levels one to five may return, but more research is needed to confirm that this happens on a larger scale. However, it is clear that working with crystal skulls, especially in developed areas like cities, towns, and communities, is important. The lines that we create through our work with crystal skulls take over the role of the lower five levels and will contribute to a rebalancing of all of the other Earth grid systems. Therefore, we need as many people as possible to contribute to the creation of new lines to replace the crystalline grid lines that have disappeared. In this way, every crystal skull caretaker can contribute to the improvement of our energetic environment and help to create an optimal condition for an expansion of our collective consciousness.

Creating Your Own Crystalline Vortex

Working with crystals and crystal skulls will always create crystalline vortexes. These vortexes normally dissolve after a couple of days, but that does not mean you have lost the energies that were created. These energies will move into either the different grids or the different fields. However, the vortex itself will be gone after a few days. Of course, you can create a new one any time you want.

To make a vortex part of the crystalline grid, you need to create a permanent vortex. To create a permanent crystalline vortex, you need to take a number of points into account. I will summarize these points:

- Meditate with your crystal or crystal skull on a regular basis.
- Do your meditations at a fixed place inside or outside. Some people like to create an altar as the basis of such a place.
- When finished with the meditation, make sure that you always place your crystal skull back to anchor the vortex. You can also use a crystal or stone to anchor the energies so you can bring your crystal skull to other places.
- You can create your crystalline vortex inside your house or anywhere outside as long as the place is used regularly and you use a stone or crystal as an anchor.
- Use this vortex for your crystal skull activations. That will increase the frequency and power of the energies in the vortex. This makes it possible to create connections with other higher-frequency vortexes in the grid.
- Whenever possible, meditate with others at your vortex in creation. This will bring in more energy and stabilize the vortex faster. In addition, it will hold a larger diversity of energies — more than you can create alone. Therefore, it will create a more powerful contribution to the crystalline grid with more opportunities to connect with other vortexes.
- Realize that you are responsible for the quality of the vortex you are taking care of. Work or connect with the vortex only from a place of love, and ask others to do the same. Use the oneness meditation (chapter 4) when you work with others.

When your vortex in creation becomes permanent depends on many factors. When you are alone and you meditate three to four times a week, your vortex will most likely become permanent after six to eight weeks. Once you have created a permanent vortex, it has become part of the crystalline grid and you have added an important quality to your work with crystal skulls. The effect of everything you do while sitting on your vortex is an important contribution to healing and transforming everything that no longer serves the collective. It is our responsibility to transform and heal everything we have messed up when we were disconnected from both the physical and spiritual aspects of ourselves and the world around us. Crystal skulls are excellent tools to support us in this process.

A Final Statement

We have a responsibility to fulfill: We came here to remember and help others remember that we are spiritual beings having a human experience. We came here with the handicap of forgetting who we are. This seems to be part of entering this physical reality. The process of remembering what it means to be a spiritual being in a physical form is challenging because we are faced with a collective amnesia. Fortunately, all the information we need is present in the different energy and information fields. One of the most important fields is the collective crystal skull field. Working with crystal skulls helps us access information that helps us remember. Once we remember, we will be able to change and transform any negative energy in any other energy system, supporting the process even more.

When we work with all these energies from a place of love, we stimulate shifts of consciousness. We need these shifts because our current state of collective consciousness restricts our development as a species and that of our planet and all that lives on her. Because we are part of a galaxy, and even of a universe, we will even have an effect on the development of the galaxy and of the universe. Everything is connected and all things affect one another. This may be the reason why the different extraterrestrial beings of all levels of consciousness have so much interest in our process and why they are contributing so much to it. As we have seen, one of the ways they support us is through crystal skulls. May your crystal skull guide you to contribute optimally to this process.

ADDENDUM I:

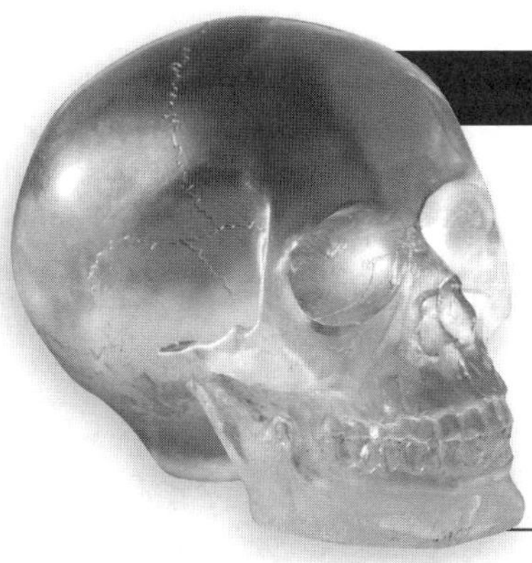

Overview of the "Awakened" Crystal Skulls

Earlier in this book, I described the different energies of crystal skulls — in particular, those that are related to the awakening of crystal skulls by various people in the past. These "ancient and old" crystal skulls help us understand different levels of activation. They are like beacons on the road to help us awaken the potential of the contemporary crystal skulls. These beacons have different powers and shine light of different intensities, but they are all part of the journey of awakening. In this addendum, I will give short descriptions of the crystal skulls that function as beacons. I have added two contemporary crystal skulls because their characteristics are similar to the energies of ancient crystal skulls. Describing their energies and the differences from the ancient crystal skulls should prevent confusion.

The given descriptions are incomplete. For many of the crystal skulls presented in this addendum, a whole chapter or even a book could be written. I will restrict the descriptions to some basic elements that will help you understand the unique aspects of each of these crystal skulls. I will give references whenever possible for those who would like more information.

There are more crystal skulls known than are described in this addendum. Over time crystal skulls have appeared and disappeared. With a few exceptions, the crystal skulls that are no longer available to the public have not been included. Also, crystal skulls in private collections are not included if the information is very limited or the caretaker desires anonymity.

Over time, many crystals skulls have been studied by the Society of Crystal Skulls International, headed by the late Nick F.R. Nocerino. Nick and the society collected a great deal of information of which the majority is not available. Some of the information has been published by Pelton Publications[1].

As I mentioned earlier, there are crystal skulls that are claimed to be ancient but do not have energies that support this claim. I have not included these crystal skulls in this overview unless there is a reasonable possibility they could be old. I did this on purpose and not as a consequence of lack of knowledge of their existence. Of course, more genuine ancient crystal skulls may be discovered.

1. Mitchell-Hedges Crystal Skull

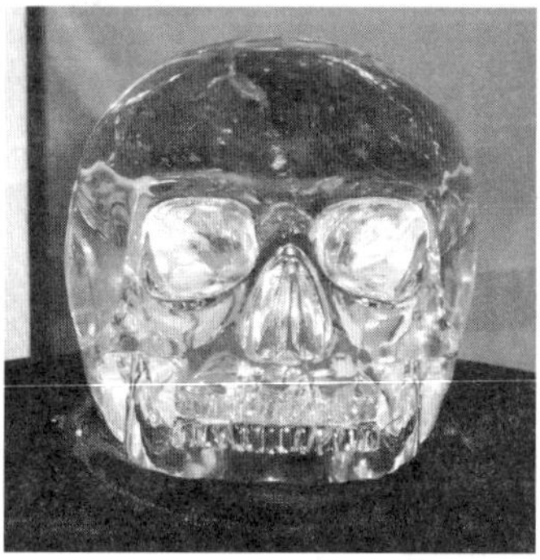

The Mitchell-Hedges crystal skull is considered to be the most exquisitely carved crystal skull. During many years of her long life (she became 100 years old), Anna Mitchell-Hedges made this crystal skull available for viewing, both during events and in private settings. Frank Dorland has been investigating this crystal skull for about six years, and his research has been published by Bryant and Galde[2] and by himself[3].

Anna passed away in April 2007, and her crystal skull was passed on to Bill Homann, who is its current caretaker. For a variety of reasons, the skull has not attended larger events since 2009. Its website[4] states: "The skull is no longer available for meetings, publications, interviews, and television programs".

No other crystal skull has received so much print and film coverage. Its beautiful carving has astounded people. Its energies have led to enthusiasm even in those who later believed that the Mitchell-Hedges crystal skull is a "fake" — a contemporary crystal skull probably carved in Idar Oberstein[5].

Anna Mitchell-Hedges told the story of the discovery of this crystal skull many times. The story is found in many books, articles, websites, and interviews. The basic story is that F.A. Mitchell-Hedges was leading an archeological expedition in Lubaantun, a possible Mayan ruin in modern Belize. Anna, his adopted daughter, found the skull on January 1, 1924, on her seventeenth birthday. She saw something reflecting light in the ruins, which turned out to be the crystal skull. The skull's detachable jaw was found three months later. According to the story, Mitchell-Hedges gave the skull to a man named Barney as collateral for a loan. Barney put it up for sale at an auction in 1943. Mitchell-Hedges bought it back at that auction.

The story is not backed up with any proof — no pictures, no papers. The earliest existing "proof" is that Barney put the skull up for sale and Mitchell-Hedges bought it in 1943. It stayed in his and Anna's possession until Anna died and Bill Homann became the skull's caretaker.

The fact that the story of Anna Mitchell-Hedges cannot be verified has been a strong argument for Nick Nocerino and later Stephen Mehler to define it as a "hoax"[6]. However, any suggestion about what the true story could be is pure speculation, and there is no shortage of that[7]. Jane Walsh of the Smithsonian Institute determined that the skull was carved with lapidary rotary tools[8]. This has added scientific weight to the belief that the skull is a hoax.

The stories and discussions bring more questions than answers. "Incorrect" stories surrounding the origins of crystal skulls are given occasionally in order to protect the caretakers who hold privately ancient artifacts. None of these cases are scrutinized in the same way as the story of the Mitchell-Hedges crystal skull.

Another question that has been raised and that cannot be answered is why Barney never revealed the source of the skull. The suggestion that the skull was carved in Idar Oberstein is not supported by any information. Also, there is no documentation that carvers in Idar Oberstein carved any crystal skulls in the past. Carvers in Idar Oberstein try to promote the quality of their work, and recently they carved a crystal skull. They refer to the fact that they used quartz from Madagascar and Brazil in the past[9], but they do not state that they actually carved crystal skulls at that time.

Jane Walsh postulated the possibility that the Mitchell-Hedges skull is a more sophisticated copy of the British Museum skull[10]. However, to make such an accurate copy, you need either measurements or a lot of pictures taken from different angles. In both cases, the carvers would have needed to approach the British Museum and would have been noticed by others. In both situations, some kind of record would have been available.

The points I raise are not meant to criticize any researcher or any article — only to help you realize that we will not understand a crystal skull by looking at its "factual" history. There are no crystal skulls that are considered ancient that have official published records of their history. They start with stories from the moment the current caretaker received the skull, and sometimes the skull comes with a story. That is the reason metaphysical research is so important. Obtaining information about the energies of crystal skulls helps us understand the knowledge and mastery with which crystal skulls have been created and used (awakened) in the past. This adds valuable information that helps create a more complete picture of a crystal skull.

While there are many questions about the history of the Mitchell-Hedges crystal skull, there also are questions about its energies. From an energetic perspective, it has been the most difficult crystal skull for me to understand. Whenever it seemed like I understood the energies, it was unclear the next time I looked at it. It seems as if I was laughed at when I attempted to understand this crystal skull. Yes, I know that this is a strange statement, but it reflects the feeling I often had after studying the energies of this crystal skull.

The biggest question may be: Who activated the Mitchell-Hedges skull in such a way that it already had thirty-six layers activated with a widened thirty-sixth layer with a bluish shimmer when it was sold in 1943? I base this energetic description on photos from that time. The level of activation of this skull reflects mastery, because of its widened thirty-sixth layer with a bluish shimmer. It seems unlikely that Barney had these abilities; a person with such a deep connection must have had a deep love for this skull and would never sell it at an auction. So who worked with this crystal skull at such a high metaphysical level? Most likely, we will never know the answer, but the fact that the Mitchell-Hedges crystal skull is so highly activated may explain the enthusiasm of Nick Nocerino and his team when they did research on it[11].

In summary, this crystal skull has fulfilled an important function in the past by bringing a lot of attention to the subject of crystal skulls. Based on its uniqueness, it will always be an important part of the crystal skull energy field. That uniqueness has been described extensively and beautifully by Nick Nocerino in an interview published in *Mysteries of Crystal Skulls Revealed*[12]. I like to refer to it because there is little I can add.

2. ET

The crystal skull "ET" is a smoky quartz skull that was found in 1906 in Guatemala by a Mayan family while they were digging on their property. The skull is slightly larger than a human skull. Its shape is rather unusual and quite different from other well-known crystal skulls. It has a slightly pointed head and an overbite and therefore looks rather alien, hence its name. As with all ancient crystal skulls, the story of how the caretaker came into possession of this crystal skull is rather peculiar. In

1991, Joky van Dieten, who at that time lived in Costa Rica, intuitively felt that she needed to call a particular store near Los Angeles to ask for a crystal skull. At the moment that Joky called, the store did not have a crystal skull. She asked them to call her back if they ever received one. Surprisingly for the store — but not for Joky — a few days later its owners were offered a crystal skull from Guatemala. When they called Joky, she bought the skull — unseen — became its caretaker, and named it ET. Joky used ET to help herself heal from a complex operation in which a large tumor was removed from her head.

In May, 1999, ET was acknowledged by Mayan representatives as a lost Mayan skull during a sunrise ceremony at a Crystal Healing Conference in Sedona, Arizona, organized by Dr. Chet Snow and his wife, Kallista. According to these Mayans, ET came from the Pleiades[13]. In that sunrise ceremony, the Mayan representatives confirmed that Joky was the rightful guardian[14].

Joky collected more crystal skulls and traveled the world with them, making them available for display in exhibitions like "Unsolved Mysteries" in Vienna[15]. During that time, ET was studied by Dr. Distelberger, a stone processing specialist. He believed that ET was most likely more than 500 years old[16].

Due to her health, Joky has been unable to travel much in the last years of her role as caretaker. She has received visitors at home, but ET has lost a lot of its activity and its activity levels have diminished. With the help of friends, Joky brought her skulls to the 11–11–11 event "Crystal Skulls World Mysteries Gateway" in Los Angeles[17]. After that event, she did not take the crystal skulls back home to the Netherlands but instead gave them to her son, Johannes, who is currently functioning as their caretaker.

ET is an interesting crystal skull. ET and Synergy (see crystal skull 3) are the only ones in the group of "accepted ancient" crystal skulls that hold Lemurian harmonic frequencies. ET has thirty-six layers, but compared to the other ancient skulls, it has a smaller widened thirty-sixth layer and a less intense bluish shimmer. Does this mean that its activation was never completed, or that it was created in a more recent period? The skull has a barrier at the twenty-fourth layer, suggesting that there was a certain level of mastery when this crystal skull was activated. This is a level of mastery beyond what people today are able to reach.

3. Synergy

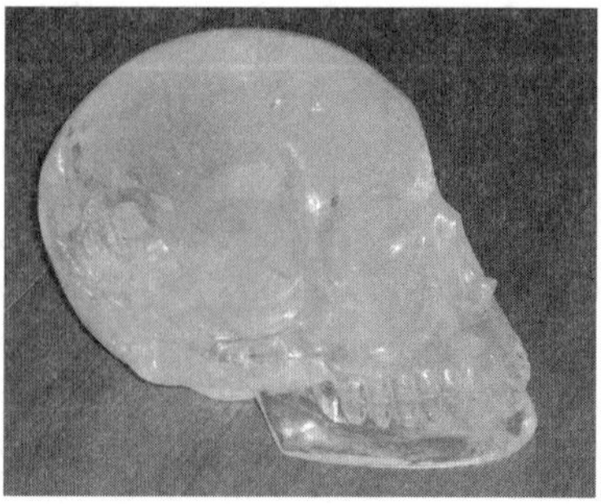

Of all of skulls that have a widened thirty-sixth layer with a bluish shimmer, Synergy has the most extensive history. Its story has unfolded over time as more information has become available. Sherry Whitfield, Synergy's current caretaker, received the skull in 2001 as a gift from a European businessman named George. George acquired Synergy around 1986-1987 from an old native man in a tiny village in the Andes, near the borders of Peru, Bolivia, and Chile.

When Sherry began to travel around and presented Synergy to those who were ready to meet this crystal skull, she met a person who helped her to obtain more information about Synergy. What follows is a summary of what Sherry has shared on Synergy's website[18].

The story of Synergy began to unfold in 2005 when a representative of an indigenous tribe that lives on an island in Micronesia was in the United States. He saw a picture of Synergy in a newspaper. He came to meet Synergy, and for him it was like a special reunion.

When the man returned to the island, he took a picture of Synergy and a small crystal skull that had been with Synergy. The tribe recognized Synergy as the crystal skull that had been sent out by their ancestors from the island across the Pacific in a reed boat. It was sent to the "People of the Sky" in South America. There it would await the person who would bring it further on its journey.

The tribe was very excited. They have the twin of Synergy named Harmony. According to their story, the skulls were not carved by them but were passed on to them from a "lost civilization" (Micronesia is considered to have been part of Lemuria).

Sherry received information from two Hawaiian kahunas that Synergy had been in Hawaii when it traveled from the island in Micronesia to the People of the Sky. Remnants of the reed boat are still present on the islands of Hawaii as proof of this story.

There is no doubt that the enfolding of such a story is exciting. Most stories about crystal skulls are either limited or seem to come from psychic sources, so it is refreshing to hear a story that comes from people with oral traditions that go back over longer time periods. It is even more exciting that there are people who "know" Synergy from their oral traditions.

The fact that Synergy holds the Lemurian harmonic frequencies strengthens the story that it comes from an area that is considered to have been part of Lemuria. It is a crystal skull with a widened thirty-sixth layer with a bluish shimmer. Without any doubt, Synergy was activated during a time when people still mastered crystal skull activation and the awakening of a crystal skull to its optimal level. Synergy and ET are the only known skulls from the past that hold a barrier at the twenty-fourth layer.

Another interesting aspect is that Synergy has ancient runes carved on its underside. Specialists have studied these runes and translated them. Sherry will decide when that information will become public.

Synergy holds Pleiadean energies and is, in my opinion, the most powerful skull for connecting with the Divine Feminine. Because many people are more strongly connected with masculine energies, they may miss the special energies that this crystal skull holds. I consider it to be a unique skull in many ways.

4. Sha Na Ra

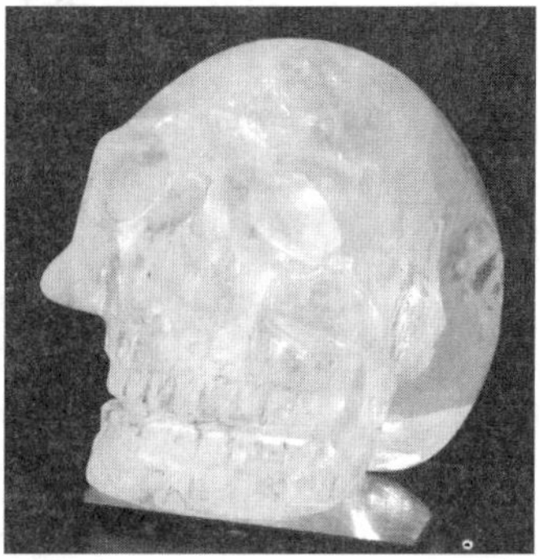

Michele Nocerino is the current caretaker of Sha Na Ra. She became the caretaker after her father, F.R. Nick Nocerino, passed away. Nick has become a legend in the world of crystal skulls because of his knowledge of them and his unique psychic abilities. Nick named this crystal skull Sha Na Ra in honor of one of his several ethereal teachers/healers. Chuck Pelton, who closely worked together with Nick Nocerino, mentions that research at the Society of Crystal Skulls International has indicated that the skull has been used in ritualistic healing ceremonies[19].

Sha Na Ra was found in 1995 in the Guerrero state in Mexico[20], although it was suggested in *The Mystery of the Crystal Skulls* that Sha Na Ra came from a dig in the 1950s[21]. It is special that the crystal skull was found in an actual dig, and the way it was found is unusual — it was located by Nick using psychic archeology, which means that it was found through psychic guidance. When Nick said to the diggers, "Dig here," they found a terracotta basket containing Sha Na Ra[22].

Sha Na Ra has been tested in the British Museum as part of the famous BBC documentary that inspired Chris Morton and Ceri Louise Thomas to write *The Mystery of the Crystal Skulls*. During the tests, the British Museum skull and the Smithsonian skull were found to be modern carvings, although no official information was given about the results of the research on Sha Na Ra and Max. The official comment was: "I am afraid that we are unable to comment on the other two skulls"[23].

Sha Na Ra's carving is unique and is called "primitive." However, this is a powerful crystal skull. It has thirty-six fully activated layers, which means it has a widened thirty-sixth layer with a bluish shimmer. It also has a barrier at the eighteenth layer. The activity level of this skull is among the highest found, so it is wonderful that Michele is willing to bring this special crystal skull out into the world again.

Sha Na Ra has its own website[24] if you'd like to learn more.

5. Max

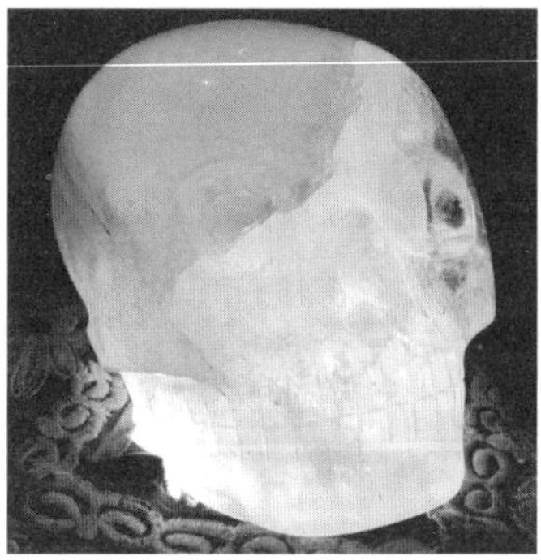

Max, also called the Texas skull, is responsible for inspiring many people's interest in crystal skulls. JoAnn Parks, who lives in Houston, Texas, has been Max's caretaker since 1980 and has shared this crystal skull extensively with the world.

JoAnn has shared the story of Max many times. It starts between 1924 and 1926 when the skull was purportedly found in a tomb in Guatemala, where it was used by Mayan priests for healing, rituals, and prayers[21]. Norbu Chen, a Tibetan Red Hat Lama, studied with Mayan priests in Guatemala. During that period, he met Max. When he left, the Maya gave him the crystal skull to support him on his journey as a healer. Norbu ended up in Houston, Texas, where he started a healing foundation. The crystal skull sat on his altar as a healing and spiritual tool.

JoAnn Parks and her husband Carl met Norbu in 1973 through their family doctor. JoAnn started to work for Norbu and was with him until his death in 1980. Before he passed away, he handed her the crystal skull, telling her that she would know what to do with it. She placed it in a closet in a box for about seven years. She kept hearing messages, one of which led to the name "Max." Other messages made her search for "the man." In 1987 JoAnn learned about Nick Nocerino after watching a television program. She knew that he was "the man," so she contacted him, and Nick recognized Max as the skull he had heard about in 1949 and had been searching for ever since[22].

Nick helped JoAnn to understand what and who Max was. That started her on a journey to share Max with the world, especially with people in the United States. She has been traveling extensively for about twenty-four years, making Max the record traveler among the crystal skulls. Rightfully, JoAnn is honored by many for her service to the crystal skulls through making people aware of their message.

Max was tested by the British Museum in 1996, together with Sha Na Ra, and as I mentioned in the section about Sha Na Ra, the British Museum did not want to comment on the obtained results.

Max has thirty-six layers with a widened thirty-sixth layer with a bluish shimmer, making it one of the special beacons on our journey. Max also has a barrier at the eighteenth layer. From an energetic point of view, Max has similarities to skulls like Sha Na Ra, Einstein, and the two amethyst skulls (Addendum I, skulls 7 and 8). Because of its intense use, Max is a highly activated crystal skull with a strong focus on healing.

In JoAnn's booklet, she mentions that Max is the largest of the thirteen crystal skulls known to man[27]. In more recent statements, it is said that Max *is* the thirteenth crystal skull, the skull that holds the information of all[28]. This information has been channeled by James Tyberonn, who channels Archangel Metatron. This statement has spread and is shared on several other websites. In this channeling, Tyberonn also said that Max is not from this Earth but originated in the Pleiades.

Based on the energies of Max, it seems unlikely to me that Max is something other than a crystal skull carved on Earth. There is no doubt that Max is special; however, I am unclear as to which other skulls Max is supposed to be the thirteenth of. It is interesting that if we place Max in one of the twelve star nations, its energy undoubtedly belongs to the Pleiades. However, from my perspective, the fact that its energy resonates with the Pleiades does not mean that it actually comes from there. As I mentioned in chapter 9, every crystal skull resonates with one of the twelve star nations.

6. Einstein

Somebody once described Einstein as a "new" ancient crystal skull. That somebody was referring to the fact that Einstein appeared publicly for the first time at the 10–10–10 crystal skull conference in New York. Carolyn Ford presented Einstein to a large public gathering after having been its caretaker for around twenty years. Its appearance was impressive. Einstein

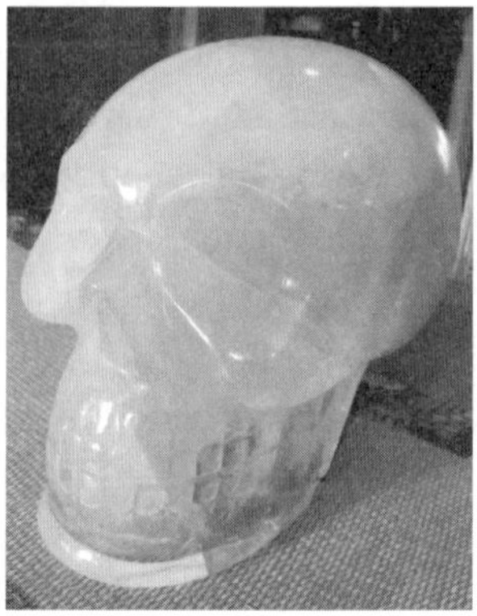

weighs around thirty-three pounds, making it the largest ancient crystal skull known — a title that had been held by Max since 1987.

It is interesting to note that crystal skull researchers seem to have no doubt that Einstein is ancient. The fact that Nick Nocerino, who studied Einstein in 1991, also considered it ancient is of course helpful.

The story of Einstein most likely is very long, but only the last part is known. After having a positive experience with crystal skulls, Carolyn started to look for one of her own. She contacted a friend who had a crystal and mineral store, telling him that she was looking for a skull with a size of two to three inches. The next day her friend called her and told her that he had a crystal skull that she would like to see, even though it was "a bit larger" than she had originally requested. Meeting Einstein makes it difficult to say no, so Carolyn acquired the skull in 1990. According to Carolyn's friend, a businessman had come to his shop just that morning looking to sell some artifacts he received from the estate of an explorer. These pieces had been brought back in the '30s and '40s from various expeditions in different parts of the world[29].

Einstein's shape is quite similar to the Mayan crystal skull (see skull 9). Both skulls have a noticeable circular indentation. This is a feature that is found in more crystal skulls, but the sizes vary quite a bit. Stephen Mehler, who has studied both crystal skulls, mentioned that their similarity makes it possible for Einstein to be the central skull of a group of thirteen and the Mayan skull could be part of that group[30].

Einstein is another crystal skull with thirty-six layers and a widened thirty-sixth layer that has a bluish shimmer. It also has a barrier at the eighteenth layer. Since the skull has been made available to the public, its activity level has increased, showing more of its power and gifts to humanity.

Carolyn calls Einstein "the skull of consciousness." It was included in Chuck Pelton's publication as the "32-pound Aztec skull." It said that the skull is classified as pre-Columbian, most probably Aztec or Mixtec[31]. Nobody doubts that it is pre-Columbian, but the statement that it is probably Aztec or Mixtec is not supported at this time.

When Einstein visited the crystal skull circle in our house, I understood why this crystal skull could be seen as a central skull: The way Einstein activated and amplified the crystal skull circle was beyond anything those present had experienced. The specific role of Einstein is only partly understood. It seems to bring crystals, crystal skulls, and stones into a harmonious energy field that gives the impression of oneness. Possibly this explains its name "one stone" (which is the German translation of "ein stein" and the meaning of the skull's name) — because Einstein brings many "stones" together to function as one. I believe that Einstein will impress many in the future.

Einstein and Carolyn have their own website[32] with general information and information about their activities.

7. Ami, the Amethyst Skull
(San Jose, California)

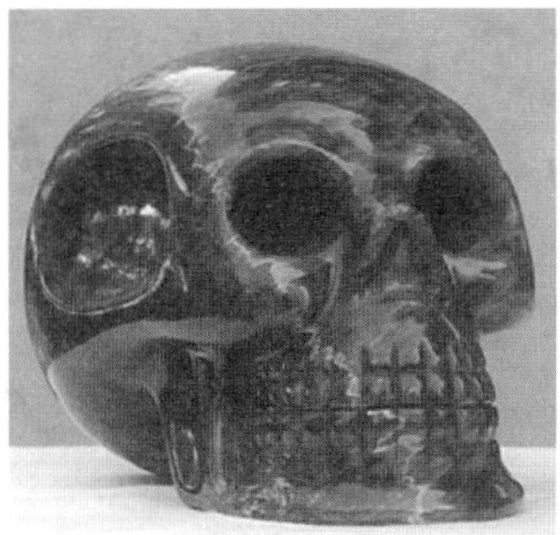

The amethyst crystal skull was extensively studied by Nick Nocerino and Stephen Mehler while it was in San Jose, California[33]. This skull has always been included in the list of ancient crystal skulls. Even when the skull was for sale and locked up in a vault, it kept its fame as one of the important crystal skulls. I do not know where the nickname "Ami" came from, but it has been used so often that most people now know this skull only by this name.

This skull seems to have been part of a collection that lay on the desk of President Porfirio Diaz of Mexico somewhere between 1876 and 1910. In the year 1910, the Mexican revolution removed President Diaz and the skull went to the Lascurian family in Mexico. It stayed there until Francisco Reyes, a Mayan priest, purchased the skull in 1979. According to Reyes, the Mayan priesthood had possession of this skull in the Oaxaca area of Mexico[34]. As an agent for Reyes, John Zamora brought the amethyst skull to the United States. In 1983, a group of nine businessmen gave a loan to Zamora. The loan was never repaid, and in 1985 this group assumed the role of caretaker and offered it for sale for one million dollars. In 2009 the skull was purchased and left the vault. However, the name of the new owner is unknown, and unfortunately the new caretaker has not yet been willing to share this skull with the world.

It is considered to be a skull for healing and makes a deep impression on those who have seen it. The skull is characterized by a circular indentation at the temples and a white squiggly line that goes around the circumference of the skull. The circular indentation is similar to that of Einstein and the Mayan skull. This led Stephen Mehler to mention that it is possible that these three skulls were part of the same group[35].

The amethyst skull has thirty-six layers and a widened thirty-sixth layer with a bluish shimmer. There is a barrier at the eighteenth layer. The activity level of this skull is low at the moment, based on the last public photos (image I.7), but the skull is so powerful that I have no doubt that it will return to its full potential as soon as it is worked with again.

8. Amethyst Skull

This crystal skull is also an amethyst skull carved from one piece. It was found in Mexico in a tomb dating from the ninth or tenth century. Based on other items that were found together with it, it was dated as being older than the third century. Pelton wrote in his book: "The skull projects a great number of images, while scrying or doing psychometry, of what could be called battles and rituals of various cultures such as the Toltecs, Mayan, Incas, and Aztecs. This skull has too much perversion; entire scenes were of sacrifices and the vibrations made one feel death. The so-called Mayan priest that had it would, for a price, remove anyone you wished to have removed. It was his power tool"36.

I have not seen this skull but scanned the picture in Pelton's book[37] to determine its energies. This is a crystal skull that not only shows negative images but also has been programmed by people who use black magic. This is especially scary because it has thirty-six layers with a widened thirty-sixth layer that has a bluish shimmer. It also has a barrier at the eighteenth layer. The "perversions" were brought in (programmed) later. Let us be glad that this crystal skull is not available at the moment and that its current whereabouts are unknown.

9. Mayan Skull

The Mayan skull is often mentioned together with the amethyst skull, Ami. This is not so surprising because they look similar and were both brought into the United States in 1979 by the same person: John Zamora. The Mayan skull and the amethyst skull were studied by Nick Nocerino (for three months) and by Stephen Mehler[38].

The Mayan skull is similar in appearance to Ami but is made of clear

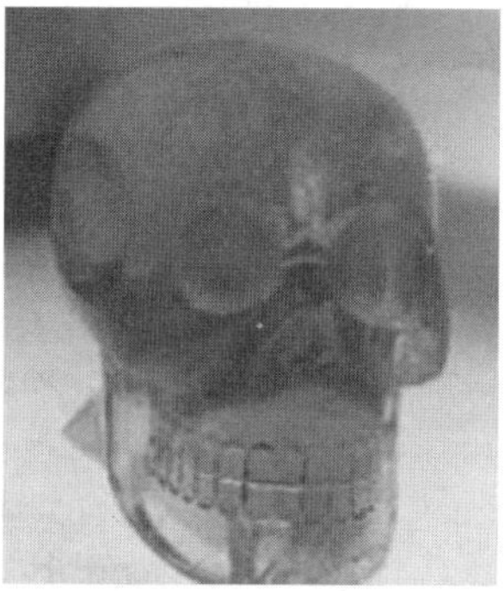

quartz. It has round indentations at the temples similar to Ami's. It is even more similar to Einstein, seeming to be a miniature version of it. John Zamora was the agent of the Mayan Priest Francisco Reyes, who owned both the Mayan skull and Ami. According to this Mayan priest, the Mayan skull was found in the Mayan site of Copan, Guatemala, in 1912.

In 1980 John Zamora received a loan from a lawyer in Texas in which he used the Mayan skull as collateral. The loan was never repaid. The current whereabouts of the Mayan skull remain unknown.

The Mayan skull has thirty-six layers. It has a slightly widened thirty-sixth layer but not as much as the previously mentioned skulls. This may be the reason why the bluish shimmer is weaker than that of other ancient skulls. Like the previous skulls, this one has a barrier at the eighteenth layer. This seems to suggest that the Mayan skull was either carved later than Einstein and Ami, or its activation process was not completed to the same level. According to psychic researchers, this skull also shows images of human sacrifice[39].

10. Lucy

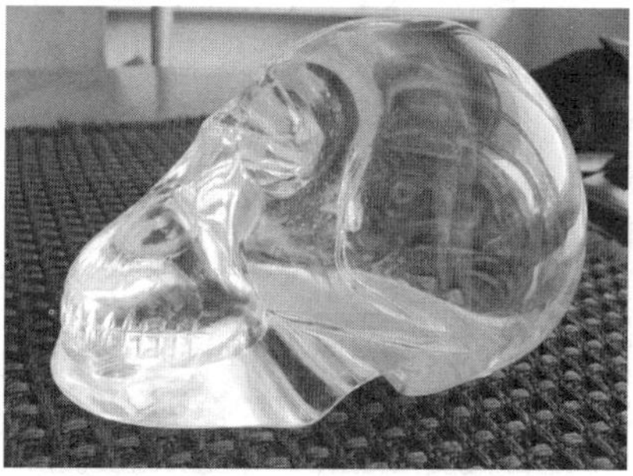

Lucy is different from the previously mentioned crystal skulls. Its shape is not that of a human crystal skull but more of a Simian (ape- or monkey-like). The fact that it does not look like a human skull brings up the question whether it has the crystal skull harmonic frequencies, but there is no doubt that the skull has these frequencies. From an energetic point of view, the similarity of these energies is enough to make Lucy a real crystal skull.

The skull is about seven inches long and is made from very clear quartz. It has hardly any inclusions. At first look, it seems to be a modern carving; however, the energies defy that. Lucy has thirty-six activated layers, with the thirty-sixth being wide with a bluish shimmer. I have not seen any contemporary crystal skull with these characteristics, so it is unlikely that it is a contemporary crystal skull. However, contrary to the previous crystal skulls, it does not have a barrier. In that sense, Lucy is similar to the Mitchell-Hedges skull. It differs from the Mitchell-Hedges crystal skull in not having any Atlantean harmonic frequencies. This skull is a riddle to me — energetically, it does not fit anywhere.

Basically, nothing is known about this crystal skull. The current caretaker, Kirk Landauer, bought this crystal skull in 1991 from the same person he bought Ixchel (see skull 12) from. While there is more history connected with Ixchel, no information about Lucy is available. The skull is mentioned in Chuck Pelton's publication as "Tibet Skull"[40]. But all of the information sent to Nick Nocerino came from Kirk and he has no idea why this skull was connected to Tibet in Pelton's publication.

11. ShiRaEl and ShaRaEl

These two crystal skulls are described under the same heading because their story is connected — they are made from the same material and their energetic characteristics are similar. These two crystal skulls do not seem to belong to the groups we have described so far in this addendum, but their energies suggest that they should be included.

The material these skulls are made from is different from that of any other crystal skull and could be defined as glass, which is exactly what Jeanne and I thought when we saw them for the first time.

Someone called and told us that he had some special skulls and wanted to show them to us. Initially I was not very open, but at his second attempt we decided to meet him. He showed us three skulls, and at first we thought that they were made of glass. However, their carving was very unusual, and when we held them, the energy we felt was not that of glass at all.

This man told us that these three skulls were bought by his brother in Egypt from a man who had acquired them in Tibet. The brother was an archeologist and had become very fond of these skulls. Before he died, he gave them to his brother, this man who had called us. Although the brother asked him to never separate these three skulls, he had decided to sell two of them. He wanted to keep the third. After quite some hesitation, we bought the two he offered, feeling that they were worth further study. That proved to be true.

Although there is no way to verify the truth of the story, many people who have seen these skulls and worked with them are impressed with their energies. They are especially interesting because they also have monatomic element harmonic frequencies. This is not surprising, given that they have thirty energy layers with a widened thirtieth layer that has a bluish shimmer. Because I have not met anybody who can create this bluish shimmer, these crystal skulls must have been in the hands of people who understood crystalline energies. This makes it unlikely that these skulls are contemporary skulls.

We have tried to determine the material ShaRaEl and ShiRaEl are made of, and it seems that the material is is made by heating volcanic ash. We know this type of material from Mount St. Helen, the Krakatau, Mexico (we have material from this place but do not know the exact location in Mexico), and California (known as Andara stones). However, none of these materials are capable of creating more than twelve energy layers, let alone thirty. Some of them have monatomic element harmonic frequencies, such as most Andara stones and about one-third of the material I have seen from Mexico. However, none of these materials holds energy in a similar way to the material of these two skulls. Quartz can exhibit such energies, but in the case of this green material, it is a riddle.

Who are the creators of these skulls? Information obtained using techniques like psychometry suggests that the material may have been made or altered in an alchemical way. I have no doubt that further study of these two skulls may reveal interesting information.

The two crystal skulls are not very large, and although their shape is quite different from each other, their sizes are the same — length: $3^{3}/_{5}$″ (9 cm), height: 3″ (7.5 cm) and width: $2^{4}/_{5}$″ (7 cm). The third one was slightly larger but looked similar to ShaRaEl.

12. Ixchel

Ixchel came into public awareness during the 11–11–11 crystal skull event in Los Angeles. Its current caretaker, Kirk Landauer, is also the caretaker of Lucy (see skull 10). Kirk bought this skull around 1990 from a man named Chuck Sillo. Chuck got the skull from his father, Carmen, who was a collector of artifacts. Carmen bought the skull in 1939 from F.T. Johnson from Tennessee for

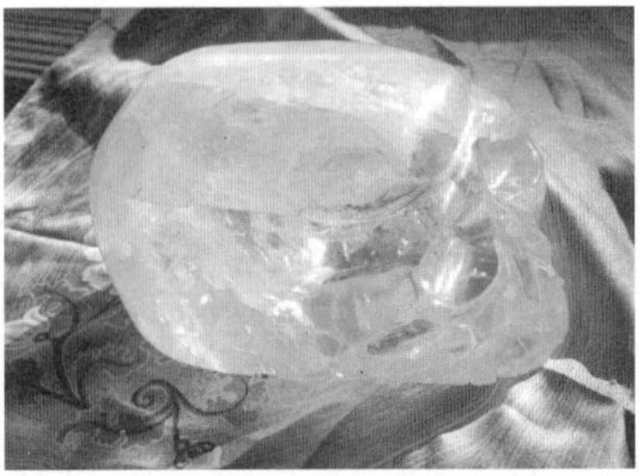

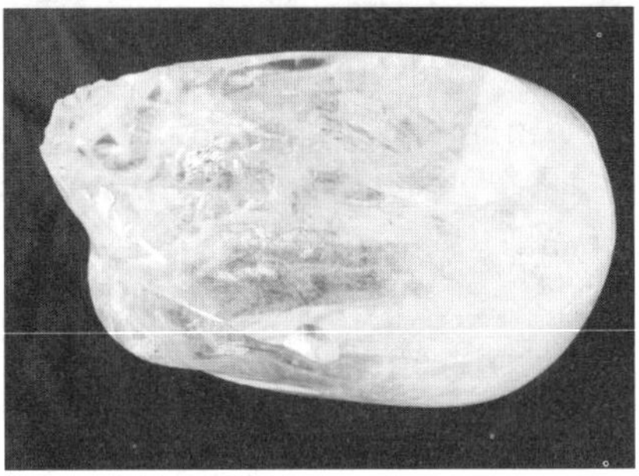

$2,000. Johnson had had it since 1916. Johnson's source is unknown, although it seems that it came from somewhere in Central America. Kirk has a written statement for the transaction between Carmen and Johnson.

Kirk contacted Nick Nocerino and sent him pictures of the skull, which may be the reason Ixchel and Lucy are mentioned in Chuck Pelton's publication. In this publication, Ixchel is named "Mayan (New York)"[40]. One day Thomas Morton called Kirk and invited him to bring his two crystal skulls to the British Museum in London for the BBC documentary, but at the last moment Kirk was told not to come.

Kirk gave me the opportunity to study Ixchel for about three months. This crystal skull has twenty-four layers, and the widened twenty-fourth has a bluish shimmer. I have no doubt that this state of activity was created on purpose. The skull has energies and images that suggest it was first used by women for ceremonies and healing and later corrupted by men who used it to support their black magic practices. These energies have been cleared, opening the door for this skull to share its gifts with the world. I have no doubt that this skull will attain its rightful place among the other well-known crystal skulls. The skull is $7^{1}/_{2}''$ long. It seems that its lower jaw is missing but like it was created this way on purpose.

13. Madre

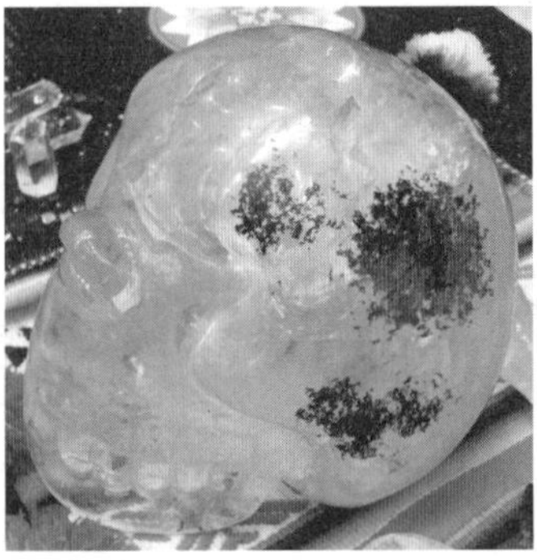

Madre is another ceremonial and healing skull that has twenty-four activated layers with a widened twenty-fourth layer with a bluish shimmer. Its current caretaker is Laurie Walker, the wife of DaEl Walker. According to Pelton, Madre was found near the location where Sha Na Ra was discovered[41]. However, on the website for the

11-11-11 crystal skull event, it is said that DaEl bought the skull from a private collection[42].

Madre is described by Laurie as the "clan mother of the dolphin skulls ... a powerful, heart-centered Lemurian skull. Madre is a sweet, loving energy and a wisdom keeper"[43]. The nose of the skull when seen from the side does indeed look like a dolphin. Laurie believes that the skull is connected with water, and in her presentations, she shows pictures demonstrating this connection. Although Madre is claimed to be a Lemurian skull, it does not have the Lemurian harmonic frequencies.

Madre is a human-sized skull that weighs thirteen pounds. It is a wonderful crystal skull, and it is great that Laurie brings this skull out for people to connect with it. It demonstrates that every crystal skull is unique and that every caretaker develops a special relationship with their crystal skull.

14. Pancho

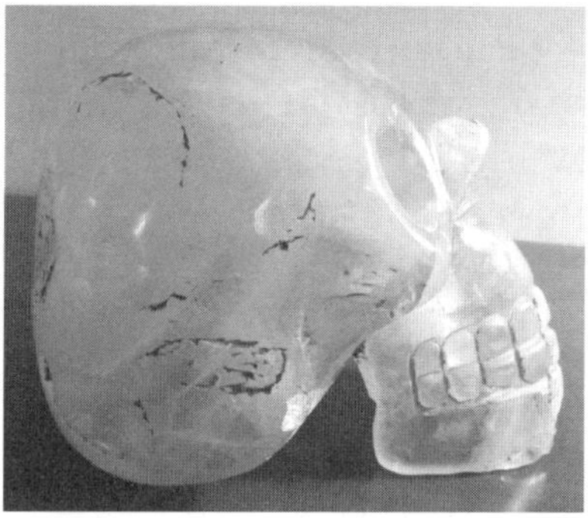

From the moment Mario Bojorquez became the caretaker of Pancho, he felt that he needed to perform ceremony with the skull. Of all the ceremonial skulls (or the skulls with twenty-four layers) this skull seems to invite ceremony more than any of the others.

According to Pancho's origin story[44], Alberto and Delfina, Mario's grandparents, lived in Mexico City. They started to organize tours to archeological sites. During one of their visits to Monte Alban, they met a person who showed them a crystal skull — Pancho — and ultimately gave it to them. The skull is believed to have originated from the Zapotecas who lived in the Oaxaca area in pre-Columbian times.

Before Delfina passed away in 2009, she gave Pancho to her grandson, Mario. He felt that it was important to bring this skull out into the world, so he quickly gathered a group of enthusiastic people around it. In 2010, during the 10-10-10 crystal skull event in New York, Pancho was shown at a large gathering for the first time[45]. During the event, the left side of its jaw was damaged.

Pancho is a hollow skull of about human size. From the moment it was shown, people were excited about it. It has twenty-four layers fully awakened with a widened twenty-fourth layer with a bluish shimmer.

In 2011, Mario left Pancho in a taxicab in New York City. The crystal skull has not resurfaced.

15. Paco

I have seen Paco only one time. This was during the first Mexican crystal skull conference, called "Prophecies of the Crystal Skulls"[46] in Mexico City in 2009. I learned that people are still finding crystal skulls in Mexico but are careful about publicly announcing the finds. These people are afraid that they may lose the skulls; therefore, there is often a request not to give details.

Paco is a large skull — larger than human-size — made of cloudy clear quartz. It has the typical characteristics of a ceremonial crystal skull with twenty-four layers activated and a widened twenty-fourth layer that has a bluish shimmer.

16. Ichabod

The name of this skull is also written as "Icabod." This skull was with the Society of Crystal Skulls International. It was brought to the Wolf Song IX gathering in 1998 by Kathy Grimshaw, who also took it to the UK after the gathering[47].

In Pelton's publication, Ichabod is described as "a very dirty Amethyst skull with a slightly damaged cranium, possibly by a shovel or pick during excavation. The skull was purchased from a digger in the mountains of Guerrero, Mexico. It was found along a wall about twenty feet high and slanted toward a tunnel, which went about twenty feet into the mountain. It is about 7″ long"[48]. According to this publication, Ichabod is in the hands of a private collector. Currently this skull is not available for viewing and studying. The only image I have seen is in this publication, which unfortunately is not readily available.

The skull has twenty-four layers activated with a widened twenty-fourth layer with a bluish shimmer and seems to be another ceremonial skull.

17. Redo Skull and Cross

This skull is named "the Redo skull" because it has belonged to the Redo family since the 1840s. This skull was part of the research when the British Museum tested a number of crystal skulls in the BBC documentary I have mentioned a number of times. For an image of this skull, see *The Mystery of the Crystal Skulls*[49]. At that time, Norma was the caretaker on behalf of the Redo family. According to her, it was not clear how her great-grandfather acquired the skull other than he got it when the government took over the properties of the church[50]. The skull is smaller than an average human skull and has a monkey-like face. The strangest aspect of it, however, is a large cross on top that is so much larger than the skull that it gives the impression of a system that is out of balance. It is not known how old the skull is, although the Redo family believes that it is old. The cross, however, has a date carved on the base — 1571 — that seems to have been placed on the skull more recently.

The results of the tests done on this skull at the British museum were very interesting. At the teeth and at the top of the skull where the cross has been placed, there are signs of rotary tools. But the rest of the skull is definitely hand carved and displays characteristics of pre-Columbian work[51]. Dr. Rankin found that the quartz the cross was made of may have come from Brazil, but the quartz of the skull seems to be similar to that of the crystal goblet found at Monte Alban that is presumably made from quartz from Central America. This crystal goblet was included in the tests as a reference and is estimated to be over 1,000 years old[52]. Jane Walsh of the Smithsonian Museum was part of the research team for the British Museum and BBC documentary. Although this research established that the Redo crystal skull is ancient, she has forgotten this part of the research when she expresses her belief that there are no pre-Columbian crystal skull artifacts[53].

The skull was most likely a ceremonial skull, given the fact that it has twenty-four layers, the twenty-fourth widened with a bluish shimmer.

When I met Norma Redo in Mexico City in 2009, she shared that the family had decided to sell the skull with the cross. There is no recent information on its whereabouts.

18. Amar

Of all the crystal skulls that do not have a widened twenty-fourth or thirty-sixth layer with a bluish shimmer, Amar is the most impressive that I have met to date. It has all thirty-six layers fully activated and is a

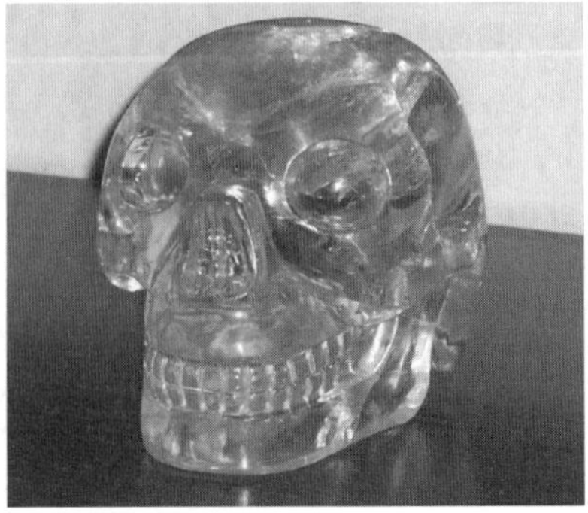

very powerful skull. Its size and beauty contribute to its impressiveness. Grace and Maurice Dunner are the caretakers of this special skull, which is used to charge up all the other skulls sold by crystalskulls.com[54].

Amar is a Tibetan crystal skull. According to the skull's website, a Tibetan high lama undertook a dangerous journey when he carried the twenty-two-pound revered crystal skull Amar by hand from Tibet to Nepal in order to protect it from the Chinese. Tibetan Buddhist priests used this crystal skull for healing and divination[55].

If not ancient, Amar is considered at least old. I am unfamiliar with the energies of other crystal skulls from Tibet. Therefore, I do not know whether it was important for them to fully activate a crystal skull. The ones I have discussed that have a bluish shimmer at a widened layer are, with the exception of Synergy, all from Mesoamerica. Are the crystal skulls from the East different? Or are there no ancient crystal skulls that have surfaced from that part of the world?

ShiRaEl and ShaRaEl are said to have come from Tibet, but there is no evidence to support that. However, if they are from the Tibetan area, it indicates that there were people who had the ability to fully activate crystal skulls, since both skulls have a widened layer with a bluish shimmer. Hopefully more crystal skulls from that area will surface, helping us understand the energies of these skulls.

Whatever the case, Amar is an important and wonderful part of the crystal skull community.

19. Rainbow

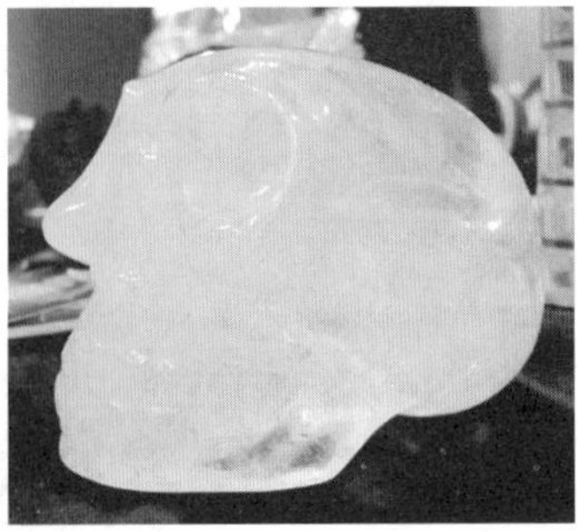

Rainbow is a cloudy quartz crystal skull that seems to have been found in Mexico, as per Pelton's publication. Pelton mentions that it was found in ruins near where Sha Na Ra was found[56]. However, on May 24, 1998, DaEl Walker, Rainbow's caretaker, wrote that Rainbow came to him three years ago: "It was a trade for some other material I had. The trader said it came down to him from his Grandfather and was given to him by two priests from Guatemala. I have not been able to verify this"[57]. On his own website DaEl is more careful, saying, "The Rainbow crystal skull came from Mesoamerica, perhaps Guatemala or Mexico. No one knows"[58]. Whatever the story is, Rainbow seems to have come from Central America.

DaEl has brought this crystal skull to many events. He has taken many pictures of images in the skull, which he loves sharing during lectures.

Rainbow looks very different from the crystal skull Madre, of which DaEl's wife, Laurie, is the caretaker. Although it feels like a ceremonial skull, Rainbow does not belong to the group with twenty-four layers of which the twenty-fourth is wider and has a bluish shimmer. This means that, most likely, it is less old than Madre and may not be as old as is generally believed. Chuck Pelton also believes that Rainbow is a ceremonial skull[59]. He mentions that Rainbow seems to have a connection with Atlantis, but the energies of this skull do not support this notion.

20. Zar

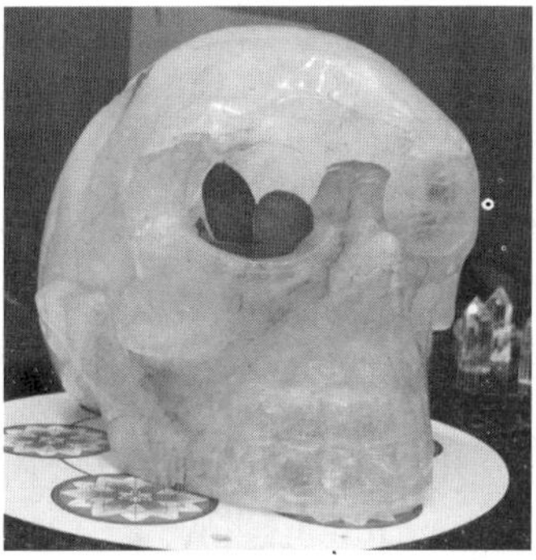

Zar is a hollow skull that in many ways is unique in appearance. Its caretaker is DaEl Walker, who on his website to announce the 11-11-11 crystal skull event in Los Angeles mentions Zar as an alien skull. He says, "He may be as much as 4,000,000 years old. Come see the skull that expert stone carvers consider 'impossible.' What is it? Is it a 'hybrid between humans and aliens'? Did it come from another star system? Come see for yourself and form your own opinion"[60].

There is not much information about this skull. It is without any doubt a nice skull, but it is not very active. There is no widened layer and no bluish shimmer. The number of layers is less than twenty-four, which indicates that this skull is either contemporary or a was carved in a time when activate abilities were no longer used or available. Undoubtedly, it is not as old as DaEl suggests.

21. Nefertiti

Nefertiti is an amethyst crystal skull, another one of DaEl Walker's. He has brought this crystal skull to events in 2010 and 2011, and Stephen Mehler was excited about it because it screamed "antiquity" to him[61].

Not much is known of this skull's story. From an energetic perspective, it does not seem to be old. It does not belong to the groups with thirty-six or twenty-four layers; it does not have a widened layer and therefore has no bluish shimmer. Nefertiti does not have many activated layers, and it seems that not much work has been done with this skull.

22. Jesuit Skull

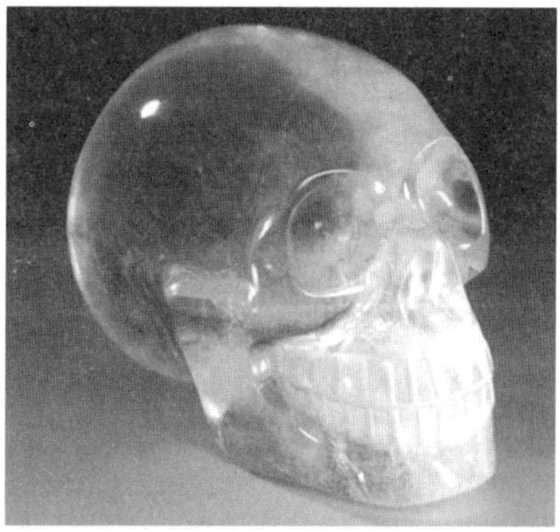

The Jesuit skull is one of the ten skulls of which Joky van Dieten is the caretaker. We have already discussed one of them: ET (see skull 2). Both on Joky's website[62] and in a booklet that she published[63], she says about the Jesuit: "This skull, made of clear quartz crystal, came into Joky's possession in August 1993. It is thought to have a connection with St. Francis of Assisi, who is well known for his love of animals. It has been known since 1534. This crystal skull was offered to Joky by the abbot of an American monastery which urgently needed money."

The Jesuit is a clear quartz skull that is smaller than the crystal skulls mentioned so far, being 6″ (15 cm) long. The story about the connection to St. Francis of Assisi was narrated by the abbot of the order who had the Jesuit for 400 years. However, the priests contend that it is much older.

According to Pelton, research from the Society of Crystal Skulls International appears to confirm that the Jesuit skull has been worked with by a religious order, going back to the 1500s. There is little information that came as a result of scrying from before that time — with the exception of normal crystal activity[64]. This is not completely in alignment with what has been described in another Pelton publication, written by Joky van Dieten[65]. In *this* publication, Nick Nocerino describes in a scrying session that he sees the year 975 with native people and scenes with human sacrifice. Chuck Pelton himself reports that in a scrying session he estimated the skull to be from between the third and the fifth century AD[66]. He believes that it was never buried under stones in ruins but always in someone's possession.

When I look at the energies of this crystal skull, it seems that it has not been used by people who knew how to fully activate it. When I met the Jesuit for the first time, I did not know its history. I estimated it to be around 500 years old at that time. It seems that there is a general agreement that it is not very old. That may explain why it has less than twenty-four layers and no completeness of activation at any level.

23. Janus

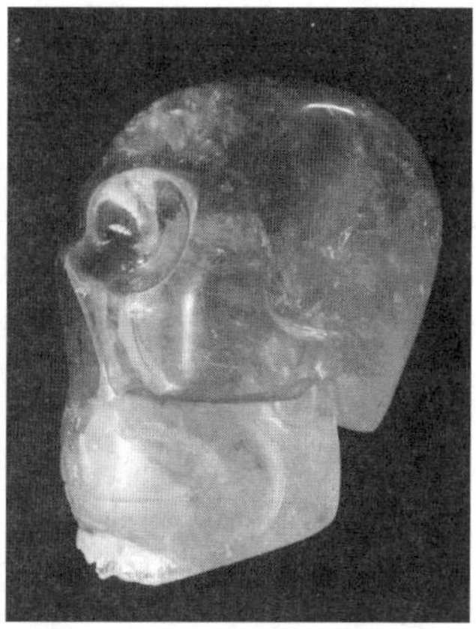

Janus is another skull in the collection of Joky van Dieten. It actually is a crystal skull she acquired recently — in 2007. It is a smoky quartz skull with a shape that is quite different from most crystal skulls. Joky got it from a family in Montenegro. As is mentioned on her website, "Mrs. Vesna Kilibarda of Monenegro said that the skull has been in her family for many years, but since she is getting older, she wanted to pass it on to some friends who promised that it would be in loving hands in the future and [that] its history [would be] preserved"[67]. It is believed that this skull is connected to the history of the kingdom of Illyria, which comprised the actual territories of Dalmatia, Croatia, Bosnia and Herzegovina, Montenegro, and Northern and Central Albania, with a large part of modern Serbia, but in the course of its development, it extended all along the eastern part of the Adriatic Sea. The earliest known king of Illyria was Hyllus who is allegedly recorded to have died in the year 1225 BC. According to legend, the people of Illyria took the head of King Hyllus to battle and won every battle. It is believed that Janus is this head crystallized in the form of a skull[68].

It was interesting for me to meet this skull. Although it is supposed to have energies associated with war and killing, that was not the impression I received. It is actually a pleasant crystal skull with energies that I could not define. Although I can accept that this skull was not carved recently, it does not come from a time or a place in which people knew how to fully activate a crystal skull. It has less than twenty-four layers, and therefore there is no completion — no widened layer with a bluish shimmer — at any level.

24. Baby Luv

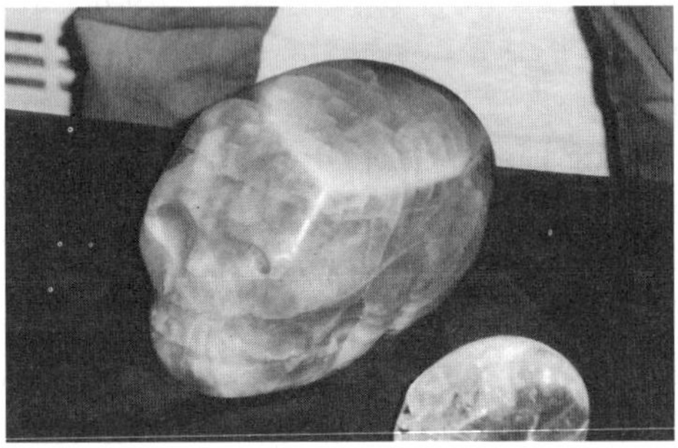

Baby Luv is a rose quartz skull that was the third that came into the collection of Joky van Dieten. This skull was found in Ukraine in the early 1700s by a Russian Monk who was walking in the woods near Lvov. The monk saw something shining in a mound that had been built by the Scythians in 700 BC. In the mound, he found a crystal skull and lots of jewelry. The monks gave all the jewelry to the government but kept the crystal skull. The skull was bought in 1872 by a Russian archaeologist when the monks needed money to repair their monastery. Nothing is known of what happened since. When the iron curtain was lifted, the skull was in the possession of a Russian family who were ancestors of the archaeologist. There were only children left in the family, and the purchase was handled through an executor[69].

This skull has a unique shape. It has a rather long head. Joky suggested that it could be based on the shape of the skulls of the people from early civilizations who had been conquered by the Scythians[70].

A skull that old could have had a completion of activation on some level, at least. However, it does not. Does this mean that people in parts of the world other than Central America did not know how to activate crystal skulls? Or was it irrelevant for these civilizations? If so, what was the purpose of the crystal skulls for them?

25. Shui Ting Er

Shui Ting Er is the first crystal skull described in this Addendum that is not a quartz skull. It is made from amazonite and is the second crystal skull that Joky van Dieten acquired. She describes the story on her website and in her booklet as follows: "This amazonite skull originates from South-West Mon-

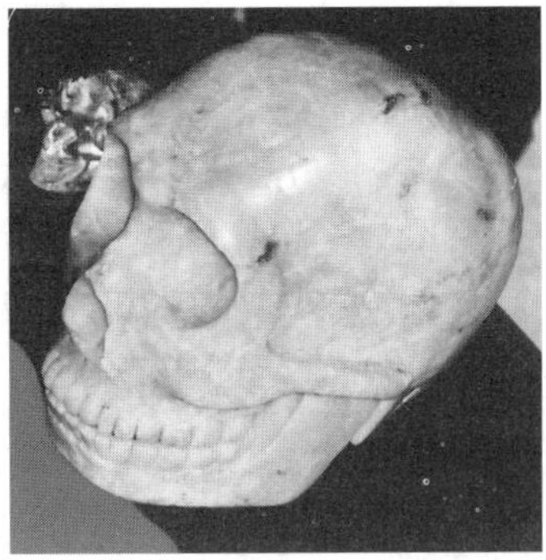

golia, near the Chinese border. It was discovered there 140 years ago by a Chinese archeologist named Yeng Fo Huu. In the 1930s a Danish missionary, Pastor Utkielen, was able to buy this unique skull from the archeologist's family. Pastor Utkielen's family offered Joky the skull in 1992"[71].

I have enjoyed meeting this skull. It is no effort to feel that this is an old skull. However, it is not a quartz skull, so it can have only twelve energy layers. All these twelve layers have been activated. I believe that a skull like this may have been ceremonial or part of a shrine. It was not designed to store information, or its carvers would have used quartz.

26. British Museum Skull

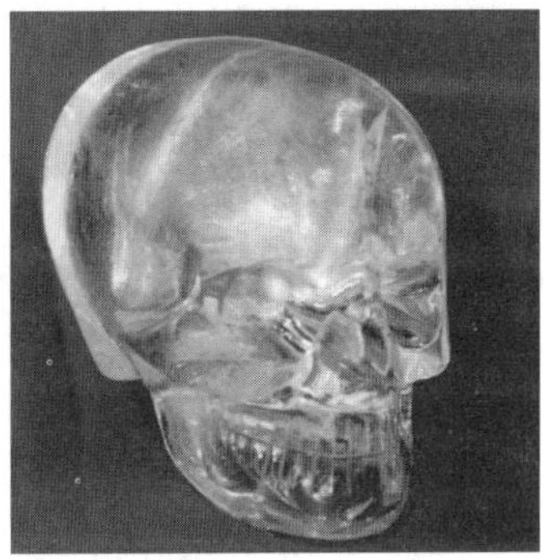

The British Museum skull is a clear quartz skull that was bought by the museum from Tiffany's in 1898. It is a clear quartz skull that, according to Pelton, appears to be an attempt to imitate the Mitchell-Hedges skull in shape and size[72]. This is interesting in light of later comments from the Society of Crystal Skulls International stating that the Mitchell-Hedges skull is not ancient crystal, and Stephen Mehler describes this extensively in his book[73]. Jane Walsh believes that it is the other way around — that the Mitchell-Hedges crystal skull is an elaborate copy of the British Museum skull[74]. Given the times of discovery that seems to be the most logical explanation; the British Museum skull was "found" first (bought in 1898 versus the Mitchell-Hedges skull being reportedly found in 1924). However, there is no information about someone measuring the size of the British Museum skull in order to make a copy more elaborate than the "original." Given the energies of these two skulls, it is highly unlikely, if not impossible, that the Mitchell-Hedges crystal skull is a copy of the British Museum skull.

There is not much additional information about the British Museum skull. According to Jane Walsh, this skull first appeared in 1881 in Eugène Boban's Paris shop. He later exhibited it and attempted to sell it in Mexico

City in 1885 as an Aztec skull, but it was denounced by a Mexican museum curator as a fake[75].

While the energies of the Mitchell-Hedges crystal skull leave open the possibility that we are dealing with an ancient skull, it seems that the energies of the British Museum skull confirm that it was never worked with in ancient times. Although by now the skull has more than twenty-four layers, it does not have any of the characteristics that I see with older crystal skulls: barriers and a widened twenty-fourth or thirty-sixth layer with a bluish shimmer. I do not believe that tool marks lead to a final conclusion about age. However, in the case of the British Museum skull I have to agree with the results of the research: This is not an ancient skull[76].

27. Paris Skull

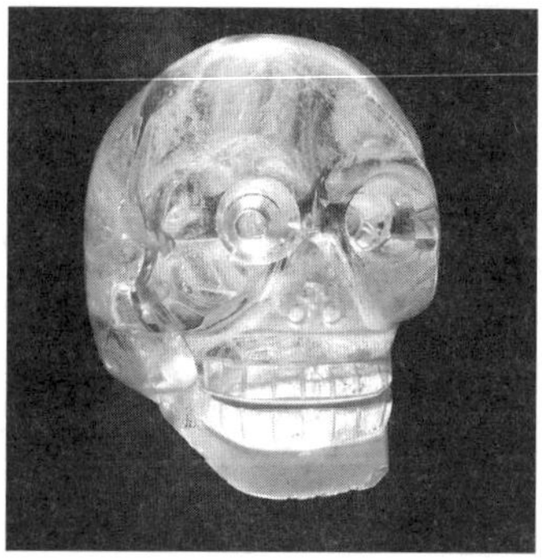

The Paris crystal skull also belongs in the group of crystal skulls that are not really contemporary but aren't ancient either. The Paris crystal skull, like the British Museum skull, came from the Mexican artifacts dealer Boban. He sold it to the ethnographer Alphonse Pinart, who donated it in 1883 to the Trocadéro Museum in Paris, no known as Musée du Quai Branly[77]. The skull was initially displayed by the museum as an Aztec skull. The Paris skull was on display for many years until the museum found out that it may not be an ancient skull and they hid it in the basement of the Louvre.

"The Paris skull is another clear quartz skull. There is a hole going through it from top to bottom which makes people believe that it was placed on a pole or maybe on a cross"[78].

The museum stopped displaying the skull because all scientific research with it leads to the conclusion that it is not a pre-Columbian artifact. The most recent research was done in 2009 by researchers of the Center for Research and Restoration of the Museums in France, or C2RMF. They wanted to determine once and for all when the Paris skull was carved. The results were published in a scientific paper[79]. By using a scanning electron microscope, they were able to find markings that indicated the use of lapidary (rotary) tools in its carving. They also used a recently developed dating method known as quartz hydration dating, which is based on the phenomenon that water at the surface of a quartz sample exposed to the natural environment penetrates progressively (meaning that the older a quartz object, the deeper the penetration). With this method, it was demonstrated that the Paris skull had been carved later than a reference quartz specimen artifact known to have been cut in 1740. Based on the results of these two testing methods, the researchers concluded that the skull was carved in the eighteenth or nineteenth century[80].

The energies of this crystal skull are in alignment with these findings. It is a crystal skull that has less than twenty-four layers and of course no widened layers or bluish shimmering.

28. Smithsonian Skull

The history of the Smithsonian skull (for an image, see Smithsonian.com[81]) is rather short. It was donated to the Smithsonian Museum in 1992 by an anonymous donor who stated that the skull was bought in 1960 in Mexico. It has been suggested that the skull is Aztec. It is a very large skull that is hollow and nonetheless weighs thirty-two pounds.

This skull was part of the testing at the British Museum in 1996 and considered not to be an ancient skull based on the finding of lapidary tool marks[82]. The researchers could not determine the source of the crystal that the skull was carved from.

The energies of the Smithsonian skull are in alignment with these findings. Only a limited number of its energy layers have been activated, suggesting it is a recently carved crystal skull. Being housed in a museum most likely will not change the skull's activity level. Although it is mentioned in the group of "older" skulls, I believe that the Smithsonian skull actually belongs with the contemporary crystal skulls.

29. Ti and Bet

These two small skulls are in my and my wife's collection. Both were bought in a shop in Pune (Poona), India. The shop owner purchased these two skulls from a person selling Tibetan artifacts that he had collected in Tibet from people needing money. That is all that is known about them.

Ti is clear quartz while Bet is citrine. They look very similar in carving, both being rather primitive. Ti is about 3″ (7.7 cm) and Bet is about 2″ (5.1 cm) tall. When we obtained these skulls, their energy showed that they had

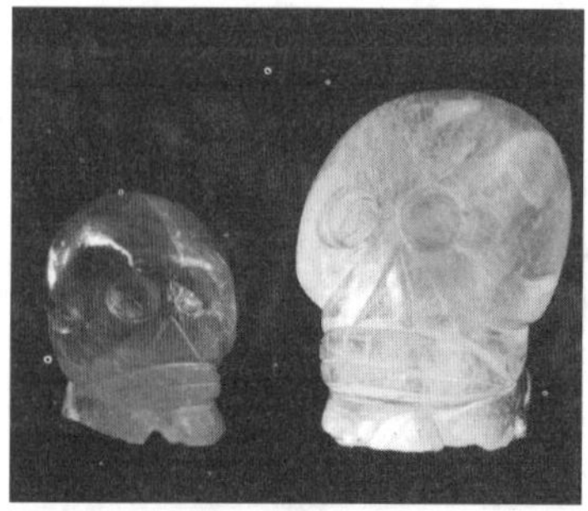

too many layers to be newly carved crystal skulls, but they did not reach the twenty-fourth layer. Now they both have thirty-six activated layers — without the characteristics of the ancient ones.

Different people have estimated the age of these two skulls. The estimation varies from maybe a couple hundred years to 1,500 years for Ti and a couple hundred years to 750 years for Bet. I personally believe that Ti may be 200 years old and Bet about 150 years old.

30. The Nepalese Skulls

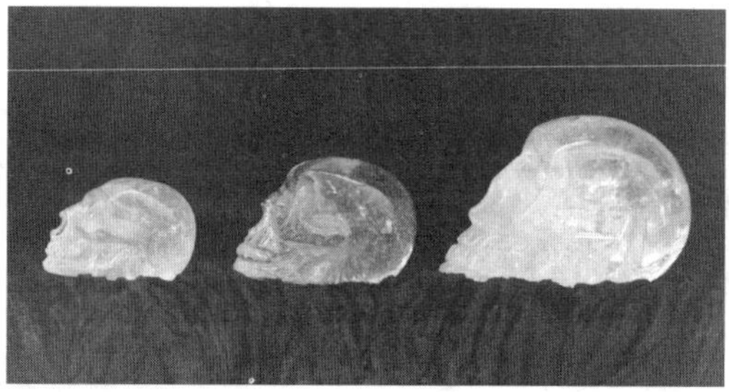

To complete the list of crystal skulls that do not belong to the recent wave of carved skulls, I would like to include three small skulls from Nepal. They were bought from a store in Kathmandu. As I mentioned in *Crystal Skulls: Interacting with a Phenomenon*, they felt fully activated, which at that time meant that they had at least twelve activated layers. This, again, does not happen with recently carved crystal skulls. I also mentioned that they were not really old — maybe around a hundred years (*CS*, 48). I still believe this to be true.

These three skulls are small — one is 3", one is 1.8" (both clear quartz), and one is 2.4" (a smoky quartz). This shows again that size does not matter, and I will not be surprised if more skulls, mostly small ones, from Tibet and Nepal surface. However, not all skulls from there are older, as there are quite a few newly carved skulls as well.

From the current understanding of activation, these skulls were not very active. When we obtained them they had less than twenty-four layers and possessed none of the characteristics of the ancient skulls.

31. Sam and AhBeSo

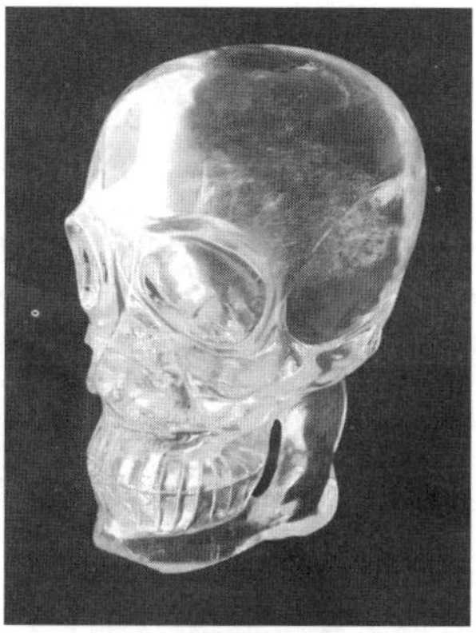

Formally, these two skulls do not belong in this addendum. They both are contemporary crystal skulls. My wife and I are the caretakers of these two skulls. I have included them because they have some characteristics that make it possible to confuse them energetically with older skulls. I believe that this will happen more frequently in the future because many people are learning how to activate their crystal skulls. An increasing number of contemporary crystal skulls are beginning to show characteristics that make them energetically even more powerful than skulls that may be a couple hundred years old.

Sam (top right) is a clear quartz crystal skull slightly smaller than human size with a rather unusual shape. Sam was carved in 1996 in Brazil by someone who had never carved a crystal skull before. AhBeSo (lower right) is a large very dark amethyst crystal skull that was carved around 2002 by the Brazilian master carver Leandro Souza. This skull is larger than human size (about 9" long). Both crystal skulls have been worked with intensely and have been key in understanding a lot of the information presented in this book.

Sam has thirty-six activated layers in addition to Atlantean harmonic frequencies. As I mentioned in chapter 5, it is a riddle how these harmonic frequencies have been induced into this crystal skull. It may have happened when Sam had an intense interaction with the Atlantean orb. However, if it was that easy, why are there not more crystals and crystal skulls that hold these Atlantean harmonic frequencies? And why doesn't Sam pass these energies on to others?

We see a similar situation with AhBeSo. This crystal skull also has thirty-six activated layers and holds Lemurian harmonic frequencies. This crystal skull has been on all the Lemurian nodes (cross points of lines) that outline the edge of the Lemurian area in the Western United States as described in *Gifts of Mother Earth* (135-138). If these Lemurian energies were induced at these sites, why is it that other crystal skulls that have been on these sites do not hold Lemurian harmonic frequencies?

We are still learning how to activate energies in crystal skulls and what determines that certain contemporary crystal skulls become holders of certain harmonic frequencies like those of Atlantis and Lemuria. Even more intriguing is whether it will be possible to activate contemporary crystal skulls to such a level that they have a widened thirty-sixth layer with a bluish shimmer.

We still have much to learn. However, we see that from an energetic point of view, the difference between older and even ancient crystal skulls and contemporary crystal skulls becomes smaller. My prediction is that over time these differences will disappear; however, at this moment we still are far away. Energetically ancient crystal skulls can still be differentiated from contemporary ones.

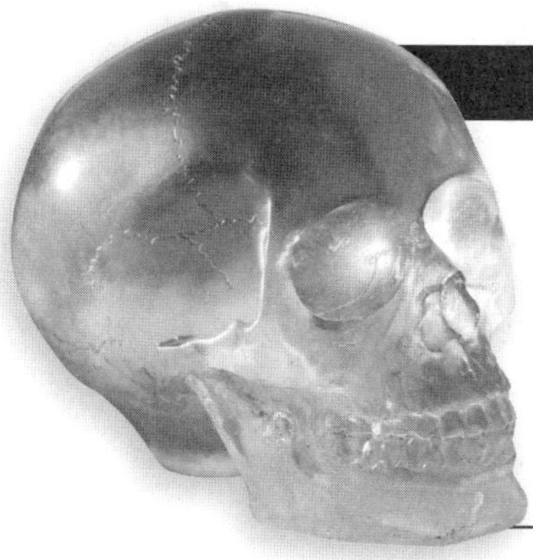

ADDENDUM II:

Thirteen Symbols of Star Nations Connected with Crystal Skulls

In this addendum, the symbols of star nations connected with crystal skulls have been printed on a large scale to make them easier to work with. I have presented each symbol both as a photo of a three-dimensional symbol made of copper wire and as a two-dimensional line drawing. Jeanne and I have experienced that people's preferences for these different presentations of the symbols differ greatly. Presenting both forms gives you the possibility to choose the one you most strongly resonate with. You can copy the page from the book and cut the paper to work with the symbol. You can then hold the symbol, look at it, or place your crystal skull on top of it with the intention of connecting with the star nation whose symbol you have selected. The beings from all twelve star nations are connected with Earth and with the shift occurring in our collective. These beings can also help you connect with energies and information that is important for you at any moment on your personal journey.

To facilitate your connection with the star nations, I have integrated two meditations from the book and present them here as one (see also the meditation CD).

Prepare your environment by placing crystals and crystal skulls in a preferred pattern. You may want to select music or light candles. Make sure you will not be disturbed. Select the star nation you want to work with and use the respective symbol from this book. The meditation follows.

Make yourself as comfortable as possible without forcing yourself into a position that seems "better," like sitting a lotus position, for example. Feeling comfortable will support your meditation better than trying to maintain an uncomfortable "ideal" position. Start with some deeper in-

halations and exhalations, and with every exhalation, allow yourself to relax a little more. Feel yourself sinking into the here and now. Realize that by choosing to meditate, nothing else matters right now.

When you feel relaxed, realize that your brain is less active. This means your system is beginning to align itself more with your heart. Now fully shift your awareness to your heart area, the area behind your breastbone. With every inhalation, bring more energy to your heart center and feel the energy of love expanding throughout your body. For now, restrict this expansion to your physical body.

Be aware that the love energy is spreading into every little corner, into every cell. This means that love is beginning to become the directing force, which makes every cell work optimally. The cells will begin to synchronize with each other. This helps the physical system to heal and balance.

Now allow the energy of love to expand beyond the physical and let it fill the whole room (if you do this outdoors, define the area — for example, create a bubble of love with a radius of 100 to 150 feet, or 30 to 45 meters.) In doing so, each person present will sit in the love energy of everyone else. Feel how that creates a strong connection with everyone present and how this field becomes a coherent field of love.

In this field of love, supported by each other, we come closer to unconditional love and, consequently, to a heartbeat frequency that is optimal. That frequency will be closer to the heartbeat of Mother Earth. We begin to resonate with her, feeling connected with her as one. When you are alone, imagine yourself resonating with Mother Earth.

When we are connected with Mother Earth through love and our system resonates with her, we will also connect with Father Sun and the other planets of the solar system, because they all are in harmony with each other through love, through the same heartbeat.

When we resonate this love with the solar system, we will by definition also resonate with our whole galaxy and, consequently, with the whole universe. Feel your connection with the whole universe, with all universes, with All That Is. Feel the oneness.

Remain in this state. Open your eyes and look at the star nation symbol you have selected. Set a clear intent to use this symbol as a key to enter the consciousness field of the beings of the star nation you have selected. Some people prefer to keep a copy of the symbol in their hands or place their skull on top of it.

Trust that you now have made a connection. Never doubt yourself, because then your vibration will go down in frequency and a connection may no longer be possible.

Allow whatever happens to happen. Being in a state of love means that you will always encounter only beings from the selected star system who live in a place of love.

When you feel complete, express your gratitude for the connection and the gifts that you have been given. By definition, every connection will bring you gifts in the form of — for example — energy, insights, information, or healing.

Take a few deep breaths and bring your awareness to your feet and your body. When you feel ready, open your eyes again.

Share or write down your experiences so that you can follow the development of your deepening connection.

Realize that connecting with these beings, their consciousness, and the connected information is a journey. Over time, you will learn their language and it will become easier to connect, even outside the setting of a meditation. Once you have experienced these connections it will be a joy to deepen them.

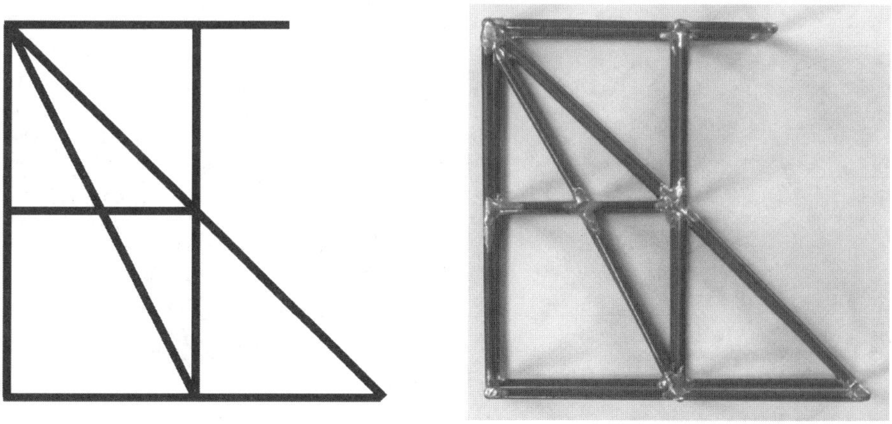

Arcturus

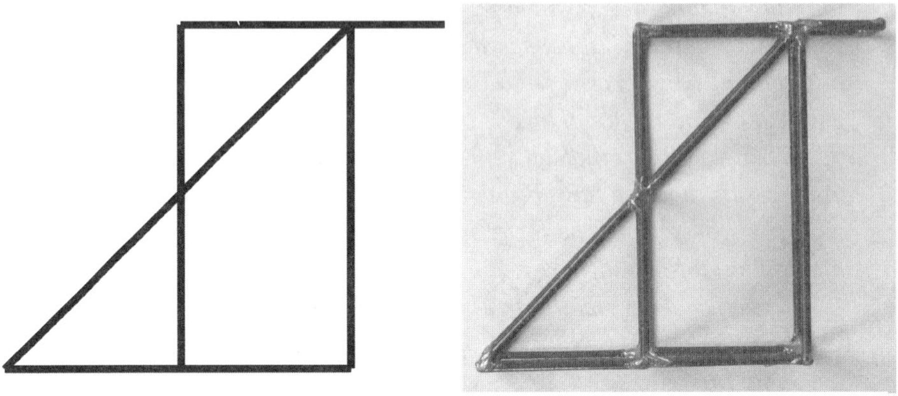

Zeta Reticuli

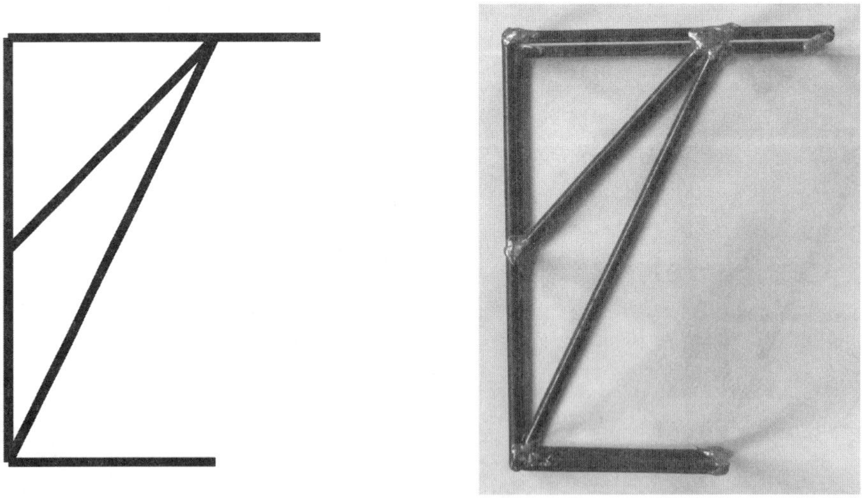

Ursa Major

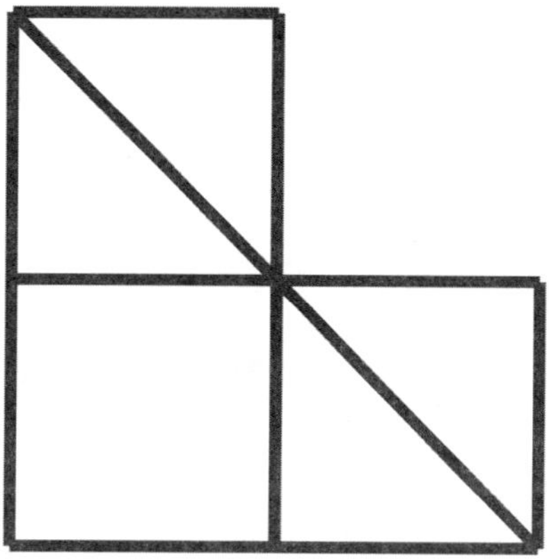

Dragon

Alpha Centauri

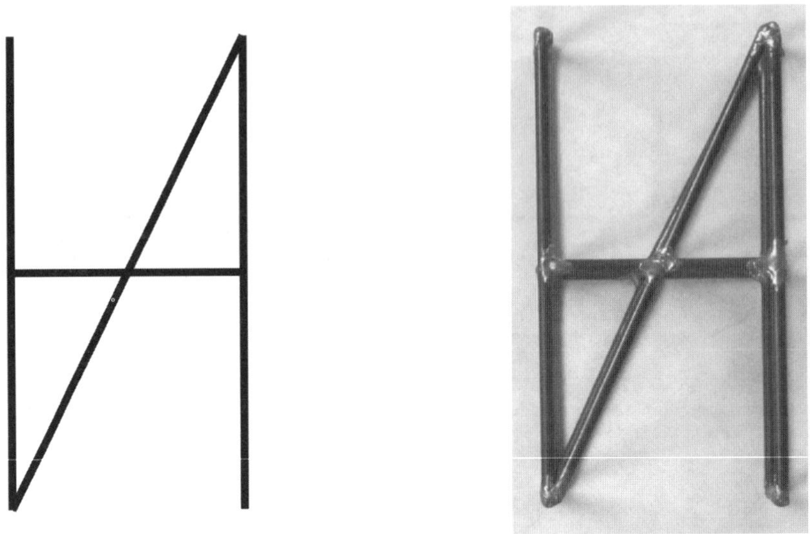

Sirius

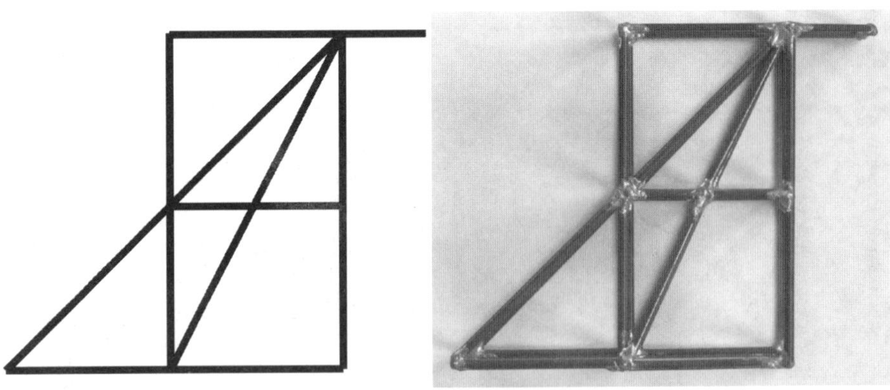

Orion

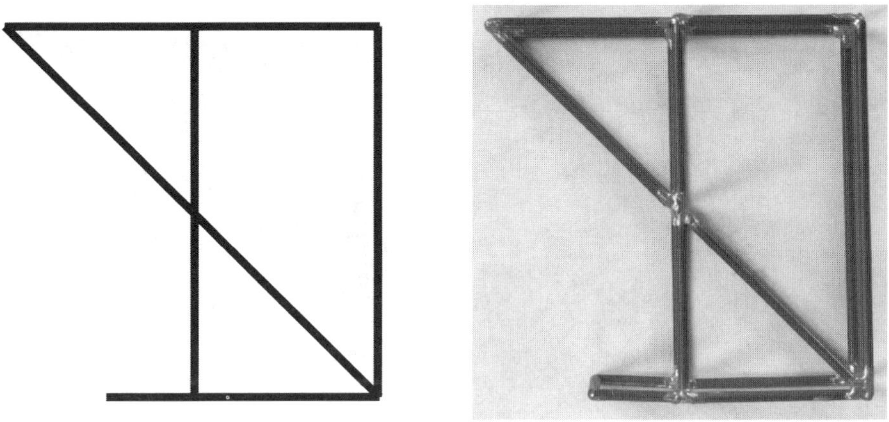

Cassiopeia

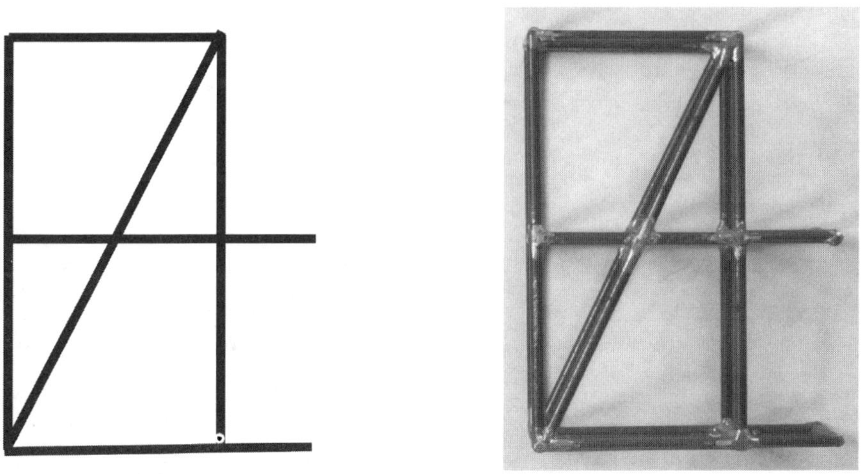

Pleiades

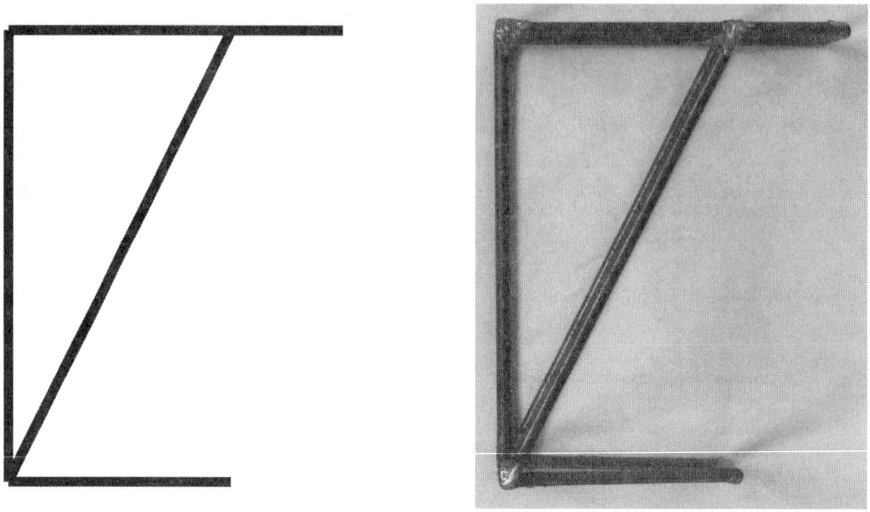

Taurus

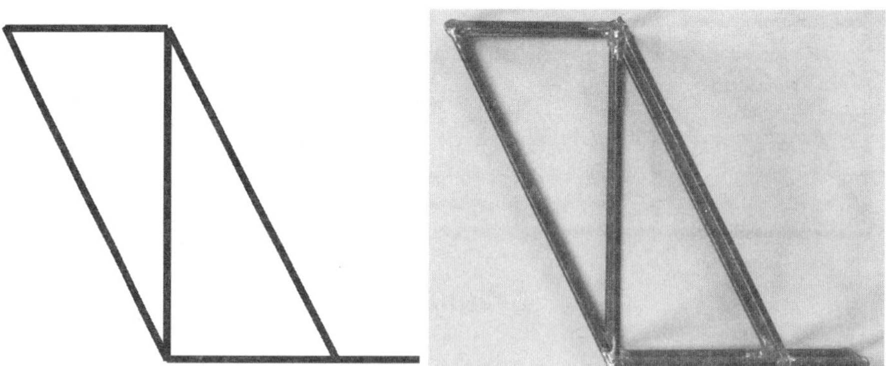

Andromeda

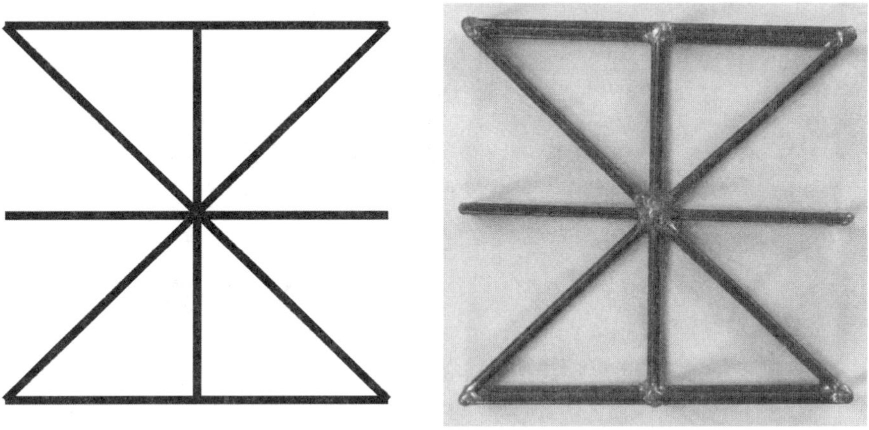

Earth

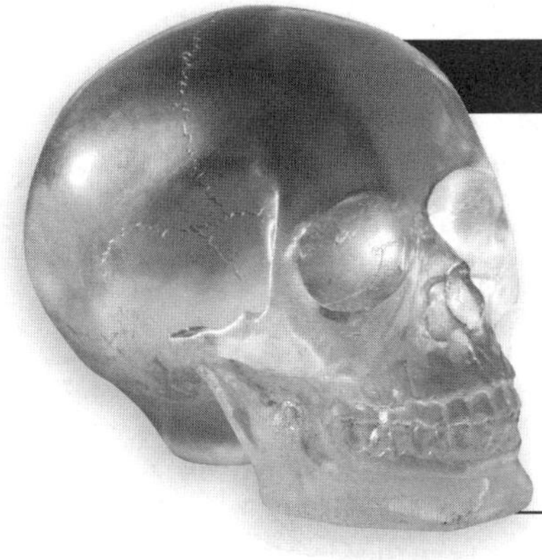

Notes

Introduction

1. Carl Johan Calleman, a Swedish researcher of the Mayan calendar, believed that the date of the shift would be October 28, 2011. This date was based on his theory that nine levels of consciousness completed at that date and so the shift occurred. This did not happen. He now believes that the ninth wave of consciousness continues. For more information, go to his website: http://www.calleman.com/
2. David Icke gives many lectures on this subject for large audiences. He has written many books, and there are many videos available on YouTube. See his website for more: http://www.davidicke.com.
3. Jaap van Etten, *Crystal Skulls: Interacting with a Phenomenon* (Flagstaff, AZ: Light Technology Publishing, 2007), xv-xvi (hereafter cited in text as CS).
4. Sandra Bowen, F.R. "Nick" Nocerino, and Joshua Shapiro, *Mysteries of the Crystal Skulls Revealed* (Pacifica, CA: J&S Aquarian Networking, 1988).
5. Joshua Shapiro's oldest website is http://www.v-j-enterprises.com/cs.html. Of course, the website has changed over time, but some of the older information is still available.
6. The website for the crystal skull event in Mexico City, Cráneos de Cristal México, is http://www.craneosdecristal.org.mx/en/index.html.
7. David Bohm has written many interesting books on the implicate order. See: David Bohm, *Wholeness and the Implicate Order* (London: Routledge, 1980) and David Bohm and Basil J. Hiley, *The Undivided Universe* (London: Routledge, 1993).
8. Vilim Kanjski and Hrvoje Zujic, *The Secrets of the Pyramids Revealed: Energetics Discovers the Truth* (Bosnia: Grafika d.o.o. Osijek, 2008), 23.
9. Ibid.
10. Dolores Cannon has written many books. In relationship to the subject of this book, I recommend especially *The Three Waves of Volunteers and the New Earth* (Huntsville, AR: Ozark Mountain Publishing, 2011).
11. Scott Mowry, "New Crop Circles Found in England May Offer Proof That a New Earth Is About to Unfold," Miracles and Inspiration, posted July 31, 2010, http://www.miraclesandinspiration.com/news_cropcircles.html.

Chapter 1

1. Jaap van Etten, *Gifts of Mother Earth: Earth Energies, Vortexes, Lines, and Grids* (Flagstaff, AZ: Light Technology Publishing, 2011), 29–88 (hereafter cited in text as *GME*).
2. Drunvalo Melchizedek, *Serpent of Light: Beyond 2012; The Movement of the Earth's Kundalini and the Rise of the Female Light, 1049 to 2013* (San Francisco: Weiser Books, 2007), 189–191.
3. Chris Morton and Ceri Louise Thomas, *The Mystery of the Crystal Skulls: Unlocking the Secrets of the Past, Present, and Future* (San Francisco: Thorsons, 1997) (hereafter cited in text as *MCS*).
4. Patricia Mercier wrote two books: *The Mayan End Times: A Spiritual Adventure; Maya Prophecies for 2012,* and *Crystal Skulls and the Enigma of Time: A Spiritual Adventure into the Mayan World of Prophecy and Discovery*, both published by Watkins Publishing, London, in 2008 and 2011, respectively.
5. Oracle Stone Productions organizes crystal skull events on the triple dates: 9–9–9, 10–10–10, 11–11–11, and 12–12–12. See http://www.crystalskullsevent.com.
6. Information shared during the event "The Journey of the Crystal Skull Guardians," held in Sedona, Arizona, September 26-28, 2008.
7. Dr. Joseph Ray, "The Legacy de Lubicz," in *The Search for Lost Origins* (Livingston, MT: Atlantis Rising Books, 1996), 37–42.
8. Sherry Whitfield, "The Crystal Skull, 'Synergy,'" http://www.angelslove.net/crystalskull/.
9. Brian Hadley-James, ed., *The Skull Speaks (through Carole Davis)* (Toronto: Amrhea Publishing, 1985).
10. Type "holographic imaging using crystals" into a search engine and you will find a great deal of technical information. For a general introduction to the principle, see: Wikipedia, s.v. "Holography," last modified November 14, 2012, http://en.wikipedia.org/wiki/Holography.

Chapter 2

1. Many books on the qualities of crystals have been published. However, I have been unable to resonate with more than 75 percent of the content. Therefore, I have chosen not to make any recommendations.
2. Kirsten Hilling, *Kristallschädel: Anleitung zur Energiearbeit mit Kristallschädeln* [Crystal skull: Introduction to energy work with crystal skulls] (Leipzig, Germany: Bohmer Verlad, 2011), 28. (Book only available in the German language.)

Chapter 3

1. The use of smudging comes from the practices of shamanism, derived from North American native traditions. (For an example, see: Wikipedia, s.v. "Smudge stick," last modified October 12, 2012, http://en.wikipedia.org/wiki/Smudge_Stick.)

   Incense may have been used for thousands of years, but its origin is uncertain. Nowadays, the use of incense is a general practice. (For an example, see: Wikipedia, s.v. "Incense," last modified November 4, 2012, http://en.wikipedia.org/wiki/Incense.)

   Copal is a resin that was used and is still in use in ceremonies in Meso-America — by the Maya, for example. (For examples, see: Wikipedia, s.v. "Copal," last modified November 2, 2012, http://en.wikipedia.org/wiki/Copal and Brian Stross, "Mesoamerican Copal Resins," *U-Mut Maya 6*, 177-186, http://www.utexas.edu/courses/stross/papers/copal.htm.)
2. DaEl Walker, *The Crystal Book* (Sunol, CA: Crystal Co., 1983), 19–20.
3. Nick F.R. Nocerino used this method in certain cases. See *The White Knight*, a quarterly publication produced by The Pelton Foundation of Applied Paranormal Research, in association with White Knight Productions and *The Society of Crystal Skulls International*, volume 2, no. 4, 4.

Chapter 4

1. Dowsing is the use of certain tools, like a pendulum or rod, to see answers to questions. The movement of the tool signals a yes, no, or neutral answer. It is a method to make extrasensory information visible that otherwise could not be received and perceived. It is a method that requires thorough training and preparations, which is why mastering brainwaves is important in dowsing.
2. Antoine Lutz et al., "Long-Term Meditators Self-Induce High-Amplitude Gamma Synchrony during Mental Practice," *Proceedings of the National Academy of Sciences of the United States of America* 101, no. 46 (November 16, 2004), doi: 10.1073/pnas.0407401101. A summary was also published in the *Washington Post* by Marc Kaufman on January 2, 2005 under the title "Meditation Gives Brain a Charge, Study Finds." See http://www.washingtonpost.com/wp-dyn/articles/A43006-2005Jan2.html.
3. Gerald O'Donnell, *The Complete Remote Influencing Training System* (Boca Raton, FL: Academy of Remote Viewing and Remote Influencing, 2006). See also http://www.ProbableFuture.com.
4. Check for the availability of the CD at http://www.lemurantis.com/publications.html or http://www.lemurantis.com/shop.html.
5. Shelley Kaehr, PhD, *Crystal Skull Consciousness* (Dallas: Out of This World, 2007), 45–52; Kirsten Hilling, *Kristallschädel: Anleitung zur Energiearbeit mit Kristallschädeln* [Crystal skull: Introduction to energy work with crystal skulls] (Leipzig, Germany: Bohmer Verlad, 2011): 76–104.
6. Joshua Shapiro and DesyRainbow Roodnat-Shapiro, *Kristallen Schedels: Een Groot Mysterie Nader Bekeken* (Eeserveen, the Netherlands: Uitgeverij Akasha, 2006): 137–169.
7. Ibid.
8. For meridians see 45–59 and for chakras 61–88.
9. Drunvalo Melchizedek, *Serpent of Light: Beyond 2012; The Movement of the Earth's Kundalini and the Rise of the Female Light, 1049 to 2013* (San Francisco: Weiser Books, 2007): 189–191.

Chapter 5

1. David Hatcher Childress and Stephen Mehler, *The Crystal Skulls: Astonishing Portals to Man's Past* (Kempton, IL: Adventures Unlimited Press, 2008): 155.
2. For information on the composition of nebula stone, go to http://www.nebulastone.com.
3. Wikipedia, s.v. "Sarsen," last modified August 23, 2012, http://en.wikipedia.org/wiki/Sarsen_stone.
4. Hatcher Childress and Mehler, *The Crystal Skulls*, 177, 180, and 208.
5. Kirby Seid, "The Light Labyrinth," Ancient Technologies, http://www.ancient-technologies.com/liminal.html.

Chapter 6

1. In December 2011, a replica of the Mitchell-Hedges skull was offered for sale. It was carved in China. In this case it was indicated clearly that this was a replica. Later, replicas of this skull made from smoky quartz and rose quartz were offered. However, there are many "replicas" from so-called ancient skulls for sale that are suggested or stated to be ancient — for example, from the Hongshan period. Unfortunately, people believe these stories and buy the skulls, spreading the stories even further. This book is not intended to expose all these misleading activities. Ultimately, it does not make any difference because crystal skulls are wonderful tools to work with, but the contemporary ones need to be activated.

   It is different when the "crystal skulls" are made from artificial materials like resin, often mixed with quartz powder. There are many of these fake skulls being offered as "ancient." When you become more sensitive, you will be able to feel whether a skull is made of natural material or not.

2. When we are looking at stories of ancient skulls, it is easy to note that some of these stories are false. These stories have been created to protect the ancient artifacts and prevent possible claims from those who may claim them for a variety of reasons. Of these stories, the one that has been discussed most extensively is that of the Mitchell-Hedges skull. Trying to understand why the story has been presented the way it has will most likely be in vain since the "players" may have taken the "true story" with them. It is surprising that only the story of the Mitchell-Hedges crystal skull has been scrutinized and others have been ignored. This has happened most likely for the same reason we have chosen not to go into these details: What is important is what crystal skulls do for us on our journey and not about what we do to the crystals skulls. Crystal skulls will amplify whatever exists, giving us the opportunity to learn from our creation.
3. There is a lot of information and speculation about technologies used in Egypt and especially in Puma Punku. Here I offer a few references as a starting point.

   For Egypt: Global Education Project, "Spirit and Stone: Showcasing the Extraordinary of Old Kingdom Egypt," http://www.theglobaleducationproject.org/egypt/articles/stonetech.php/. For Puma Punku: Dave Early, "Ancient Mysteries Puma Punku in Tiahuanaco," March 10, 2009, http://daveearly.hubpages.com/hub/Ancient-Mysteries-Puma-Punku-in-Tiahuanaco.

   For general information: in the TV series *Ancient Aliens*, attention is given to technology in many episodes. See: http://www.history.com/shows/Ancient-aliens.
4. Margaret Sax et al., "The Origins of Two Purportedly Pre-Columbian Mexican Crystal Skulls," *Journal of Archeological Science* 35, no. 10 (October 2008): 2,751-2,760, doi: 10.1016/j.jas.2008.05.007.
5. Frank Thadeusz, "German Artisans Lay Claim to a Mysterious Tradition," *Der Spiegel*. Published electronically in English October 7, 2011, http://www.spiegel.de/international/spiegel/0,1518,790456,00.html.
6. Jane MacLaren Walsh, "Legend of the Crystal Skulls: The Truth behind Indiana Jones's Latest Quest," *Archaeology* 61, no. 3 (May/June 2008), http://www.archaeology.org/0805/etc/indy.html.
7. Publishing Archaeology, "Aztec Crystal Skulls," blog entry by Michael E. Smith, May 19, 2008, http://publishingarchaeology.blogspot.com/2008/05/blog-post.html.
8. Wigholt Vleer, Leylijnen en Leycentra in *de Lage Landen: 200 Heilige Plaatsen in Nederland en Vlaanderen* (The Netherlands: Ankh-Hermes, 1992): 27–31.
9. See for example: "Atlantean Sphere," Dr. Ray Brown, Scribd, http://www.scribd.com/doc/25498910/Atlantean-Sphere-Dr-brown.
10. "Interview with Lemurian Crystal Dealer, uploaded by "SenseiDennis," October 15, 2009, http://www.youtube.com/watch?v=hGWkOzmVj7c.
11. Katrina Raphaell, "Lemurian Seed Crystals," *Crystal Buzz*, 12 (Spring 2000): 1, 3, and 6.
12. "David Hudson Lectures," Ascension Alchemy, http://www.asc-alchemy.com/hudson.html.
13. Robert E. Cox, T*he Elixir of Immortality: A Modern-Day Alchemist's Discovery of the Philosopher's Stone* (Rochester, VT: Inner Traditions, 2009).
14. Nicholette Zeliadt, "Silver Beware: Antimicrobial Nanoparticles in Soil May Harm Plant Life," *Scientific American*, August 9, 2010, http://www.scientificamerican.com/article.cfm?id=silver-beware-antimicrobial-nanoparticles-in-soil-may-harm-plant-life.
15. See note 12 above.
16. Robert E. Cox, *The Elixir of Immortality: A Modern-Day Alchemist's Discovery of*

the Philosopher's Stone (Rochester, VT: Inner Traditions, 2009): xiii. This is the main subject of this book.

17. There are several sources for purchasing Andara stones. One of them is http://www.ladynellie.com. Be aware, though — a lot of what is sold as Andara is actually colored glass.
18. See, for example: "Featuring Mount St. Helens Emerald Jewelry (Obsidianite, Helenite)," Mount St. Helen's Gift Shop, http://www.mt-st-helens.com/obsidianite.html.
19. Ibid.
20. Richard Boylan, "Star Nations," http://www.drboylan.com/starnations.html.
21. Richard Boylan, "Elders Reveal Centuries of Extraterrestrial Contact Lore," 1996, http://www.drboylan.com/strknrpt2.html.
22. Chief Golden Light Eagle/Standing Elk, "Chief Shares Knowledge about Star Nations, UFOs," uploaded by "GreenGuerrillas" June 13, 2010, http://www.youtube.com/watch?v=JLYW2RC8LIY.
23. Richard Boylan, PhD, "Return of the Star Nations during our Time of Purification: Report on the Star Knowledge Conference in Sedona," 1998, http://www.think-aboutit.com/Spiritual/return_of_the_star_nations_durin.htm.
24. Edgar Evans Cayce, *Edgar Cayce on Atlantis*, (New York: Castle Book, 1968): 87–91.
25. See maps in: W. Scott-Elliott, *Legends of Atlantis and Lost Lemuria* (Wheaton, IL: Quest Books, 1990). A map is also available online: Wikipedia, s.v. "Map of William Scott-Elliott," last modified September 10, 2010, http://en.wikipedia.org/wiki/File:Map_of_Lemuria.jpg.
26. Stephen S. Mehler, "Crystal Skulls: The Adventure Continues," *World Explorer* 6, no. 1 (August 2011): 36–41.
27. Chuck Pelton, *The Crystal Skulls: A Legacy of Past Civilizations or Prophets of our Future* (Pinole, CA: Pelton Publications, 1997): 18.
28. See "The 10–10–10 World Mysteries Crystal Skull Event," http://www.crystalskullsevent.com/101010.html.
29. See "The 9–9–9 Crystal Skulls World Mysteries Event," http://www.crystalskullsevent.com/999.html.
30. See note 18 above.
31. See "The 11–11–11 Crystal Skulls World Mysteries Gateway in L.A. Event," http://www.crystalskullsevent.com/111111.html.
32. See the gallery at http://www.craneosdecristal.org.mx/en/index.html. In pictures 10 and 11, Paco is the largest crystal skull on the table.
33. Jade was highly valued in Central America and China. For example see: "Jade," International Colored Gemstones Association, http://www.gemstone.org/index.php?option=com_content&view=article&id=121:sapphire&catid=1:gem-by-gem&Itemid=14.
34. See pictures 10 and 11 in the gallery at http://www.craneosdecristal.org.mx/en/index.html. There are three crystal skulls of this group on the table, but for privacy reasons I have not specifically indicated their positions.
35. Go to http://www.eBay.com and search for "Hongshan skull."

Chapter 7

1. Brian Hadley James, *The Skull Speaks* (Kitchener, Ontario: Anna Mitchell-Hedges Research and Exploration Association, 1985).
2. Ibid., 9.
3. Brian Hadley-James, *Beyond the Veil of Time ... with Carole Davis-Wilson* (Ontario: Like-Minds Publishing, 2000): 14 and 50.
4. Hatcher Childress and Mehler, *The Crystal Skulls*, 178–179.
5. Wikipedia, s.v. "Crystallographic defect," last modified September 29, 2012, http://en.wikipedia.org/wiki/Crystallographic_defect.
6. Wikipedia, s.v. "Maxwell's equations," last modified November 12, 2012,

http://en.wikipedia.org/wiki/Maxwell's_equations.
7. Konstantin Meyl, "Scalar Waves: Theory and Experiments," *Journal of Scientific Exploration* 15, no. 2 (2001): 199–205. http://www.scientificexploration.org/journal/jse_15_2_meyl.pdf.
8. Nicole Loeffler, "The Effects of a Conditioned Space Called the 'Scalar Room' on the Experience of Meditation" (doctor of theology dissertation, Holos University, 2007), 26–40, http://www.holosuniversity.net/pdf/NLoeffler_Dissertation.pdf.
9. Ibid., 39.
10. James Dacey, "Atoms Teleport Information over Long Distance," Institute of Physics, January 22, 2009, http://physicsworld.com/cws/article/news/37450.
11. See note 4 above.
12. Hatcher Childress and Mehler, *The Crystal Skulls*, 174.
13. Wikipedia, s.v. "Scrying," last modified November 10, 2012, http://en.wikipedia.org/wiki/Scrying.
14. Wikipedia, s.v. "Psychometry (Paranormal)," last modified October 15, 2012, http://en.wikipedia.org/wiki/Psychometry_(paranormal).
15. Sandra Bowen, F.R. "Nick" Nocerino, and Joshua Shapiro, *Mysteries of the Crystal Skulls Revealed* (Pacifica, CA: J&S Aquarian Networking, 1988): 16-21.
16. Hatcher Childress and Mehler, *The Crystal Skulls*, 211–227.
17. Jaap van Etten, Lecture presented during the 11–11–11 event. This lecture will soon be available on DVD. See http://www.crystalskullsevent.com.
18. Ibid.
19. Konstantin Meyl, "Scalar Waves: Theory and Experiments," *Journal of Scientific Exploration* 15, no. 2 (2001): 199–205.
20. Nicole Loeffler, "The Effects of a Conditioned Space Called the 'Scalar Room' on the Experience of Meditation," (DTh diss., Holos University, 2007), 39.
21. Glen Rein, PhD, "Biological Effects of Quantum Fields and Their Role in the Natural Healing Process," *Frontier Perspectives* 7 (1998): 16–23. http://www.item-bioenergy.com/infocenter/BiologicalEffectsofQuantumFields.pdf.
22. David Bohm has written many interesting books on the implicate order. See *Wholeness and the Implicate Order* (New York: Routledge, 2002) and *The Undivided Universe* (New York: Routledge, 1995).
23. Glen Rein, PhD, "Biological Effects of Quantum Fields and Their Role in the Natural Healing Process," *Frontier Perspectives* 7 (1998): 2. http://www.item-bioenergy.com/infocenter/BiologicalEffectsofQuantumFields.pdf.

Chapter 8

1. Rhonda Byrne, *The Secret* (Hillsboro, OR: Beyond Words Publishing, 2006).
2. Esther and Jerry Hicks, *The Law of Attraction: The Basics of the Teachings of Abraham* (New York: Hay House, 2006).

Chapter 9

1. Bowen, Nocerino, and Shapiro, *Mysteries of the Crystal Skulls Revealed*, 16 and 21.
2. Cal Garrison, "The 13 Crystal Skulls Will Arrive in San Francisco on 11–11–11," Before It's News, Monday October 24, 2011, http://beforeitsnews.com/story/1275/074/The_13_Crystal_Skulls_Will_Arrive_In_San_Francisco_On_11-11-11.html.
3. "Important News: An Update on the Crystal Skull Journey with Mayan Daykeeper, Hunbatz Men," Ma'at Magazines (November 2011), http://www.spiritofmaat.com/crystall_skulls_update_en.html.
4. Aryeh Kaplan, *Sefer Yetzirah: The Book of Creation* (Boston: Weiser Books, 1997): 146. The book focuses much attention on this process.
5. Chief Golden Light Eagle/Standing Elk, "Chief Shares Knowledge about Star Nations, UFO's," uploaded by "GreenGuerrillas" June 13, 2010, http://www.youtube.com/watch?v=JLYW2RC8LIY.

6. There are many images of Boötes that all vary slightly. See: Wikipedia, s.v. "Boötes," last modified November 2, 2012, http://en.wikipedia.org/wiki/Bootes, and "Boötes, the Herdsman," StarDate, http://stardate.org/nightsky/constellations/bootes.
7. Without making a complete list and without detailed references, I mention books from Barbara Marciniak: *Bringers of the Dawn, Earth,* and *Family of Light*; Amorah Quan Yin: *The Pleiadian Workbook: Awakening Your Divine Ka,* and *Pleiadian Perspectives on Human Evolution*; and Barabara Hand Clow: *The Pleiadian Agenda: A New Cosmology for the Age of Light,* and *Heart of the Christos: Starseeding from the Pleiades.*
8. Satguru Sivaya Subramuniyaswami, *Lemurian Scrolls: Angelic Prophecies Revealing Human Origins* (Hawaii: Himalayan Academy, 1998).
9. "Mayan Astronomy," last modified January 28, 2011, http://www.authenticmaya.com/maya_astronomy.htm.
10. James W. Deardorff, "The Pleiades," http://www.tjresearch.info/pleiades.htm.
11. "About the Pleaideans," last modified February 3, 2011, http://www.4truthseekers.org/articles/about_the_pleaideans.php.
12. Robert K.G. Temple, *The Sirius Mystery: Was Earth Visited by Intelligent Beings from a Planet in the System of the Star Sirius?* (Rochester, VT: Destiny Books, 1987).
13. Ibid., 209-210.
14. Wikipedia, s.v. "Dogon people," last modified October 31, 2012, http://en.wikipedia.org/wiki/Dogon_people.
15. M. Temple Richmond, *Sirius* (Mariposa, CA: Source Publications, 1997).
16. Ibid., 49.
17. "Hopi Prophecies," Crystalinks, http://www.crystalinks.com/hopi2.html.
18. Vigilant Citizen, "The Mysterious Connection between Sirius and Human History," Secret Arcana, http://secretarcana.com/hiddenknowledge/the-mysterious-connection-between-sirius-and-human-history/.
19. Murry Hope has written several books that all seem to have some connection with Sirius, like *The Sirius Connection, The Lion People,* and *The Paschats and the Crystal People.*
20. James Mullaney, "Celebrating the Universe," Edgar Cayce's Association for Research and Enlightenment, posted May 6, 2011, http://www.edgarcayce.org/are/blog.aspx?id=4645&blogid=445.
21. Dr. Norma J. Milanovich, *We, the Arcturians* (Albuquerque, NM: Athena Publishing, 1990).
22. Lyssa Royal and Keith Priest, *The Prism of Lyra: An Exploration of Human Galactic Heritage* (Phoenix: Royal Priest Research Press, 1992): 61–62.
23. Robert Bauval and Adrian Gilbert, *The Orion Mystery: Unlocking the Secrets of the Pyramids* (New York: Crown Trade Paperbacks, 1994).
24. Philip Coppens, *The New Pyramid Age: Worldwide Discoveries of New Pyramids Challenge Our Thinking* (Washington: O Books, 2007): 59.
    See also: "Teotihuacán," Ancient Wisdom, http://www.ancient-wisdom.co.uk/mexicoteotihuacan.htm.
25. Gary A. David, *The Orion Zone: Ancient Star Cities of the American Southwest* (Colfax, WI: Hayriver Press, 2005).
26. Ibid., 48.
27. Exopædia, s.v. "Centauri," http://www.exopaedia.org/Centauri.
28. Andrew Collins, *The Cygnus Mystery: Secrets of Life's Origins and the Cosmos* (London: Watkins Publishing, 2010).
29. Andrew Collins, "The Cygnus Mystery: Have Cosmic Rays Affected Human Evolution?," in *Lost Knowledge of the Ancients: A Graham Hancock Reader, ed. Glenn Kreisberg* (Rochester, VT: Bear and Company, 2010): 114.
30. Ibid., 122–123.
31. Philip Jacobsen, *De Kathedralenbeer* (Amsterdam: Frontier, 2000): 19–20. Available only in Dutch.

32. Dolores Cannon, *The Three Waves of Volunteers and the New Earth* (Huntsville, AR: Ozark Mountain Publishing, 2011).

Chapter 10

1. "Genocide in the 20th Century," The History Place, 2000, http://www.historyplace.com/worldhistory/genocide/index.html.
2. Shirley MacLaine, *The Camino: A Journey of Spirit* (New York: Pocket Books, 2000): 215.
3. Brian Hadley-James, *Beyond the Veil of Time ... with Carole Davis-Wilson* (Ontario: Like-Minds Publishing, 2000): 151.
4. Radu Cinamar with Peter Moon, *Transylvanian Moonrise* (New York: Skybooks, 2011): 130.
5. The Kogis extensively express their way of thinking and their worries about the actions of us, the "little brother," and the pending destruction of our world in: Alan Ereira, *The Elder Brother's Warning* (UK: Tairona Heritage Trust, 2008), http://www.taironatrust.org.

Addendum I

1. Chuck Pelton, *The Crystal Skulls: A Legacy of Past Civilizations or Prophets of Our Future?* (Pinole, CA: Pelton Publications, 1997). (Publication no longer available.)
2. Alice Bryant and Phyllis Galde, *The Message of the Crystal Skull: From Atlantis to the New Age* (St. Paul, MN: Llewellyn Publications, 1991).
3. Frank Dorland, *Holy Ice: Bridge to the Subconscious* (St. Paul, MN: Galde Press, 1992).
4. The website of the Mitchell-Hedges crystal skull is http://mitchell-hedges.com/en/home.html. The announcement quoted here is made on the home page under "Future" (accessed July 2012).
5. Hatcher Childress and Mehler, *The Crystal Skulls*, 225.
6. Ibid., 211–227.
7. For examples, see: Sibley S. Morill, Ambroce Bierce: *F.A. Mitchell-Hedges and the Crystal Skull* (San Francisco: Cadleon Press, 1972) or, more recently, Philip Coppens, "The Mitchell-Hedges Crystal Skull Mystery," *Nexus* 15, no. 4 (June/July 2008), http://www.philipcoppens.com/mitchellhedges_origin.html.
8. Jane MacLaren Walsh, "The Skull of Doom: Under the Microscope," *Archaeology*, January 26, 2010, http://www.archaeology.org/online/features/mitchell_hedges/microscope.html.
9. Frank Thadeusz, "The Kingdom of the Crystal Skull: German Artisans Lay Claim to a Mysterious Tradition," *Der Spiegel* 40 (2011), http://www.spiegel.de/international/spiegel/0,1518,790456,00.html.
10. See note 8 above.
11. Bowen, Nocerino, and Shapiro, *Mysteries of the Crystal Skulls Revealed*, 15–39.
12. Ibid.
13. Joky van Dieten, "ET," http://www.jokys-peacemission.com/et.htm.
14. In addition to the website above, also see Joky van Dieten's self-published booklet called *Messengers of Ancient Wisdom*, a story about her crystal skulls narrated by ET.
15. Joky van Dieten, *Messengers of Ancient Wisdom*, 19.
16. Ibid.
17. The website for the event is http://www.crystalskullsevent.com. Photos can be viewed through the event's Facebook page, https://www.facebook.com/media/set/?set=a.203720163036952.50478.136907959718173&type=3.
18. The website with more information on Synergy is http://www.angelslove.net/crystalskull/history_of_this_skull.htm.
19. Pelton, *The Crystal Skulls*, 16.
20. "Ancient Crystal Skull Sha Na Ra, Not Shanara," http://www.crystalskulls.com/shanara-crystal-skull.html.
21. Chris Morton and Ceri Louise Thomas, *The Mystery of the Crystal Skulls: Unlocking the Secrets of the Past, Present and Future* (San Francisco: Thorsons, 1997): 224.

22. Ibid.
23. Ibid., 222.
24. The new website of Sha Na Ra and its caretaker, Michele Nocerino, is: "Sha Na Ra: Portal of the Ancients," http://www.shanaracrystalskull.com.
25. "Crystal Skull: Max," http://www.crystalskulls.com/max-crystal-skull.html.
26. JoAnn Parks, *The Story of Max: The Texas Crystal Skull* (Privately printed by JoAnn Parks, 1990): 6.
27. Ibid., 8.
28. "Information About Crystals," http://fourthdimensionhigherawareness.com/about.html.
29. Stephen S. Mehler, "Crystal Skulls: The Adventure Continues," *World Explorer* 6, no. 1 (August 2011): 36–41.
30. Ibid.
31. Pelton, *The Crystal Skulls*, 25.
32. The website of Einstein and its caretaker Carolyn Ford is http://www.einsteinthecrystalskull.com.
33. Hatcher Childress and Mehler, *The Crystal Skulls*, 164–165. See also the interview with Stephen Mehler in: Bowen, Nocerino, and Shapiro, *Mysteries of the Crystal Skulls Revealed*, 104–135.
34. Pelton, *The Crystal Skulls*, 17.
35. Mehler, "Crystal Skulls," 36–41.
36. Pelton, *The Crystal Skulls*, 18.
37. Ibid.
38. Hatcher Childress and Mehler, *The Crystal Skulls*, 164-165.
39. Pelton, T*he Crystal Skulls*, 24.
40. Ibid., 23.
41. Ibid., 27.
42. "Laurie Walker and Madre," Oracle Stone Productions, http://crystalskullsevent.com/laurie.html.
43. This text has been used to announce workshops by Laurie Walker. For example, see: "Crystal Skull Presentation and Healings with Laurie Walker and Crystal Skull Madre," Skull4U Blog, http://www.crystalskulls.eu/blog/.
44. "About Pancho," Pancho: The New Generation Skull, http://panchocrystalskull.blogspot.com/p/about-pancho.html and "Guardians of Pancho," Pancho: The New Generation Skull, http://panchocrystalskull.blogspot.com/p/bojorquez-family-panchos-guardians.html.
45. "The 10–10–10 World Mysteries Crystal Skulls Event," Oracle Stone Productions, http://www.crystalskullsevent.com/101010.html.
46. Previous Events: October 2009, Cráneos de Cristal México, http://www.craneodecristal.org.mx/en/index.html.
47. "Wolf Song IX: UK Tour of World Peace Elders and Sacred Ancient Crystal Skulls Sept. '98," Rainbow Network Cambridge, http://www.cam.net.uk/home/aaa315/events/WOLFS_UK.HTM
48. Pelton, *The Crystal Skulls*, 30.
49. Morton and Thomas, *The Mystery of the Crystal Skulls*, Color plates 14 and 26.
50. Ibid., 151.
51. Ibid., 221.
52. Ibid., 222.
53. Jane MacLaren Walsh, "Legend of the Crystal Skulls: The Truth Behind Indiana Jones's Latest Quest," *Archaeology* 61, no. 3 (May/June 2008), http://www.archaeology.org/0805/etc/indy.html.
54. "Rare Crystal skull from Tibet: Amar," http://www.crystalskulls.com/tibet-crystal-skull.html.
55. Ibid.
56. Pelton, *The Crystal Skulls*, 19.
57. DaEl Walker, "The Rainbow Crystal Skull," Journeys of the Crystal Skull Explorers, last modified May 24, 1998, http://www.v-j-enterprises.com/daelw.html.
58. DaEl Walker, "Rainbow," Crystal Awareness Institute, last modified in 1998, http://www.crystalawareness.com/crystal-skulls/index.html.
59. See note 56 above.
60. See notes 57 and 58 above.
61. Mehler, "Crystal Skulls," 37–38.
62. Joky van Dieten, "The Jesuit," http://www.jokys-peacemission.com/jesuit.htm
63. Joky van Dieten, *Messengers of Ancient Wisdom*, 11.

64. Pelton, *The Crystal Skulls*, 21.
65. Joky "the Guardian" van Dieten, Messengers of Ancient Wisdom: An Odyssey of Crystal Skulls, (Pelton Publications, Pinole, California, 1995): 26–28.
66. Ibid., 29.
67. Joky van Dieten, "Janus: The Mysterious Illyrian Skull from Montenegro," http://www.jokys-peacemission.com/janus.htm
68. Ibid.
69. Joky "the Guardian" van Dieten, *Messengers of Ancient Wisdom*, 20.
70. Ibid.
71. Joky van Dieten, "Shui Ting Er," http://www.jokys-peacemission.com/shuiting.htm; Joky van Dieten, *Messenger of Ancient Wisdom*, 7.
72. Pelton, *The Crystal Skulls*, 14.
73. Hatcher Childress and Mehler, *The Crystal Skulls*, 211–227.
74. Jane MacLaren Walsh, "The Skull of Doom: Just the Facts," *Archeology*, January 26, 2010, http://www.archaeology.org/online/features/mitchell_hedges/facts.html.
75. Ibid.
76. Morton and Thomas, *The Mystery of the Crystal Skulls*, 221.
77. Wikipedia, s.v. "Crystal skull," last modified November 12, 2012, http://en.wikipedia.org/wiki/Crystal_skull.
78. Pelton, *The Crystal Skulls*, 11.
79. Thomas Calligaro et al., "Dating Study of Two Rock Crystal Carvings by Surface Microtopography and by Ion Beam Analyses of Hydrogen," *Applied Physics A: Materials Science & Processing* 94, no.4 (March 2008): 871–878. doi: 10.1007/s00339-008-5018-9. http://www.springerlink.com/content/p53g67m845762616/
80. Ibid.
81. Owen Edwards, "The Smithsonian's Crystal Skull," *Smithsonian*, May 30, 2008, http://www.smithsonianmag.com/history-archaeology/The_Smithsonians_Crystal_Skull.html.
82. Morton and Thomas, *The Mystery of the Crystal Skulls*, 221.

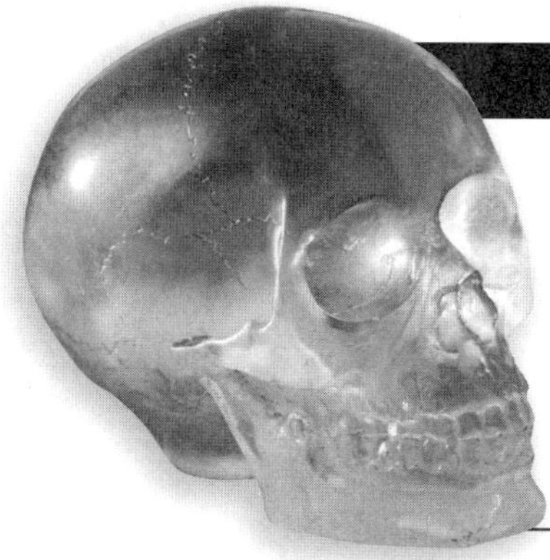

Bibliography

Amorah, Quan Yin. *The Pleiadian Workbook: Awakening Your Divine Ka*. Santa Fe, NM: Bear & Company Publishing, 1995.

Amorah, Quan Yin, and Barbara Hand Clow. *Pleiadian Perspectives on Human Evolution*. Santa Fe, NM: Bear & Company Publishing, 1996.

Bauval, Robert, and Adrian Gilbert. *The Orion Mystery: Unlocking the Secrets of the Pyramids*. New York: Crown Trade Paperbacks, 1994.

Bohm, David, and Basil J. Hiley. *The Undivided Universe*. New York: Routledge, 1995).

———. *Wholeness and the Implicate Order*. New York: Routledge, 2002 .

Bowen, Sandra, F.R. "Nick" Nocerino, and Joshua Shapiro, *Mysteries of the Crystal Skulls Revealed*. Pacifica, CA: J&S Aquarian Networking, 1988.

Boylan, Richard. "StarNations." http://www.drboylan.com/starnations.html.

———. "Elders Reveal Centuries of Extraterrestrial Contact Lore." 1996. http://www.drboylan.com/strknrpt2.html.

———. "Return of the Star Nations during our Time of Purification: Report on the Star Knowledge Conference in Sedona." 1998. http://www.think-aboutit.com/Spiritual/return_of_the_star_nations_durin.htm.

Bryant, Alice, and Phyllis Galde. *The Message of the Crystal Skull: From Atlantis to the New Age*. St. Paul, MN: Llewellyn Publications, 1991.

Byrne, Rhonda. *The Secret*. Hillsboro, OR: Beyond Words Publishing, 2006.

Cannon, Dolores. *The Three Waves of Volunteers and the New Earth*. Huntsville, AR: Ozark Mountain Publishing, 2011.

Cayce, Edgar Evans. *Edgar Cayce on Atlantis*. New York: Castle Book, 1968.

Calligaro, Thomas, Yvan Coquinot, Ina Reiche, Jacques Castaing, Joseph Salomon, Gerard Ferrand, and Yves Le Fur. "Dating study of two rock crystal carvings by surface microtopography and by ion beam analyses of hydrogen." *Applied Physics A: Materials Science & Processing* 94, no. 4 (March 2008): 871–878. Doi: 10.1007/s0039-008-5018-9.

Cinamar, Radu, and Peter Moon. *Transylvanian Moonrise*. New York: Skybooks, 2011.

Collins, Andrew. *The Cygnus Mystery: Secrets of Life's Origins and the Cosmos*. London: Watkins Publishing, 2010.

Collins, Andrew. "The Cygnus Mystery: Have Cosmic Rays Affected Human Evolution?" in *Lost Knowledge of the Ancients: A Graham Hancock Reader*, edited by Glenn Kreisberg, 102–127. Rochester, VT: Bear and Company, 2010.

Coppens, Philip. *The New Pyramid Age: Worldwide Discoveries of New Pyramids Challenge Our Thinking*. Washington: O Books, 2007.

———. "The Mitchell-Hedges Crystal Skull Mystery." *Nexus* 15, no. 4 (June/July 2008). http://www.philipcoppens.com/mitchellhedges_origin.html.

Cox, Robert E. *The Elixir of Immortality: A Modern-Day Alchemist's Discovery of the Philosopher's Stone*. Rochester, VT: Inner Traditions, 2009.

Dacey, James. "Atoms Teleport Information over Long Distance." *Institute of Physics*. January 22, 2009. http://physicsworld.com/cws/article/news/37450.

David, Gary A. *The Orion Zone: Ancient Star Cities of the American Southwest*. Colfax, WI: Hayriver Press, 2005.

Dorland, Frank. *Holy Ice: Bridge to the Subconscious*. St Paul, MN: Galde Press, 1992.

Early, Dave. "Ancient Mysteries: Puma Punku in Tiahuanaco." March 10, 2009. http://daveearly.hubpages.com/hub/Ancient-Mysteries-Puma-Punku-in-Tiahuanaco.

Edwards, Owen. "The Smithsonian Crystal Skull." *Smithsonian*. May 30, 2008. http://www.smithsonianmag.com/history-archaeology/The_Smithsonians_Crystal_Skull.html.

Ereira, Alan. *The Elder Brother's Warning*. UK: Tairona Heritage Trust, 2008. http://www.taironatrust.org.

Hadley-James, Brian, ed. *The Skull Speaks (through Carole Davis)*. Toronto: Amrhea Publishing, 1985.

Hadley-James, Brian. *Beyond the Veil of Time ... with Carole Davis-Wilson*. Ontario: Like-Minds Publishing, 2000. Ebook.

Hand Clow, Barbara. *Heart of the Christos: Starseeding from the Pleiades*. Santa Fe, NM: Bear and Company, 1989.

———. *The Pleiadean Agenda: New Cosmology for the Age of Light*. Santa Fe, NM: Bear and Company Publishing, 1995.

Hatcher Childress, David, and Stephen S.Mehler. *The Crystal Skulls: Astonishing Portals to Man's Past*. Kempton, IL: Adventures Unlimited Press, 2008.

Hicks, Esther, and Jerry Hicks. *The Law of Attraction: The Basics of the Teaching of Abraham*. New York: Hay House, 2006.

Hilling, Kirsten. *Kristallschäedel: Anleitung zur Energiearbeit mit Kristallschädeln* [Crystal skull: Introduction to energy work with crystal skulls]. Leipzig, Germany: Bohmer Verlad, 2011. (Book only available in the German language.)

Hope, Murry. *The Lion People: Intercosmic Messages from the Future*. Loughborough, Great Britain: Thoth Publications, 1992.

———. *The Paschats and the Crystal People*. Loughborough, Great Britain: Thoth Publications, 1988.

———. *The Sirius Connection: Unlocking the Secrets of Ancient Egypt*. Rockport, MA: Elements Books, 1997.

Hudson, David, "Lectures." Ascension Alchemy. http://www.asc-alchemy.com/hudson.html.

International Colored Gemstones Association. "Jade. "http://www.gemstone.org/index.php?option=com_content&view=article&id=121:sapphire&catid=1:gem-by-gem&Itemid=14.

Kaehr, Shelley. *Crystal Skull Consciousness*. Dallas: Out of This World Production, 2007.

Kanjski, Vilim, and Hrvoje Zujoc. *The Secrets of the Pyramids Revealed: Energetics Discovers the Truth*. Bosnia: Grafika d.o.o. Osijek, 2008.

Kaplan, Aryeh. *Sefer Yetzirah: The Book of Creation*. Boston: Weiser Books, 1997.

Loeffler, Nicole. "The Effects of a Conditioned Space Called the 'Scalar Room' on the Experience of Meditation." DTh diss., Holos University, 2007. http://www.holosuniversity.net/pdf/NLoeffler_Dissertation.pdf.

Lutz, Antoine, Lawrence Greischner, Nancy Rawlings, Matthieu Ricard, and Richard J. Davidson. "Long-Term Meditators Self-Induce High-Amplitude Gamma Synchrony during Mental Practice." *Proceedings of the National Academy of Sciences of the United States of America* 101, no. 46 (November 16, 2004). doi:10.1073/pnas.0407401101. http://www.pnas.org/content/101/46/16369.full.

MacLaine, Shirley. *The Camino: A Journey of Spirit*. New York: Pocket Books, 2000.

MacLaren Walsh, Jane. "Legend of the Crystal Skulls: The Truth behind Indiana Jones's Latest Quest." *Archaeology* 61, no. 3 (May/June 2008). http://www.archaeology.org/0805/etc/indy.html.

———. "The Skull of Doom: Under the Microscope." *Archaeology*. January 26, 20120. http://www.archaeology.org/online/features/mitchell_hedges/microscope.html.

———. "The Skull of Doom: Just the Facts." *Archaeology*. January 26, 2010 http://www.archaeology.org/online/features/mitchell_hedges/facts.html.

Marciniak, Barbara. *Bringers of the Dawn: Teachings from the Pleiadians*. Santa Fe, NM: Bear and Compan, 1992.

Marciniak, Barbara, with Karen Marciniak and Tera Thomas. *Earth: Pleiadian Keys to the Living Library*. Santa Fe, NM: Bear and Company, 1995.

———. *Family of Light: Pleiadian Tales and Lessons in Living*. Santa Fe, NM: Bear and Company, 1999.

Mehler, Stephen S. "Crystal Skulls: The Adventure Continues." *World Explorer* 6, no. 1 (August 2011).

Melchizedek, Drunvalo. *Serpent of Light: Beyond 2012; The Movement of the Earth's Kundalini and the Rise of the Female Light, 1049 to 2013*. San Francisco: Weiser Books, 2007.

Mercier, Patricia. *The Mayan End Times: A Spiritual Adventure; Maya Prophecies for 2012*. London: Watkins Publishing, 2008.

———. *Crystal Skulls and the Enigma of Time: A Spiritual Adventure into the Mayan World of Prophecy and Discovery*. London: Watkins Publishing, 2011.

Meyl, Konstantin. "Scalar Waves: Theory and Experiments." *Journal of Scientific Exploration* 15, no. 2 (2001): 199–205.

Milanovich, Dr. Norma J. *We, The Arcturians*. Albuquerque, NM: Athena Publishing, 1990.

Morill, Sibley S. Ambroce Bierce: *F.A. Mitchell-Hedges and the Crystal Skull*. San Francisco: Cadleon Press, 1972.

Morton, Chris, and Ceri Louise Thomas. *The Mystery of the Crystal Skulls: Unlocking the Secrets of the Past, Present, and Future*. San Francisco: Thorsons, 1997.

Mowry, Scott. "New Crop Circles Found in England May Offer Proof That a New Earth Is About to Unfold." Miracles and Inspiration, posted July 31, 2010. http://www/miraclesandinspiration.com/news_cropcircles.html.

Mullaney, James. "Celebrating the Universe." Edgar Cayce's Association for Research and Enlightenment, posted May 6, 2011. http://www.edgarcayce.org/are/blog.aspx?id=4645&blogid=445.

"Nebula Stone." http://www.nebulastone.com.

O'Donnell, Gerald. *The Complete Remote Influencing Training System*. Boca Raton, FL: Academy of Remote Viewing and Remote Influencing, 2006.

Parks, JoAnn. *The Story of Max: The Texas Crystal Skull*. Privately printed by JoAnn Parks, 1990.

Pelton, Chuck. *The Crystal Skulls: A Legacy of Past Civilizations or Prophets of our Future?* Pinole, CA: Pelton Publications, 1997. (Publication no longer available.)

———. *The White Knight* 2, no. 4. (Quarterly publication produced by The Pelton Foundation of Applied Paranormal Research in association with White Knight Productions and The Society of Crystal Skulls International.)

Raphaell, Katrina. "Lemurian Seed Crystals." *Crystal Buzz* 12 (Spring 2000).

Ray, Dr. Joseph. "The Legacy de Lubicz." *In The Search for Lost Origins*. Livingston, MT: Atlantis Rising Books, 1996.

Rein, Glen. "Biological Effects of Quantum Fields and Their Role in the Natural Healing Process." *Frontier Perspectives* 7 (1998): 16–23. http://www.item-bioenergy.com/infocenter/BiologicalEffectsofQuantumFields.pdf.

Royal, Lyssa, and Keith Priest. *The Prism of Lyra: An Exploration of Human Galactic Heritage*. Phoenix: Royal Priest Research Press, 1992.

Satguru Sivaya Subramuniyaswami. *Lemurian Scrolls: Angelic Prophecies Revealing Human Origins*. Hawaii: Himalayan Academy, 1998.

Sax, Margaret; Jane M. Walsh; Ian C. Freestone; Andrew H. Rankin; and Nigel D. Meeks. "The Origins of Two Purportedly Pre-Columbian Mexican Crystal Skulls." *Journal of Archaeological Science* 35, no. 10 (October 2008): 2,751–2,760. doi: 10.1016/j/jas.2008.05.007.

Scott-Elliott, W. *Legends of Atlantis and Lost Lemuria*. Wheaton, IL: Quest Books, 1990.

Seid, Kirby. "The Light Labyrinth." Ancient Technologies. http://www.ancienttechnologies.com/liminal.html.

Shapiro, Joshua, and DesyRainbow Roodnat-Shapiro. *Kristallen Schedels: Een Groot Mysterie Nader Bekeken*. Eeserveen, the Netherlands: Uitgeverij Akasha, 2006.

Smith, Michael E. "Aztec Crystal Skulls." *Publishing Archaeology*. May 19, 2008. http://publishingarchaeology.blogspot.com/2008/05/blog-post.html.

Stross, Brian. "Mesoamerican Copal Resins." *U-Mut Maya* 6, 177–186. http://www.utexas.edu/courses/stross/papers/copal.htm.

Temple, Robert K.G. *The Sirius Mystery: Was Earth Visited by Intelligent Beings from a Planet in the System of the Star Sirius?* Rochester, VT: Destiny Books, 1987.

Temple Richmond, M. *Sirius*. Mariposa, CA: Source Publications, 1997.

Thadeusz, Frank. "The Kingdom of the Crystal Skull: German Artisans Lay Claim to a Mysterious Tradition." *Der Spiegel* 40 (2011). http://www.spiegel.de/international/spiegel/0,1518,790456,00.html.

Vigilant Citizen. "The Mysterious Connection between Sirius and Human History." *Secret Arcana*. http://secretarcana.com/hiddenknowledge/the-mysterious-connection-between-sirius-and-human-history/.

van Dieten, Joky. *Messengers of Ancient Wisdom*. (A story narrated by ET, self-published, year unknown.)

van Dieten, Joky "the Guardian." *Messengers of Ancient Wisdom: An Odyssey of Crystal Skulls*. Pinole, CA: Pelton Publications, 1995.

van Etten, Jaap. *Crystal Skulls: Interacting with a Phenomenon*. Flagstaff, AZ: Light Technology Publishing, 2007.

van Etten, Jaap. *Gifts of Mother Earth: Earth Energies, Vortexes, Lines, and Grids*. Flagstaff: AZ: Light Technology Publishing, 2011.

Vleer, Wigholt. *Leylijnen en Leycentra in de Lage Landen: 200 Heilige Plaatsen in Nederland en Vlaanderen*. The Netherlands: Ankh-Hermes, 1992.

Walker, DaEl. *The Crystal Book*. Sunol, CA: The Crystal Company, 1983.

Whitfield, Sherry. "The Crystal Skull, 'Synergy.'" http://www.angelslove.net/crystal-skull/.

Zeliadt, Nicholette. "Silver Beware: Antimicrobial Nanoparticles in Soil May Harm Plant Life." *Scientific American*. August 9, 2010. http://www.scientificamerican.com/article.cfm?id=silver-beware-antimicrobial-nanoparticles-in-soil-may-harm-plant-life.

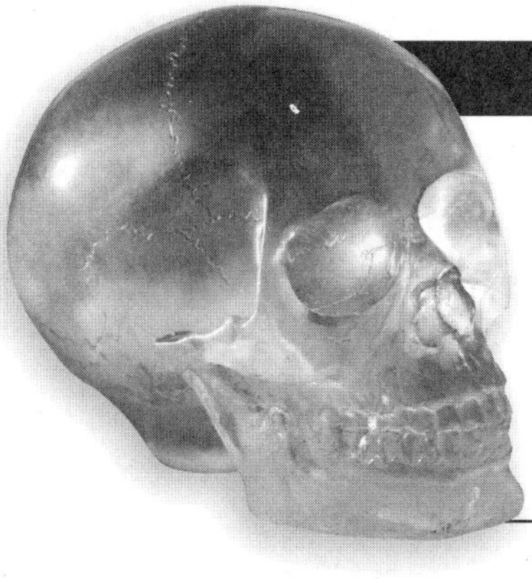

About the Author

Jaap van Etten, PhD was born and educated in the Netherlands. He received his PhD in biology in Amsterdam, specializing in ecology. For the past twenty years his focus has been on metaphysical ecology. He studies and teaches about human energies, Earth energies, energies of stones, crystals, and crystal skulls, and how these energies interact. He is the author of *Crystal Skulls: Interacting with a Phenomenon* and *Gifts of Mother Earth.* In this book, he focuses on crystal skulls and how their energies support our journey of remembering and fully becoming our true selves. Since 1998, he has lived in the United States with his wife, Jeanne Michaels. They currently reside in Sedona, Arizona.

Light Technology PUBLISHING **Presents**

TO ORDER PRINT BOOKS
Visit LightTechnology.com, Call 928-526-1345 or 1-800-450-0985,
or Check Amazon.com or Your Favorite Bookstore

BOOKS THROUGH JAAP VAN ETTEN

Gifts of Mother Earth

Earth Energies, Vortexes, Lines, and Grids

We live in a sea of energies that are part of the Earth we live on. Most people are not aware of these energies and consequently are not aware that they hold many gifts. These gifts help us to heal, balance, expand consciousness (awareness), and support spiritual evolution. Our ancestors knew the gifts of Mother Earth and used these energies to support their lives and spirituality in many ways. We, modern humans, have mostly forgotten that they exist.

$25.00 • 256 PP. • Softcover
978-1-891824-36-4

Crystal Skulls: Interacting with a Phenomenon

Discover your energetic connection with crystal skulls. Learn how to utilize these energies for your own personal growth and how these special energies affect your awareness and expand your consciousness.

This book reveals the skulls' ancient mysteries, their different characteristics and special energies, and the effects they have on humans and on Earth.

Enhanced by 16 pages of color photos, this book invites you to delve deep into the mystical world of the crystal skulls.

$19.95 • 240 PP. • Softcover
978-1-891824-64-7

All Our Books Are Also Available as eBooks from Amazon, Apple iTunes, Google Play, Barnes & Noble, and Kobo.

Light Technology PUBLISHING

TO ORDER PRINT BOOKS

Visit LightTechnology.com, Call 928-526-1345 or 1-800-450-0985,
or Check Amazon.com or Your Favorite Bookstore

BOOKS THROUGH JAAP VAN ETTEN

Birth of a New Consciousness

Dialogues with the Sidhe

We usually base our perception of reality on what our five main senses receive, particularly our visual interpretation of the world, but the world we live in actually consists of many different worlds, most of which are invisible to us. All these worlds are part of Gaia and make up the reality we live in.

This book contains dialogues with the Sidhe, a race of human-like beings who are our direct relatives. Invisible to us, they occupy one of the subtle worlds of Gaia.

As the Sidhe and the author share their views on their respective worlds, explore the similarities and differences and gain a different perspective. Learn to recognize our respective gifts and self-induced limitations.

By collaborating with beings from the subtle realms, such as nature spirits and unicorns, we can create a new consciousness — and a new world. Embark on the journey available to every soul who comes to Earth, and raise your vibration and expand your view of reality.

$16.95 • Softcover • 6 x 9 • 192 PP.
ISBN 978-1-62233-033-1

CHAPTERS INCLUDE

- Meeting the Sidhe
- Getting to Know Each Other
- Our Origins and the Influence of the Stars
- The Separation
- Thoughts and Emotions
- Energy Systems and Healing
- Procreation and Hereditary Factors
- Teaching and Learning: the Education Systems
- Relationships with Plants and Animals
- Crystalline Energies

COMING SOON!

Dragons: Guardians of Creative Powers

All Our Books Are Also Available as eBooks from Amazon, Apple iTunes, Google Play, Barnes & Noble, and Kobo.

Light Technology PUBLISHING Presents

TO ORDER PRINT BOOKS

Visit LightTechnology.com, Call 928-526-1345 or 1-800-450-0985,
or Check Amazon.com or Your Favorite Bookstore

BOOKS THROUGH DRUNVALO MELCHIZEDEK

THE ANCIENT SECRET OF THE FLOWER OF LIFE, VOLUME 1

Also available in Spanish as *Antiguo Secreto Flor de la Vida, Volumen 1*

Once, all life in the universe knew the Flower of Life as the creation pattern, the geometrical design leading us into and out of physical existence. Then from a very high state of consciousness, we fell into darkness, and the secret was hidden for thousands of years, encoded in the cells of all life.

$25.00 • 240 PP. • Softcover • ISBN 978-1-891824-17-3

THE ANCIENT SECRET OF THE FLOWER OF LIFE, VOLUME 2

Also available in Spanish as *Antiguo Secreto Flor de la Vida, Volumen 2*

Drunvalo shares the instructions for the Mer-Ka-Ba meditation, step-by-step techniques for the re-creation of the energy field of the evolved human, which is the key to ascension and the next dimensional world. If done from love, this ancient process of breathing prana opens up for us a world of tantalizing possibility in this dimension, from protective powers to the healing of oneself, others, and even the planet.

$25.00 • 272 PP. • Softcover • ISBN 978-1-891824-21-0

Includes
Heart
Meditation CD

LIVING IN THE HEART

Also available in Spanish as *Viviendo en el Corazón*

Long ago we humans used a form of communication and sensing that did not involve the brain in any way; rather, it came from a sacred place within our hearts. What good would it do to find this place again in a world where the greatest religion is science and the logic of the mind? Don't I know this world where emotions and feelings are second-class citizens? Yes, I do. But my teachers have asked me to remind you who you really are. You are more than a human being, much more. Within your heart is a place, a sacred place, where the world can literally be remade through conscious cocreation. If you give me permission, I will show you what has been shown to me.

— Drunvalo Melchizedek

$25.00 • 144 PP. • Softcover • ISBN 978-1-891824-43-2

All Our Books Are Also Available as eBooks on Amazon, Apple iTunes, Google Play, Barnes & Noble, and Kobo.

Light Technology PUBLISHING Presents

TO ORDER PRINT BOOKS

Visit LightTechnology.com, Call 928-526-1345 or 1-800-450-0985,
or Check Amazon.com or Your Favorite Bookstore

BOOKS THROUGH TOM T. MOORE

THE GENTLE WAY

A SELF-HELP GUIDE FOR THOSE WHO BELIEVE IN ANGELS

This self-help guide introduces a new way to connect with guardian angels and create benevolent outcomes in every area of life.

$14.95 • Softcover • 160 PP. • 978-1-891824-60-9

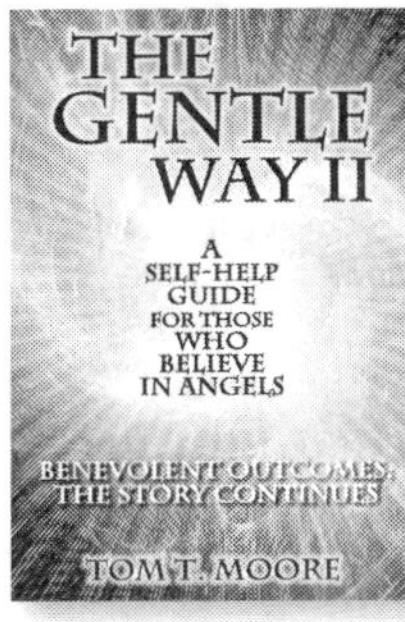

THE GENTLE WAY II

BENEVOLENT OUTCOMES: THE STORY CONTINUES

This inspirational self-help book explains how to access a more benevolent world. Tom explains how to bypass old patterns, fears, and belief systems to create an ideal life.

$16.95 • Softcover • 320 PP. • 978-1-891824-80-7

THE GENTLE WAY III

MASTER YOUR LIFE

This follow-up is filled with even more stories from people all over the world who benefit from requesting most benevolent outcomes.

$16.95 • Softcover • 352 PP. • 978-1-62233-005-8

FIRST CONTACT

CONVERSATIONS WITH AN ET

Revel in the story of how Tom was introduced to and communicates with his "brother from another planet," an ET named Antura.

$15.95 • Softcover • 224 PP. • 978-1-62233-004-1

ATLANTIS & LEMURIA

THE LOST CONTINENTS REVEALED!

Sixty thousand years ago, two continents existed: Atlantis and Lemuria. Why are they no longer there?

$16.95 • Softcover • 256 PP. • ISBN 978-1-62233-037-9

All Our Books Are Also Available as eBooks from Amazon, Apple iTunes, Google Play, Barnes & Noble, and Kobo.

Light Technology PUBLISHING Presents

TO ORDER PRINT BOOKS

Visit LightTechnology.com, Call 928-526-1345 or 1-800-450-0985,
or Check Amazon.com or Your Favorite Bookstore

Books through David K. Miller

Arcturians: How to Heal, Ascend, and Help Planet Earth
Included here are new interpretations of the Kaballistic Tree of Life, which has been expanded to embrace 5D planetary healing methods.
$16.95 • Softcover • 352 PP.
978-1-62233-002-7

Biorelativity
Biorelativity describes telepathic communication between humans and the spirit of Earth. The goal is to influence the outcome of natural events, such as volcanoes and earthquakes.
$16.95 • Softcover • 352 PP.
978-1-891824-98-2

Connecting with the Arcturians
Many have talked about the ascension process, but few really understand what it means. This book answers all the common ascension questions.
$17.00 • Softcover • 256 PP.
978-1-891824-94-4

Connecting with the Arcturians, Volume 2
This follow-up to the popular first volume contains the most updated information on personal and planetary healing and ascension.
$16.95 • Softcover • 288 PP.
978-1-62233-052-2

Connecting with the Arcturians, Volume 3
With hopeful, helpful, and healing messages, the Arcturians integrate physics with spirituality to provide personal and planetary thoughts on preparing for our future and for the ascension.
$17.95 • Softcover • 288 PP.
978-1-62233-063-8

Expand Your Consciousness
Humankind must develop higher consciousness to heal itself and to experience life more meaningfully. Explore the fascinating multidimensionality that is yours for the taking.
$16.95 • Softcover. • 288 PP.
978-1-62233-036-2

Fifth-Dimensional Soul Psychology
In a series of lectures from Vywamus, explore the meaning and usefulness of soul psychology and how it relates to modern psychology.
$16.95 • Softcover • 288 PP.
978-1-62233-016-4

Kaballah and the Ascension The author explains how studying the Kaballah allows for a unique understanding of the concept of higher consciousness.
$16.95 • Softcover • 176 PP.
978-1-891824-82-1

All Our Books Are Also Available as eBooks from Amazon, Apple iTunes, Google Play, Barnes & Noble, and Kobo.

Light Technology PUBLISHING Presents

TO ORDER PRINT BOOKS

Visit LightTechnology.com, Call 928-526-1345 or 1-800-450-0985,
or Check Amazon.com or Your Favorite Bookstore

Books Through David K. Miller

New Spiritual Technology for the Fifth-Dimensional Earth

Information is featured about native ceremonies to connect to Earth healing energies, thought projections, and thought communication.

$19.95 • Softcover • 240 pp.
978-1-891824-79-1

Teachings from the Sacred Triangle, Volume 3

Learn how to use holographic technology to project energies in the most direct and transformative way throughout Earth.

$16.95 • Softcover • 288 pp.
978-1-891824-23-4

Raising the Spiritual Light Quotient

The spiritual light quotient, one's ability to understand spiritual concepts, is similar to the intelligence quotient (IQ) test. Learn how to raise your SLQ.

$16.95 • Softcover • 384 pp.
978-1-891824-89-0

A New Tree of Life for Planetary Ascension

WITH MORDECHAI YASHIN

David Miller has teamed up with Torah expert Mordechai Yashin to provide a unique, expanded perspective on the Tree of Life.

$16.95 • Softcover • 336 pp.
978-1-62233-012-6

Teachings from the Sacred Triangle, Volume 1

This book offers an understanding of the soul, soul evolution, and how the human species is advancing toward the next evolutionary step.

$16.95 • Softcover • 272 pp.
978-1-62233-007-2

Enseñanzas del Sagrado Triángulo Arcturiano

Los capitulos incluyen:

- Los Principios de la Biorelatividad
- La Conciencia y Conexiones de Grupo
- La Estructura Etérea de la Tierra

$19.95 • 416 páginas
978-1-62233-264-9

Teachings from the Sacred Triangle, Volume 2

The teachings continue in this second volume of the *Sacred Triangle* series, focusing on the importance of energy bridges.

$16.95 • Softcover • 288 pp.
978-1-891824-19-7

David K. Miller has an extensive background in psychology and psychotherapy. After thirty-five years of conventional practice, David now focuses exclusively on soul psychology. He has developed several therapy techniques, penned many articles, and authored several books. David is also the founder of the international meditation group known as the Group of Forty. To learn more, go to GroupofForty.com.

All Our Books Are Also Available as eBooks from Amazon, Apple iTunes, Google Play, Barnes & Noble, and Kobo.

Light Technology PUBLISHING Presents

TO ORDER PRINT BOOKS

Visit LightTechnology.com, Call 928-526-1345 or 1-800-450-0985,
or Check Amazon.com or Your Favorite Bookstore

THROUGH ROBERT SHAPIRO

ETs on Earth, Volume 1
Explorer Race Book 18

This book explores the ET phenomenon with chapters on the blue spiral light over Norway, crop circles, and much more.

$16.95 • Softcover • 352 PP.
978-1-891824-91-3

ETs on Earth, Volume 2
Explorer Race Book 21

Read about who the beings in UFOs are in this fun and gentle reminder that ETs are just friends from another "neighborhood."

$16.95 • Softcover • 416 PP.
978-1-62233-003-4

ETs on Earth, Volume 3
Explorer Race Book 22

Many of you are ready to welcome ETs. In this book, you will find many reminders of who you might have been or might become in other lives.

$16.95 • Softcover • 352 PP.
978-1-62233-044-7

ETs from UFO Casebook's Best Pictures Speak

Explorer Race Book 25

This book is for those who are interested in things that are new, different, exciting, or mysterious. Perhaps you will discover your likes and dislikes are not only associated with Earth and your personality, family, and friends. Some of it might actually be associated with your extraterrestrial roots!

All of you on Earth, all you human beings, have extraterrestrial roots. If you trace the Earth-human DNA back far enough, it goes to other planets. The reason you're not aware of this or able to prove it scientifically in published papers is that what little is known about this on your planet is largely kept secret.

As you read these pages, you will discover that your brothers, sisters, cousins, aunties, uncles, friends, and relations are not only on Earth. They are on other planets too.

— Zoosh

$16.95 • Softcover • 320 PP.
978-1-62233-058-4

All Our Books Are Also Available as eBooks from Amazon, Apple iTunes, Google Play, Barnes & Noble, and Kobo.

Light Technology PUBLISHING **Presents**

TO ORDER PRINT BOOKS
Visit LightTechnology.com, Call 928-526-1345 or 1-800-450-0985,
or Check Amazon.com or Your Favorite Bookstore

SHAMANIC SECRETS SERIES THROUGH ROBERT SHAPIRO

Shamanic Secrets: Lost Wisdom Regained

Due to wars, natural disasters, a shaman not being able to train a successor, and many other reasons, Isis (through Robert) says that 95 percent of the accumulated shamanic wisdom has been lost. Now it is important to regain this wisdom as young people who are able to learn and use these processes are being born now.

Beings who lived as shamans and healers on Earth at various times now speak through Robert Shapiro and bring these lost teachings and techniques to a humanity waking up and discovering it has the talents and abilities to use this wisdom for the benefit of all.

$16.95 • Softcover • 352 PP. • ISBN 978-1-62233-049-2

Shamanic Secrets for Material Mastery

Explore the heart and soul connection between humans and Mother Earth. Through that intimacy, miracles of healing and expanded awareness can flourish.

$19.95 • Softcover • 528 PP.
978-1-891824-12-8

Shamanic Secrets for Physical Mastery

The purpose of this book is to explain the sacred nature of the physical body and some of the magnificent gifts it offers.

$25.00 • Softcover • 608 PP.
978-1-891824-29-6

Shamanic Secrets for Spiritual Mastery

Spiritual mastery is the underpinnings of multiple ways of being, understanding, appreciating, and interacting in harmony with your world.

$29.95 • Softcover • 768 PP.
978-1-891824-58-6

All Our Books Are Also Available as eBooks from Amazon, Apple iTunes, Google Play, Barnes & Noble, and Kobo.

Light Technology PUBLISHING Presents

SEDONA JOURNAL OF Emergence

Find Answers to Satisfy Your Heart and Inspire Your Life in the #1 Channeled Magazine for Spiritual Guidance

In the *Sedona Journal of Emergence*, channeled lightbeings explain the process of your movement toward becoming your natural self and regaining your natural talents and abilities, and they offer guidance to help you feel and express love and benevolence and to encourage you to make a difference in ensuring your expansion in consciousness as you move into another level of Earth — into the new reality.

The *Sedona Journal of Emergence* is the one monthly magazine you'll want to keep on hand!

- Mine the annual PREDICTIONS issue for insights on the coming year.
- Discover channeled information and inspired guidance intended to improve your body, mind, and soul.
- Learn how to improve yourself and, by default, help the planet.

DON'T DELAY — SUBSCRIBE TODAY!

SIGN UP ONLINE AT **SEDONAJOURNAL.COM**,
CALL 1-800-450-0985 OR 1-928-526-1345,

OR EMAIL **SUBSCRIPTIONS@LIGHTTECHNOLOGY.COM.**
(ELECTRONIC SUBSCRIPTIONS AVAILABLE)

Light Technology PUBLISHING Presents

EASY ORDER

Order ONLINE!
www.LightTechnology.com
Email:
customersrv@lighttechnology.com

Order by Mail
Send to
Light Technology Publishing
PO Box 3540
Flagstaff, AZ 86003

Order by Phone
800-450-0985
928-526-1345

Order by Fax
928-714-1132

Available from your favorite bookstore or

LIGHT Technology PUBLISHING

MasterCard VISA AMERICAN EXPRESS DISCOVER PayPal

LightTechnology.com
We Offer the Best Channeled and Inspired Books of Wisdom.
Use Our Secure Checkout.
In-Depth Information on Books, Including Excerpts and Contents.
Use the Links to Our Other Great Sites. See Below.

SedonaJournal.com
Read Excerpts of Monthly Channeling and Predictions in Advance.
Use Our Email Links to Contact Us or Send a Submission.
Electronic Subscriptions Available — with or without Print Copies.

BenevolentMagic.com
Learn the techniques of benevolence toward self and benevolence toward others to create global peace. Download all the techniques of benevolent magic and living prayer for FREE!

ExplorerRace.com
All humanity constitutes the Explorer Race, volunteers for a grand and glorious experiment. Discover your purpose, your history, and your future. Download the first chapter of each book for FREE!

ShamanicSecrets.com
What we call shamanism is the natural way of life for beings on other planets. Learn to be aware of your natural self and your natural talents and abilities. Download the first chapter of each book for FREE!